POCKET MAP

PARIS

TOP SIGHTS · LOCAL EXPERIENCES

**CATHERINE LE NEVEZ,
CHRISTOPHER PITTS, NICOLA WILLIAMS**

Contents

Plan Your Trip

Welcome to Paris................4

Top Sights......................6

Eating 10

Drinking & Nightlife..........12

Shopping......................14

Museums 16

Architecture 18

History 20

Parks & Gardens...............22

Riverside Activities..........23

Tours.........................24

Cooking & Wine-Tasting Courses.....25

For Kids 26

LGBT+.........................27

Four Perfect Days.............28

Need to Know 30

Paris Neighbourhoods..........32

Arc de Triomphe (p54)
MISCELLANEOUSTOCK/ALAMY ©

914,
436
PA
2018

Explore Paris 35

Eiffel Tower &
Les Invalides.....................37

Arc de Triomphe &
the Champs-Élysées 53

Louvre, Tuileries &
Opéra.............................67

Sacré-Cœur &
Montmartre 93

Centre Pompidou &
Le Marais 111

Notre Dame &
the Islands 135

The Latin Quarter 153

Musée d'Orsay
& St-Germain
des Prés 175

Worth a Trip

Père Lachaise..................132

Versailles 198

Survival Guide 203

Before You Go 204

Arriving in Paris 205

Getting Around 208

Essential Information ... 210

Language 215

Special Features

Eiffel Tower....................... 38

Musée Rodin..................... 40

Arc de Triomphe 54

Louvre 68

Sacré-Cœur...................... 94

Centre Pompidou 112

Notre Dame 136

Musée d'Orsay 176

Jardin du Luxembourg...178

B+T 1/26/19 unt

Welcome to Paris

Named for its leading role in the Age of Enlightenment, *la ville lumière* (the City of Light) is famed for its monument-lined boulevards, treasure-packed museums, classic bistros and *haute couture* (high fashion) houses. Today they're enhanced by a new wave of multimedia galleries, design shops and tech start-ups that are reasserting Paris' position as a visionary global city.

Notre Dame (p136)

Top Sights

THITIPHAN PAKSEESUWAN/SHUTTERSTOCK ©

Eiffel Tower
Quintessentially Paris. **p38**

Musée Rodin

Museum with a sculpture-studded garden. **p40**

Arc de Triomphe

A monument to past glories. **p54**

Louvre

The mother of all museums. **p68**

PAWEL LIBERA/GETTY IMAGES ©

LEFT: NATTEE CHALERMTIRAGOOL/SHUTTERSTOCK © RIGHT: SAILORR/SHUTTERSTOCK ©

Sacré-Cœur

Sacré-Cœur's dove-white domes crown Montmartre. **p94**

Centre Pompidou

Europe's largest collection of modern art. **p112**

Notre Dame

French Gothic masterpiece. **p136**

Jardin du Luxembourg

Playground of Paris. **p178**

Musée d'Orsay

Art in an upcycled train station. **p176**

LEFT: BADAHOS/SHUTTERSTOCK ©; RIGHT: JULIA OGRODOWSKI/SHUTTERSTOCK ©

SALVADOR MANIQUIZ/SHUTTERSTOCK ©

Eating

France pioneered what is still the most influential style of cooking in the Western world and Paris is its showcase par excellence. Colours, textures and garnishes are impeccably arranged everywhere from simple restaurants to haute cuisine establishments. The city doesn't have its own 'local' cuisine but is the crossroads for France's regional produce and flavours.

Evolving Trends

In addition to classical French fare, look out for cuisines from around the globe. Neobistros offer some of Paris' most exciting dining options. Generally small and relatively informal, they're run by young, talented chefs who aren't afraid to experiment. Exclusively vegetarian and vegan establishments are increasing, as are places offering gluten-free dishes.

Dining Times

Petit déjeuner (breakfast; usually a baguette with butter and jam, and strong coffee) is seen as a mere precursor to *déjeuner* (lunch; the traditional main meal, starting around 12.30pm). Most restaurants open for *dîner* (dinner) around 7pm or 7.30pm. Some high-end restaurants close at weekends, and many places close in August.

Menus

Restaurants usually serve a *plat du jour* (dish of the day) at lunch (and occasionally at dinner), as well as *menus* (fixed-price meals) of an *entrée* (starter), *plat* (main course) and *fromage* (cheese) or dessert or both. These offer infinitely better value than ordering à la carte. Meals are often considerably cheaper at lunch than dinner.

Best Classic Bistros

Le Chardenoux Listed historical monument where celebrity chef Cyril Lignac preserves French culinary traditions. (p127)

Le Bistrot Paul Bert Legendary address with perfectly executed classic dishes. (p123)

Chez Paul The Paris of yesteryear. (p126)

BRIAN JANNSEN/ALAMY ©

Chez Dumonet The quintessential Parisian bistro experience, lace curtains and all. (p189)

Best Gastronomic Extravaganzas

Restaurant Guy Savoy A red-carpeted staircase leads to this once-in-a-lifetime destination. (p187)

Septime A beacon of modern cuisine. (p125)

Lasserre Fine dining and flawless service beneath a retractable roof. (p62)

Best Neobistros

Richer Brilliant-value bistro fare but no reservations, so arrive early. (p81)

Clover Watch the chefs at work in the combined dining space–kitchen. (p188)

Le Servan Daily changing creations in a neighbourhood bistro near Père Lachaise. (p122)

Best Picnic Fare

Ladurée Picnic Gourmet picnics from the famed macaron creator. (p47)

La Grande Épicerie de Paris Dazzling gourmet emporium. (p196)

La Maison Plisson Premium deli fare. (p121)

Top Tips for Parisian Dining

o Midrange restaurants will usually have a free table for lunch (arrive by 12.30pm); book a day or two in advance for dinner.

o Reservations up to one or two months in advance are crucial for lunch and dinner at popular and high-end restaurants. You may need to reconfirm on the day.

o Service is always included: a *pourboire* (tip) on top of the bill is not necessary, though rounding the bill up is common.

Drinking & Nightlife

For Parisians, drinking and eating go together like wine and cheese, and the line between a cafe, salon de thé *(tearoom), bistro, brasserie, bar and even a bar à vins (wine bar) is blurred, while the line between drinking and clubbing is often nonexistent – a cafe that's quiet mid-afternoon might have DJ sets in the evening and dancing later on.*

Coffee

If you order *un café* (a coffee), you'll be served a single shot of espresso. A *café allonge* is lengthened with hot water, a *café au lait* comes with milk and a *café crème*, lengthened with steamed milk, is the closest to a latte. Local roasteries such as Belleville Brûlerie and Coutume prime cafes citywide for outstanding brews made by professional baristas, often using cutting-edge extraction techniques.

Beer

Paris' growing *bière artisanale* (craft beer) scene is going from strength to strength, with an increasing number of city breweries. An excellent resource for hopheads is www. hoppyparis.com.

Wine

Wine is easily the most popular beverage in Paris and house wine invariably costs less than bottled water. *Les vins naturels* (natural wines) contain little or no sulphites.

Cocktails

Cocktail bars are undergoing a resurgence; many hip restaurants pair cocktails with food. Paris Cocktail Week (www.pariscocktail week.fr) takes place in late January.

Best Coffee

Beans on Fire Collaborative roastery and cafe. (p127)

La Caféothèque Coffee house and roastery plus in-house coffee school. (p128)

Coutume Café Artisan roastery with a flagship Left Bank cafe. (p49)

Honor Outdoor coffee bar in an elegant rue du Faubourg St-Honoré courtyard. (p64)

PETR KOVALENKOV/SHUTTERSTOCK ©

Best Cocktails

Bar Hemingway Legendary cocktails in the Ritz. (p84)

Tiger Gin specialist with 130 varieties. (p192)

Cod House Sake-based cocktails paired with gourmet small plates. (p192)

Danico Cocktails crafted from rare ingredients in a candlelit back room. (p84)

Little Bastards House-creation cocktails in a Latin Quarter backstreet. (p167)

Wine Bars

Le Garde Robe Affordable natural wines and an unpretentious vibe. (p84)

La Quincave Perch on wine-barrel bar stools to choose from over 200 natural wines. (p193)

Au Sauvignon Original zinc bar and hand-painted ceiling. (p192)

Best Pavement Terraces

Les Deux Magots Watch St-Germain go by from a prime position at this famous cafe's terrace. (p192)

Chez Prune The boho cafe that put Canal St-Martin on the map. (p109)

Shakespeare & Company Café Live the Parisian Left Bank literary dream. (p167)

Drinking Like a Local

○ Although most places serve at least small plates (often full menus), it's normally fine to order a coffee or alcohol if you're not dining.

○ The French rarely go drunk-wild and tend to frown upon it.

○ For clubbing events, visit www.sortiraparis.com: click on 'Soirées & Bars', then 'Nuits Parisiennes'.

Shopping

Paris has it all: broad boulevards lined with international chains, luxury avenues studded with designer fashion houses, grand department stores and lively street markets. But the real charm lies in strolling the city's back-streets, where tiny speciality shops and quirky boutiques are wedged between cafes, galleries and churches.

Fashion

Fashion shopping is Paris' forte. Parisian fashion is about style and quality first and foremost, rather than status or brand names.

A good place to get an overview is at the city's famous *grands magasins* (department stores).

Markets

The city's street markets are social gatherings for the entire neighbourhood. Nearly every little quarter has its own street market at least once a week (never Monday) where tarpaulin-topped trestle tables bow beneath fresh, cooked and preserved delicacies. *Marchés biologiques* (organic markets) are increasingly sprouting up across the city. Many street markets also sell clothes, accessories, homewares and more.

The website https://meslieux. paris.fr/marches lists every market by *arrondissement* (city district), including speciality markets such as flower markets.

Gourmet Shops

Food and drink shops make for mouthwatering shopping. Pastries might not keep, but items you can take home (customs regulations permitting) include chocolates, jams, preserves and French cheeses. Many of the best *fromageries* (cheese shops) can provide vacuum packing.

Best Department Stores

Le Bon Marché Paris' oldest department store, designed by Gustave Eiffel. (p196)

MARC BRUXELLE/SHUTTERSTOCK ©

Galeries Lafayette Has a magnificent stained-glass dome, and a Champs-Élysées store opening in 2019. (Pictured above; p87)

Le Printemps Fabulous fashion, cosmetics and French food and wine. (p88)

La Samaritaine Seine-side landmark reopening in 2019. (p88)

Best Concept & Design Stores

Merci Fabulously fashionable and unique: all profits go to a children's charity in Madagascar. (p130)

Gab & Jo Stocks only French-made items. (p195)

Empreintes Emporium showcasing some 6000 French artists and designers. (p131)

L'Exception Fashion, homewares, books and more from over 400 French designers. (p87)

Best Gourmet Shops

La Grande Épicerie de Paris Glorious food emporium. (p196)

Place de la Madeleine Single-item specialist shops and famous caterers. (p89)

La Manufacture de Chocolat Alain Ducasse's bean-to-bar chocolate factory. (p131)

La Dernière Goutte Wines from small, independent French producers. (p195)

Need to Know: Shopping Tips

● Paris' twice-yearly *soldes* (sales) generally last five to six weeks, starting around mid-January and again around mid-June.

● Most shops offer free (and very beautiful) gift wrapping – ask for *un paquet cadeau*.

● Non-EU residents may be eligible for a TVA (*taxe sur la valeur ajoutée*; value-added tax) refund.

Museums

If there's one thing that rivals a Parisian's obsession with food, it's their love of art. Hundreds of museums pepper the city, and whether you prefer classicism, impressionism or detailed exhibits of French military history, you can always be sure to find something new just around the corner.

Planning Your Visit

Most museums close one day a week, generally Monday or Tuesday; many museums also open late one or more nights a week – usually the least crowded time to visit. You'll also save time by purchasing tickets online where possible. Remember that the cut-off for entry to museums is typically half an hour to an hour before the official closing times (including times listed in this guide). Audioguides are sometimes included with admission but often incur an extra charge.

National Museums

If you can, time your trip to be in Paris on the first Sunday of the month, when you can visit the *musées nationaux* (national museums; www.rmn. fr) as well as a handful of monuments for free (some during certain months only). Temporary exhibitions, however, will still incur a charge.

City Museums

You can visit the permanent collections of most *musées municipaux* (city-run museums; www.paris. fr) for free any time. Temporary exhibitions incur a charge.

Best Impressionist Collections

Musée d'Orsay France's national museum for impressionist and related artistic movements is a must. (Pictured above; p176)

Musée de l'Orangerie Monet conceived a stunning cycle of his Water Lilies series especially for this building. (p78)

TAKASHI IMAGES/SHUTTERSTOCK ©

Musée Marmottan Monet
The world's largest Monet collection occupies a former hunting lodge. (p46)

Best Museums for Modern & Contemporary Art

Musée National d'Art Moderne The country's national modern- and contemporary-art museum, located within the striking Centre Pompidou. (p112)

Musée d'Art Moderne de la Ville de Paris Paris' modern-art museum spans the 20th century to the present day. (p61)

Palais de Tokyo Temporary exhibitions and installations. (p60)

Espace Dalí Showcases the work of the surrealist master. (p99)

L'Atelier des Lumières Paris' first digital art museum. (p119)

Best Sculpture Museums

Musée Rodin Rodin's former mansion and its rose gardens contain his masterworks. (p40)

Musée de la Sculpture en Plein Air Over 50 late 20th-century unfenced sculptures by artists including César and Brancusi. (p161)

Musée Maillol Splendid museum focusing on the work of sculptor Aristide Maillol. (p186)

Money-Saving Tips

○ Save time and money by investing in a Paris Museum Pass or Paris Passlib' (which includes public transport) to bypass (or substantially reduce) ridiculously long ticket queues.

○ Look out for museum combination tickets.

○ EU citizens under 26 years get in for free at national monuments and museums.

Architecture

Baron Haussmann's overhaul, which made way for boulevards lined by neo-classical buildings, still defines Paris today. After the art nouveau movement, additions centred on French presidents' bold grands projets (great projects). For an architectural overview, visit the Cité de l'Architecture et du Patrimoine.

Haussmann's Renovation

Paris' appearance today is largely the work of Baron Georges-Eugène Haussmann. Under Napoléon III, Haussmann completely rebuilt swathes of Paris between 1853 and 1870, replacing chaotic narrow streets (easy to barricade in an uprising) with arrow-straight, wide thoroughfares, including the 12 avenues radiating out from the Arc de Triomphe.

Rising Skyline

The controversial construction of the 1970s eyesore Tour Montparnasse (undergoing major renovations from 2019 to 2023) prompted a clampdown on skyscrapers. However, due to Paris' lack of housing space, the city council approved raising height limits to 180m in some areas. Advocates include Pritzker Prize–winning French architect Jean Nouvel.

Best Art Nouveau Splendours

Eiffel Tower Paris' 'iron lady' is art nouveau at its best. (p38)

Abbesses metro entrance Hector Guimard's finest remaining metro entrance. (p97)

Brasserie Bofinger Dine amid art nouveau brass, glass and mirrors in Paris' oldest brasserie. (p125)

Musée d'Orsay The former railway station (built in 1900) which houses this monumental museum justifies a visit alone. (p176)

Galeries Lafayette Glorious department store topped by a stunning stained-glass dome. (p87)

DMITRY ZINOVYEV/SHUTTERSTOCK ©

Le Carreau du Temple This old covered market in Le Marais is now a cutting-edge cultural and community centre. (p115)

Best Presidential Grands Projets

Centre Pompidou Former president Georges Pompidou's now-beloved cultural centre sparked furore when it was unveiled in 1977. (p112)

Louvre glass pyramid IM Pei's pyramid, instigated by former president François Mitterrand, likewise created an uproar in 1989. (p68)

Opéra Bastille Mitterrand's costly *projets* include the city's second, state-of-the-art opera house. (Pictured above; p129)

Bibliothèque Nationale de France Another Mitterrand vision, the national library's four towers are shaped like half-open books. (p173)

Best Jean Nouvel Buildings

Musée du Quai Branly President Jacques Chirac's pet *projet*, designed by Nouvel. (p44)

Institut du Monde Arabe The building that established Nouvel's reputation blends modern and traditional Arabic elements with Western influences. (p158)

Fondation Cartier pour l'Art Contemporain Stunning contemporary art space. (p186)

Best Contemporary Structures

Lafayette Anticipations Contemporary art, design and fashion space transformed in 2018 by Rem Koolhaas. (p120)

Cinémathèque Française Frank Gehry designed this postmodern stunner housing two cinema museums and presenting screenings. (p173)

Forum des Halles Central shopping mall now topped by a giant rainforest-inspired canopy. (p80)

Fondation Louis Vuitton Fine-arts centre by Frank Gehry, topped by a giant glass 'cloud'. (p60)

History

Paris' history is a saga of battles, bloodshed, grand-scale excesses, revolution, reformation, resistance, renaissance and constant reinvention. But this epic is not just consigned to museums and archives: reminders of the capital's and the country's history are evident all over the city.

Early Beginnings

Paris was born in the 3rd century BC, when the Parisii tribe of Celtic Gauls established a fishing village in the area. Julius Caesar ended centuries of conflict between the Gauls and Romans in 52 BC. Christianity was introduced in the 2nd century AD; in 508 Frankish king Clovis I united Gaul and made Paris his seat.

Conflicts

In the 12th century Scandinavian Vikings pushed towards Paris, heralding the Hundred Years' War with Norman England, which resulted in England gaining control of France in 1420. In 1429 Joan of Arc rallied French troops to defeat the English.

Revolution

The excesses of Louis XIV and his heirs triggered an uprising of Parisians on 14 July 1789, which kick-started the French Revolution. The government was consolidated in 1799 under Napoléon Bonaparte, who then conquered most of Europe before his defeat at Waterloo.

Reformation & Beyond

At the behest of Napoléon III, Baron Haussmann reshaped the cityscape. However, when Parisians heard of Napoléon III's capture in the war with Prussia in 1870, they demanded a republic. It gave rise to the glittering belle époque ('beautiful era').

Best Roman Legacies

Arènes de Lutèce
Gladiatorial 2nd-century amphitheatre. (p161)

Crypte Archéologique
Gallo-Roman remains. (p141)

MALIRA/SHUTTERSTOCK ©

Best Medieval Buildings

Notre Dame Completed in the early 14th century. (Pictured above; p136)

Louvre Vast 12th-century fort turned palace turned museum. (p68)

Sainte-Chapelle Consecrated in 1248. (p144)

Best Revolutionary Sights

Place de la Bastille Site of the former prison stormed on 14 July 1789, mobilising the Revolution. (p121)

Versailles The October 1789 March on Versailles forced the royal family to leave the château. (p198)

Place de la Concorde Louis XVI and his queen, Marie Antoinette, were among thousands guillotined where the obelisk now stands. (p79)

Conciergerie Marie Antoinette was tried and imprisoned here. (p144)

Best Burial Places

Père Lachaise Famous graves fill the world's most visited cemetery. (p132)

Les Catacombes Prowl the bone-packed tunnels of Paris' ossuary. (p185)

Panthéon Mausoleum sheltering France's greatest thinkers. (p158)

Closures & Renovations

∘ Paris' history museum, the Musée Carnavalet, in Le Marais, is closed entirely for renovations until 2020; check updates at www.carnavalet.paris.fr.

∘ In the Latin Quarter, the **Musée National du Moyen Âge** (p158) is also undergoing renovations until 2020 but will be partially open to the public.

Parks & Gardens

NIKOLPETR/SHUTTERSTOCK ©

Just as Paris' cafes are the city's communal lounge rooms, its parks, gardens and squares are its backyards. Larger parks are idyllic for strolling or simply soaking up the sunshine, with plenty of seating as well as kiosks and cafes. Small, secret gardens are tucked between historic buildings or even perched in the middle of the Seine.

Best Traditional Gardens

Jardin du Luxembourg Paris' most popular park. (p178)

Jardin des Tuileries Part of Paris' historic axis and as classical as it gets. (p78)

Versailles Designed by André Le Nôtre, the château's gardens are fit for a king. (Pictured above; p199)

Best Hidden Jewels

Square du Vert-Galant Romantically situated on the tip of the Île de la Cité. (p144)

Square René Viviani Home to Paris' oldest tree. (p159)

Île aux Cygnes A tree-shaded walkway runs the length of the city's little-known third island. (p45)

Best Parks

Jardin des Plantes Paris' botanic gardens include peonies and roses, an alpine garden and greenhouses. (p159)

Parc des Buttes Chaumont Hilly, forested haven with grottoes, waterfalls, a lake and an island. (p109)

Promenade Plantée The world's first elevated park, atop a disused railway viaduct. (p120)

Place des Vosges Paris' prettiest square, ringed by cloisters, with a park at its centre. (p121)

Visiting Paris' Green Spaces

○ Opening hours vary seasonally – check closing times posted at park gates to avoid being locked in.

○ Look out for *murs végétaux* (vertical gardens) popping up around the city, such as L'Oasis d'Aboukir (p82).

○ Eco-minded city initiatives are seeing Paris become even greener, with many open areas being created.

Riverside Activities

La ligne de vie de Paris ('the lifeline of Paris'), the Seine sluices through the city, spanned by 37 bridges. Its Unesco World Heritage–listed banks offer picturesque promenades, parks, activities and events, including sandy summertime beaches. After dark, watch the river dance with the reflections of city lights and tourist-boat floodlamps.

M.SOBREIRA/ALAMY ©

Riverbank Rejuvenation

The Seine's *berges* (banks) were reborn with the 2013 creation of a car-free 2.3km stretch of the Left Bank (p185), dotted with restaurants and bars, fitness areas, kids' play areas, and floating gardens on 1800 sq metres of artificial islands.

This was followed in 2017 by the creation of a 3.3km stretch on the Right Bank (p119) featuring cycle and walking paths, facilities for *pétanque* (a variant on the game of bowls) and other sports, along with kids' play areas, restaurants and bars.

Paris Plages

Palm trees, bars, cafes, sun lounges, parasols and water sprays line the river in high summer during the 'Paris Beaches' (www.parisinfo.com).

Best River Cruises

Bateaux-Mouches

(☎01 42 25 96 10; www.bateaux-mouches.fr; Port de la Conférence, 8e; adult/child €13.50/6; Ⓜ Alma Marceau) Departing just east of the Pont de l'Alma on the Right Bank, cruises (70 minutes) run regularly from 10am to 10.30pm April to September and every 40 minutes from 11am to 9.20pm the rest of the year. Commentary is in French and English.

Vedettes de Paris

(☎01 44 18 19 50; www.vedettesdeparis.fr; Port de Suffren, 7e; adult/child €15/7; ⊙11.30am-7.30pm May-Sep, 11.30am-5.30pm Oct-Apr; Ⓜ Bir Hakeim or RER Pont de l'Alma) These one-hour sightseeing cruises on smaller boats are a more intimate experience than the major companies. It runs themed cruises too, including imaginative 'Mysteries of Paris' tours for kids (adult/child €15/9).

Tours

PASCAL LAGESSE/SHUTTERSTOCK ©

**Parisien d'un Jour –
Paris Greeters** (https://
greeters.paris; by donation)
See Paris through local
eyes with these volunteer-
led two- to three-hour city
tours. Minimum two weeks'
notice is needed.

Paris Walks (✆01 48
09 21 40; www.paris-walks.
com; 2hr tours adult/child
€15/10) Long-established
and well-respected Paris
Walks offers two-hour
thematic walking tours
(art, fashion, chocolate, the
French Revolution etc).

Fat Tire Bike Tours
(✆01 82 88 80 96; www.
fattiretours.com; tours from
€34) Offers day and night
bicycle tours of the city,
both in central Paris and
further afield.

Set in Paris (✆09 84 42
35 79; http://setinparis.com;
3 rue Maître Albert, 5e; 2hr
tours €25; ⏱tours 10am &
3pm; Ⓜ Maubert-Mutualité)
From its cinema-style 'box
office' HQ in the Latin
Quarter, Set in Paris' movie
tours cover Parisian locations where films including
*The Devil Wears Prada, The
Bourne Identity, The Three
Musketeers,* several James
Bond instalments and many
others were shot.

Canauxrama (✆01 42
39 15 00; www.canauxrama.
com; opposite 50 bd de la
Bastille, Port de l'Arsenal,
12e; adult/child €18/9;
⏱vary; Ⓜ Bastille) Sea-
sonal canal cruises depart
from the Bassin de la Villette
near Parc de la Villette and
from the Port de l'Arsenal.
During the 2½-hour one-way
trip, boats pass through
four double locks, two swing
bridges and an underground
section.

Street Art Paris
(✆09 50 75 19 92; http://
streetartparis.fr; 2½hr tour
€20) Learn about the his-
tory of graffiti on fascinating
tours taking in Paris' vibrant
street art.

Left Bank Scooters
(✆06 78 12 04 24; www.
leftbankscooters.com; 3hr
tours per 1st/2nd passenger
from €200/50) Runs a
variety of scooter tours
around Paris, both day and
evening, as well as trips out
to Versailles and sidecar
tours. A car or motorcycle
licence is required.

L'Open Tour (✆01 42 66
56 56; www.paris.opentour.
com; 1-day pass adult/child
€33/17, night tour €27/17)
Hop-on, hop-off tours
aboard open-deck buses
with three different circuits
and 50 stops – good for a
whirlwind city tour.

Localers (✆01 83 64
92 01; www.localers.com;
tours from €49) Behind-the-
scenes urban discoveries:
pétanque, photo shoots,
market tours, cooking
classes and more.

Cooking & Wine-Tasting Courses

If dining in the city's restaurants whets your appetite, Paris has stacks of cookery schools with courses for all budgets and levels of ability. Where there's food in Paris, wine is never more than an arm's length away; plenty of places offer wine tastings and instruction for beginners through to connoisseurs.

MATT MUNRO/LONELY PLANET ©

Best Culinary Classes

Cook'n With Class (☎01 42 57 22 84; www.cooknwithclass.com; 6 rue Baudelique, 18e; ⊘2hr classes from €95; Ⓜ Simplon, Jules Joffrin) Informal small classes.

Le Cordon Bleu (☎01 85 65 15 00; www.cordonbleu.edu/paris; 13-15 quai André Citroën, 15e; Ⓜ Javel–André Citroën or RER Javel) One of the world's foremost culinary arts schools.

La Cuisine Paris (☎01 40 51 78 18; www.lacuisineparis.com; 80 quai de l'Hôtel de Ville, 4e; 2hr cooking class/walking tours from €69/80; Ⓜ Pont Marie, Hôtel de Ville) Courses on bread, croissants and macarons plus 'foodie walks'.

Best Wine Appreciation Sessions

Ô Château (☎01 44 73 97 80; http://o-chateau.com; 68 rue Jean-Jacques Rousseau, 1er; ⊘4pm-midnight Mon-Sat; 🛜; Ⓜ Les Halles or RER Châtelet–Les Halles) Young, fun company offering affordable wine and Champagne tastings.

Musée du Vin (☎01 45 25 63 26; www.museeduvinparis.com; 5 sq Charles Dickens, 16e; adult/child €13.90/free; ⊘10am-6pm Tue-Sun; Ⓜ Passy) In addition to its displays, Paris' wine museum offers instructive tastings.

Wine Tasting in Paris (☎06 76 93 32 88; www.wine-tasting-in-paris.com; 14 rue des Boulangers, 5e; tastings from €46; ⊘tastings 5-7.30pm Tue, Thu & Sat; Ⓜ Jussieu) Tastings cover methodology, vocabulary, interpreting wine labels and French wine-growing regions.

Booking a Class

● Short courses are plentiful; book well ahead.

● Many establishments run classes in English – confirm when you book.

For Kids

PAGE LIGHT STUDIOS/SHUTTERSTOCK ©

Parisians adore les enfants (children) and welcome them with open arms just about everywhere. French kids are generally quiet and polite, and you'll be expected to make sure yours are, too. But kids can still burn off plenty of energy: central Paris' residential design means you'll find playground equipment in parks and squares citywide.

Dining with Kids

Many restaurants accept little diners (confirm ahead). Children's menus aren't widespread, however, and most restaurants don't have highchairs.

Accommodation

Parisian buildings' limited space often means that apartments may be more economical. Check availability and costs for a *lit bébé* (cot).

Theme Parks

Just outside central Paris, theme parks include Disneyland Resort Paris (www.disney landparis.com), Parc Astérix (www.parcasterix.fr) and the Jardin d'Acclimatation (www. jardindacclimatation.fr).

Best Attractions for Kids

Le Grand Rex Kids can become movie stars on entertaining behind-the-scenes tours. (p86)

Jardin du Luxembourg Pony rides, puppet shows and more. (Pictured above; p178)

Vedettes de Paris Special 'Paris Mystery' Seine cruises for kids. (p23)

Galerie des Enfants Natural-history museum for six- to 12-year-olds within the Jardin des Plantes. (p160)

Getting Around with Kids

○ Children under four travel free on public transport and generally receive free admission to sights. Discounts vary for older kids.

○ Be extra vigilant crossing roads: Parisian drivers frequently ignore green pedestrian lights.

LGBT+

Paris has less of a defined gay and lesbian 'scene' than many cities. While Le Marais – particularly around the intersection of rues Ste-Croix de la Bretonnerie and des Archives – is the mainstay of gay and lesbian nightlife, venues throughout the city attract a mixed crowd.

NEIL ANTON DUMAS/SHUTTERSTOCK ©

Background

Paris was the first European capital to vote in an openly gay mayor when Bertrand Delanoë was elected in 2001. The city itself is very open – same-sex couples commonly display affection in public and checking into a hotel room is unlikely to raise eyebrows.

In 2013 France became the 13th country in the world to legalise same-sex marriage (and adoption by same-sex couples). Typically, at least one partner needs to be a resident to get married here.

Guided Tours

For an insider's perspective of LGBT+ life in Paris and recommendations on where to eat, drink, sightsee and party, take a tour with the **Gay Locals** (www.thegaylocals.com; 3hr tour from €180, 2½hr gay or lesbian bar crawl €50). English-speaking residents lead tours of Le Marais as well as private tours of other popular neighbourhoods and customised tours based on your interests.

Best LGBT+ Bars

Le Tango Mingle with a cosmopolitan gay and lesbian set in a historic 1930s dance hall. (p128)

Open Café The wide terrace is prime for talent-watching. (p128)

3w Kafé Flagship cocktail bar-pub. (p128)

Quetzal Perennial favourite; cruisy at all hours. (p128)

Four Perfect Days

Day 1

FLAVIA RADDAVERO/ALAMY ©

Stroll through the elegant **Jardin des Tuileries** (p78), stopping to view Monet's enormous *Water Lilies* at the **Musée de l'Orangerie** (p78). IM Pei's glass pyramid is the entrance to the labyrinthine **Louvre** (p68).

Browse the colonnaded arcades of the **Jardin du Palais Royal** (p79; pictured above), and pop into beautiful church **Église St-Eustache** (p78). Then head to the late-opening **Centre Pompidou** (p112) for modern and contemporary art and amazing rooftop views.

There's a wealth to see in Le Marais by day – **Musée National Picasso** (p118), **Musée des Arts et Métiers** (p118)... But it's at night that the neighbourhood really comes into its own, with a cornucopia of bars (p127).

Day 2

ZEFART/SHUTTERSTOCK ©

Climb the mighty **Arc de Triomphe** (p54) for a pinch-yourself Parisian panorama. Promenade down the glamorous **Champs-Élysées** (p53), and give your credit card a workout at **Galeries Lafayette** (p87) or **place de la Madeleine** (p89) before going behind the scenes of Paris' opulent opera house, the **Palais Garnier** (p79).

Check out global indigenous art at the **Musée du Quai Branly** (p44) and contemporary installations at the **Palais de Tokyo** (p60).

Sunset is the best time to ascend the **Eiffel Tower** (p38; pictured above), to experience dizzying daylight views and the glittering city by night.

Day 3

BRIAN KINNEY/SHUTTERSTOCK ©

Starting your day at the city's most visited sight, **Notre Dame** (p136; pictured above), gives you the best chance of beating the crowds. For more beautiful stained glass, don't miss nearby **Sainte-Chapelle** (p144). Buy a **Berthillon** (p145) ice cream before browsing Île St-Louis' enchanting boutiques.

Admire impressionist masterpieces in the magnificent **Musée d'Orsay** (p176), shop in St-Germain (p194), sip coffee on the terrace of literary cafe **Les Deux Magots** (p192) and laze in the lovely **Jardin du Luxembourg** (p178).

Scour the shelves of late-night bookshops including the legendary **Shakespeare & Company** (p169), then hit a jazz club such as **Café Universel** (p168).

Day 4

SAMANTHA OHLSEN/ALAMY ©

Montmartre's slinking streets and steep staircases lined with crooked ivy-clad buildings are enchanting places to meander. Head to hilltop **Sacré-Cœur** (p94), then brush up on the area's fabled history at the **Musée de Montmartre** (p99; pictured above).

Stroll the shaded towpaths of cafe-lined **Canal St-Martin** (p108). Sailing schedules permitting, hop on a canal cruise to Bastille.

The Bastille neighbourhood calls for a cafe crawl, especially on and around rue de la Roquette. Then salsa your socks off at the 1936 dance hall **Le Balajo** (p129) on nightlife strip rue de Lappe.

Need to Know

For detailed information, see Survival Guide (p203)

Currency
Euro (€)

Language
French

Visas
Generally no restrictions for EU citizens. Usually not required for most other nationalities for stays of up to 90 days.

Money
ATMs widely available. Visa and MasterCard accepted in most hotels, shops and restaurants; fewer accept American Express.

Time
Central European Time (GMT/UTC plus one hour)

Tipping
Already included in prices under French law, though if service is particularly good, you might tip an extra 5% to 10% in restaurants. Round taxi fares up to the nearest euro.

Daily Budget

Budget: Less than €100

Dorm bed: €25–50

Coffee/glass of wine/cocktail/*demi* (half-pint of beer): from €3/3.50/9/3.50

Excellent self-catering options, especially markets

Frequent free concerts and events

Public transport, stand-by theatre tickets

Midrange: €100–250

Double room: €130–250

Two-course meals: €20–40

Museums: free to around €12

Admission to clubs: free to around €20

Top End: More than €250

Historic luxury hotel double room: from €250

Gastronomic restaurant menus: from €40

Designer boutiques

Advance Planning

Two months before Book accommodation; organise opera, ballet or cabaret tickets; check events calendars to find out what festivals will be on; and make reservations for high-end and popular restaurants.

Two weeks before Sign up for a local-led tour and start narrowing down your choice of museums, pre-purchasing tickets online where possible.

Two days before Pack your comfiest shoes!

Arriving in Paris

Paris is well served by air and train, including Eurostar services linking London with Gare du Nord.

✈ Charles de Gaulle Airport

Around one hour northeast of central Paris.

Trains (RER B), **buses** and **night buses** to the city centre €6 to €17.

Taxis €50 to €63.25.

✈ Orly Airport

Around one hour south of central Paris.

Trains (Orlyval then RER), buses and night buses to the city centre €8.70 to €13.25.

Trams T7 to Villejuif–Louis Aragon then metro to centre (€3.80).

Taxis €30 to €40.25.

Getting Around

Walking is a pleasure, and Paris' efficient, inexpensive public transport system makes getting around a breeze.

Ⓜ Metro & RER

Metros and RER trains run from about 5.30am and finish around 12.35am or 1.15am (to around 2.15am on Friday and Saturday nights), depending on the line.

🚲 Bicycle

Virtually free pick-up, drop-off Vélib' bikes have stations citywide.

🚌 Bus

Buses are convenient for parents with prams/strollers and people with limited mobility.

⛴ Boat

The handy hop-on, hop-off Batobus boat service operates along the Seine.

🚕 Taxi

Find taxi ranks around major intersections.

Parisian *bar à vins* (wine bar)

Paris Neighbourhoods

Arc de Triomphe & the Champs-Elysées (p53)

This neighbourhood sees glamorous avenues flanked by flagship fashion houses, excellent museums and elegant restaurants.

Eiffel Tower & Les Invalides (p37)

Zipping up the spire is reason enough to visit, but this stately neighbourhood also has some unmissable museums.

◉ Arc de Triomphe

Musée d'Orsay ◉

◉ Eiffel Tower

Musée Rodin ◉

Musée d'Orsay & St-Germain des Prés (p175)

With a literary pedigree, cafe terraces and exquisite boutiques, this gentrified neighbourhood retains a cinematic quality.

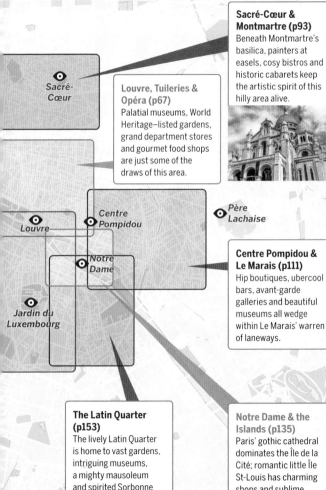

Sacré-Cœur & Montmartre (p93)
Beneath Montmartre's basilica, painters at easels, cosy bistros and historic cabarets keep the artistic spirit of this hilly area alive.

Louvre, Tuileries & Opéra (p67)
Palatial museums, World Heritage–listed gardens, grand department stores and gourmet food shops are just some of the draws of this area.

Sacré-Cœur

Père Lachaise

Louvre

Centre Pompidou

Notre Dame

Jardin du Luxembourg

Centre Pompidou & Le Marais (p111)
Hip boutiques, ubercool bars, avant-garde galleries and beautiful museums all wedge within Le Marais' warren of laneways.

The Latin Quarter (p153)
The lively Latin Quarter is home to vast gardens, intriguing museums, a mighty mausoleum and spirited Sorbonne university students.

Notre Dame & the Islands (p135)
Paris' gothic cathedral dominates the Île de la Cité; romantic little Île St-Louis has charming shops and sublime ice cream.

Explore
Paris

Eiffel Tower & Les Invalides 37

Arc de Triomphe & the Champs-Élysées ... 53

Louvre, Tuileries & Opéra 67

Sacré-Cœur & Montmartre 93

Centre Pompidou & Le Marais 111

Notre Dame & the Islands 135

The Latin Quarter 153

Musée d'Orsay & St Germain des Prés 175

Worth a Trip N

Père Lachaise 132

Versailles 198

Paris' Walking Tours N

Right Bank Covered Passages 74

Seine-Side Romantic Meander 90

Art in Montmartre 96

Exploring the Canal St-Martin 108

A Head's-Up on the Haute Marais 114

A Stroll along Rue Mouffetard 154

Southeastern Discovery 172

Left Bank Literary Loop 180

Place du Tertre (p97), Montmartre BORIS-B/SHUTTERSTOCK ©

Explore ◈
Eiffel Tower & Les Invalides

Home to very well-heeled Parisians, this grande dame of a neighbourhood stretching along the Seine's Left Bank to the west is where you can get up close and personal with magnificent architecture including the city's symbolic tower, as well as some outstanding museums that showcase history and exceptional art across myriad eras and cultures.

A river cruise is the ideal way to start (and/or end) a day in this iconic area, with several companies, such as Bateaux-Mouches (p23), stopping near the Eiffel Tower. Spend the morning exploring the Musée Rodin (p40) and its beautiful sculpture garden, then head to the Hôtel des Invalides (p44) to learn about French military history through the ages and pay homage at Napoléon's tomb. Check out the indigenous art and striking architecture of the Musée du Quai Branly (p44), then time your ascent of the Eiffel Tower (p38) for dusk for the best day and night-time views.

Getting There & Around

M Bir Hakeim (line 6) or Champ de Mars–Tour Eiffel (RER C).

M From Alma Marceau (line 9), it's an easy stroll over the Pont de l'Alma bridge.

🚢 In addition to river cruises, the hop-on, hop-off Batobus service starts and ends its run near the Eiffel Tower.

Neighbourhood Map on p42

Eiffel Tower (p38) GONZODL/SHUTTERSTOCK ©

Top Sight 📷
Eiffel Tower

There are different ways to experience the Eiffel Tower, from an evening ascent amid twinkling lights to a meal in one of its two restaurants. And even though some 6.2 million people come annually, few would dispute that each visit is unique – and something that simply has to be done when in Paris.

◎ **MAP P42, C3**

Champ de Mars, 5 av Anatole France, 7e

adult/child lift to top €25/6.30, lift to 2nd fl €16/4, stairs to 2nd fl €10/2.50

Ⓜ Bir Hakeim or RER Champ de Mars–Tour Eiffel

1st Floor

Of the tower's three floors, the 1st (57m) has the most space but the least impressive views. The glass-enclosed **Pavillon Ferrié** houses an immersion film along with a small cafe and souvenir shop, while the outer walkway features a discovery circuit to help visitors learn more about the tower's ingenious design. Check out the sections of glass flooring that proffer a dizzying view of the antlike people walking on the ground far below.

Not all lifts stop at the 1st floor (check before ascending), but it's an easy walk down from the 2nd floor should you accidentally end up one floor too high.

2nd Floor

Views from the 2nd floor (115m) are the best – impressively high but still close enough to see the details of the city below. Telescopes and panoramic maps placed around the tower pinpoint locations in Paris and beyond. Story windows give an overview of the lifts' mechanics, and the vision well allows you to gaze through glass panels to the ground. Also up here are toilets and a souvenir shop.

Top Floor

Views from the wind-buffeted top floor (276m; pictured left) stretch up to 60km on a clear day, though at this height the panoramas are more sweeping than detailed. Celebrate your ascent with a glass of bubbly (€13 to €22) from the Champagne bar (open noon to 5.15pm and 6.15pm to 10.45pm). Afterwards peep into Gustave Eiffel's restored top-level office where lifelike wax models of Eiffel and his daughter Claire greet Thomas Edison.

To access the top floor, take a separate lift on the 2nd floor (closed during heavy winds).

★ Top Tips

o Save time by buying lift tickets ahead online (www. toureiffel.paris). Choose a time slot and preprint tickets or use a smartphone that can be read by the scanner at the entrance.

o The top can be breezy; bring a jacket.

o There are extended opening hours during summer (lifts & stairs 9am-12.45am mid-Jun–Aug; lifts 9.30am-11.45pm, stairs 9.30am-6.30pm Sep–mid-Jun).

✗ Take a Break

Dine at the tower's 1st-floor brasserie **58 Tour Eiffel** (www.res taurants-toureiffel.com; menus lunch €37.20, dinner €93.70-113.70; ⏱11.30am-4.30pm & 6.30-11pm; 🖋 👪).

Savour cuisine at the Michelin-starred 2nd-floor gastronomic restaurant **Le Jules Verne** (www. lejulesverne-paris.com; 5-/6-course menus €190/230, 3-course lunch menu €105; ⏱noon-1.30pm & 7-9.30pm).

Top Sight 📷
Musée Rodin

Even if you're not an art lover, it is worth visiting this high-profile art museum to lose yourself in its romantic gardens. One of the most peaceful green oases in Paris, the formal flowerbeds and boxed-hedge arrangements framing 18th-century mansion Hôtel Biron house original sculptures by sculptor, painter, sketcher, engraver and collector Auguste Rodin. This is where he lived and worked while in Paris.

◎ MAP P42, G4

📞 01 44 18 61 10

www.musee-rodin.fr

79 rue de Varenne, 7e

adult/child €10/free, garden only €4/free

🕐 10am-5.45pm Tue-Sun

Ⓜ Varenne or Invalides

Collections

In 1908 Rodin donated his entire art collection to the French state on the proviso that they dedicate his former workshop and showroom, the 18th-century mansion Hôtel Biron (1730), to displaying his works. In addition to Rodin's own paintings and sketches, don't miss his prized collection of works by artists including Van Gogh and Monet.

The 'Rodin at the Hôtel Biron' room incorporates original furniture to re-create the space as it was when he lived and worked here.

Sculptures

The first large-scale cast of Rodin's famous sculpture **The Thinker** *(Le Penseur)*, made in 1902, resides in the garden – the perfect place to contemplate this heroic naked figure conceived by Rodin to represent intellect and poetry (it was originally titled *The Poet*).

The Gates of Hell *(La Porte de l'Enfer;* pictured left) was commissioned in 1880 as the entrance for a never-built museum, and Rodin worked on his sculptural masterpiece up until his death in 1917. Standing 6m high and 4m wide, its 180 figures comprise an intricate scene from Dante's *Inferno*.

Marble monument to love **The Kiss** *(Le Baiser)* was originally part of *The Gates of Hell*. The sculpture's entwined lovers caused controversy on completion due to Rodin's then-radical depiction of women as equal partners in ardour.

The museum also features many sculptures by Camille Claudel, Rodin's protégé and muse.

★ Top Tips

○ Prepurchase tickets online to avoid queuing.

○ Audioguides cost €6.

○ If you just want to see the outdoor sculptures, cheaper garden-only entry is available.

○ A combined ticket with the Musée d'Orsay (p176) costs €18; combination tickets are valid for a single visit to each of the museums within three months.

✖ Take a Break

Nearby *boulangeries* (bakeries) include **Besnier** (40 rue de Bourgogne, 7e; ⏱7am-8pm Mon-Sat, closed Aug; Ⓜ Varenne).

For traditional French fare, book a table at Paris' oldest and still excellent restaurant, À la Petite Chaise (p187).

Eiffel Tower & Les Invalides

For reviews see
Top Sights	p38
Sights	p44
Eating	p45
Drinking	p49
Shopping	p50

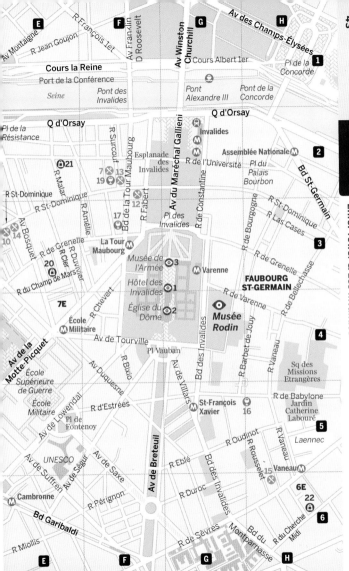

E
R François 1er
R Jean Goujon
Av Montaigne

F
Av Franklin
D Roosevelt

G
Av Winston Churchill

Av des Champs-Élysées

H
Pl de la Concorde
1

Cours Albert 1er

Cours la Reine
Port de la Conférence

Seine
Pont des Invalides

Pont Alexandre III
Pont de la Concorde

Q d'Orsay

Pl de la Résistance

Q d'Orsay

Invalides

Assemblée Nationale M

2

R Surcouf

Esplanade des Invalides

R de l'Université

Pl du Palais Bourbon

Bd St-Germain

21

R Malar
R St-Dominique

7 13
19

R de la Tour Maubourg

R St-Dominique
R Amélie

12

R Fabert

Av du Maréchal Gallieni

R de Constantine

R de Bourgogne

R St-Dominique
R Las Cases

10 14
Av Bosquet

17

Bd de la Tour Maubourg

Pl des Invalides

R de Grenelle

3

R de Grenelle
R Duvivier
R Cler

La Tour Maubourg M

Musée de l'Armée 3

Varenne M

20

R du Champ de Mars

Hôtel des Invalides 1

FAUBOURG ST-GERMAIN

R de Varenne

R de Bellechasse

7E

R Chevert

Église du Dôme 2

Musée Rodin

4

École Militaire M

Av de Tourville

Pl Vauban

Bd des Invalides

R Barbet de Jouy

R Vaneau

Sq des Missions Étrangères

Av de la Motte-Picquet

École Supérieure de Guerre

Av Duquesne

R Bixio

Av de Villars

R d'Estrées

St-François Xavier M
16

R de Babylone
Jardin Catherine Labouré

École Militaire

Av de Lowendal

Pl de Fontenoy

R Oudinot

R Rousselet

R Vaneau

Laennec

5

UNESCO

Av de Suffren
Av de Ségur
Av de Saxe

Av de Breteuil

R Eblé

Bd des Invalides

15

Vaneau M

M Cambronne

R Pérignon

R Duroc

6E

22

Bd Garibaldi

R Miollis

R de Sèvres

Bd du Montparnasse

R du Cherche Midi

6

E

F

G

H

Sights

Hôtel des Invalides

MONUMENT, MUSEUM

1 🎯 MAP P42, G3

Flanked by the 500m-long Esplanade des Invalides lawns, Hôtel des Invalides was built in the 1670s by Louis XIV to house 4000 *invalides* (disabled war veterans). On 14 July 1789, a mob broke into the building and seized 32,000 rifles before heading on to the prison at Bastille and the start of the French Revolution.Admission includes entry to all Hôtel des Invalides sights (temporary exhibitions cost extra). Hours for individual sites can vary – check the website for updates. (www.musee-armee.fr; 129 rue de Grenelle, 7e; adult/child €12/free; ⏱10am-6pm; Ⓜ Varenne, La Tour Maubourg)

Église du Dôme

CHURCH

2 🎯 MAP P42, G4

With its sparkling golden dome (1677–1735), the landmark church of Hôtel des Invalides is one of the finest religious edifices erected under Louis XIV and was the inspiration for the United States' Capitol building. It received the remains of Napoléon in 1840; the extravagant **Tombeau de Napoléon 1er** comprises six coffins fitting into one another like a Russian doll. (www.musee-armee.fr; 129 rue de Grenelle, 7e; included in Hôtel des Invalides entry; ⏱10am-7pm Jul & Aug, to 6pm Apr-Jun, Sep & Oct, to 5pm Nov-Mar; Ⓜ Varenne)

Musée de l'Armée

MUSEUM

3 🎯 MAP P42, G3

North of Hôtel des Invalides, in the Cour d'Honneur, is the Musée de l'Armée, which holds the nation's largest collection on French military history. (Army Museum; www.musee-armee.fr; 129 rue de Grenelle, 7e; included in Hôtel des Invalides entry; ⏱10am-6pm Apr-Oct, to 5pm Nov-Mar; Ⓜ Varenne, La Tour Maubourg)

Musée du Quai Branly

MUSEUM

4 🎯 MAP P42, D2

A tribute to the diversity of human culture, Musée du Quai Branly's highly inspiring overview of indigenous and folk art spans four main sections – Oceania, Asia, Africa and the Americas. An impressive array of masks, carvings, weapons, jewellery and more make up the body of the rich collection, displayed in a refreshingly unorthodox interior without rooms or high walls. Look out for excellent temporary exhibitions and performances. (☏ 01 56 61 70 00; www.quaibranly.fr; 37 quai Branly, 7e; adult/child €10/free; ⏱11am-7pm Tue, Wed & Sun, 11am-9pm Thu-Sat; Ⓜ Alma Marceau or RER Pont de l'Alma)

Parc du Champ de Mars

PARK

5 🎯 MAP P42, D4

Running southeast from the Eiffel Tower, the grassy Champ de Mars – an ideal summer picnic spot – was originally used as a parade ground for the cadets of the 18th-century **École Militaire**, the vast French-classical building at the southeastern end of the park, which counts Napoléon Bonaparte among its graduates. The steel-and-etched-glass **Wall for Peace Memorial** (http://wallforpeace.org), erected in 2000, is by Clara Halter. (Champ de Mars, 7e; Ⓜ École Militaire or RER Champ de Mars–Tour Eiffel)

Île aux Cygnes   ISLAND

6 ◎ MAP P42, A4

Paris' little-known third island, the artificially created Île aux Cygnes, was formed in 1827 to protect the river port and measures just 850m by 11m. On the western side of the Pont de Grenelle is a soaring one-quarter scale **Statue of Liberty** replica, inaugurated in 1889. Walk east along the Allée des Cygnes – the tree-lined walkway that runs the length of the island – for knock-out Eiffel Tower views. (Isle of Swans; btwn Pont de Grenelle & Pont de Bir Hakeim, 15e; Ⓜ Javel–André Citroën, Bir Hakeim)

Eating

Tomy & Co   GASTRONOMY €€

7 ✕ MAP P42, F2

Tomy Gousset's restaurant near Mademoiselle Eiffel has been a sensation since day one. The French-Cambodian chef works his magic on inspired seasonal dishes using produce from his organic garden. Winter ushers in aromatic black truffles (themed

Musée du Quai Branly

© MUSÉE DU QUAI BRANLY – JACQUES CHIRAC, PHOTO VINCENT MERCIER

tasting menu €95). The spectacular desserts – chocolate tart with fresh figs, Cambodian palm sugar and fig ice cream anyone? – are equally seasonal. Reservations essential. (📞01 45 51 46 93; 22 rue Surcouf, 7e; 2-course lunch menu €27, 3-course/tasting dinner menu €47/68, mains wine pairings €45; ⏱noon-2pm & 7.30-9.30pm Mon-Fri; Ⓜ Invalides)

Le Cassenoix   MODERN FRENCH €€

8 MAP P42, C4

The Nutcracker is everything a self-respecting neighbourhood bistro should be. *'Tradition et terroir'* (tradition and provenance) dictate the menu that inspires owner-chef Pierre Olivier Lenormand to deliver feisty dishes such as braised veal

---

Musée Marmottan Monet

The **Musée Marmottan Monet** (📞01 44 96 50 33; www.marmottan.fr; 2 rue Louis Boilly, 16e; adult/child €11/7.50; ⏱10am-6pm Tue, Wed & Fri-Sun, to 9pm Thu; Ⓜ La Muette) showcases the world's largest collection of works by impressionist painter Claude Monet (1840–1926) as well as paintings by Gauguin, Sisley, Pissarro, Renoir, Degas, Manet and Berthe Morisot. It also contains an important collection of French, English, Italian and Flemish illuminations from the 13th to 16th centuries.

---

chuck with mashed potato and caramelised onions or grilled hake with parsnips and hazelnut-parmesan crumble. Vintage ceiling fans add to the wonderful retro vibe. Book ahead. (📞01 45 66 09 01; www.le-cassenoix.fr; 56 rue de la Fédération, 15e; 3-course menu €34; ⏱noon-2.30pm & 7-10.30pm Mon-Fri; Ⓜ Bir Hakeim)

Arnaud Nicolas   FRENCH €€

9 MAP P42, D3

The upmarket hybrid restaurant and boutique of chef Arnaud Nicolas combines two natural French loves: gastronomy and charcuterie. Be it a posh pie (such as pork flavoured with herbs, or foie gras and quail with pear and pistachio), fancy terrine or a simple plate of cold cuts, this sleek address serves it to astonishing effect. End with a sublime dark-chocolate soufflé. (📞01 45 55 59 59; http://arnaudnicolas.paris/en; 46 ave de la Bourdonnais, 7e; 2-/3-course lunch menu €28/32, tasting menu €62; ⏱2-9.45pm Mon, noon-1.45pm & 2-9.45pm Tue-Sat; Ⓜ École Militaire)

Les Fables de la Fontaine   GASTRONOMY €€

10 MAP P42, E3

Prices at this Michelin-starred restaurant are a serious bargain and the lunchtime *menu* is an absolute steal. Chefs Julia Sedefdjian and David Bottreau create true works of art: on-the-shell oysters in vivid green cucumber jelly with green apple and lemon caviar;

almond-crusted veal with mashed artichokes and king trumpet mushrooms; and banana soufflé with rum ice cream. (☎01 44 18 37 55; www.lesfablesdelafontaine.net; 131 rue St-Dominique, 7e; 2-course weekday lunch menu €28, mains €21-29; ⏲noon-2.30pm & 7-10.30pm; Ⓜ École Militaire or RER Pont de l'Alma)

Café Constant
BISTRO €€

11 Ⓧ MAP P42, D3

Run by Michelin-starred chef Christian Constant, whose flagship **Le Violon d'Ingres** (☎01 45 55 15 05; 135 rue St-Dominique, 7e; 2-/3-course weekday lunch menu €49/55, tasting menu €130, mains €45-52; ⏲noon-2.30pm & 7-10.30pm) is on the same street, this traditional neighbourhood cafe with original bar and mosaic floor cooks up some fantastic staples: veal cordon bleu with mashed potato, herb-roasted chicken or beef stew followed by rice pudding. Breakfast is served until 11am, more substantial food continuously from noon until closing time. (☎01 47 53 73 34; www.maisonconstant.com; 139 rue St-Dominique, 7e; 2-/3-course weekday lunch menu €18/26, mains €18-29; ⏲7am-11pm Mon-Sat, 8am-11pm Sun; Ⓜ École Militaire or RER Pont de l'Alma)

Karamel
PASTRIES €

12 Ⓧ MAP P42, F2

Sweet-toothed gourmets won't do much better than a pit stop at the specialist boutique and *salon de thé* (tearoom) of *chef-pâtissier* Nicolas Haelewy. Exquisite rows of

Gourmet Picnic

The first of its kind, **Ladurée Picnic** (Map p42, A6; ☎01 70 22 45 20; www.laduree.fr; 16 rue Linois, 15e, Centre Commercial Beaugrenelle; breakfast/lunch menu €14.50/9.50, sandwiches/salads from €2.40/5.50; ⏲9.30am-8.30pm Mon-Sat, 10am-7pm Sun; Ⓜ Charles Michels) specialises in gourmet picnics to take away in the famous patisserie's signature peppermint-green packaging. Luxury salads include lobster or aromatic salmon; flavoured waters such as ginger and coriander and mint and cucumber are on offer; and the rainbow of cakes and macarons are out of this world.

fresh, caramel-spiked cakes jostle for the limelight with caramel-laced chocolate bars, jars of caramel spread, and chewy bite-sized caramels flavoured with vanilla and *fleur de sel* (rock salt), passion fruit or rose and raspberry. (☎01 71 93 02 94; https://karamelparis.com; 67 rue St-Dominique, 7e; ⏲8.30am-8.30pm; Ⓜ Invalides, Tour Maubourg)

Restaurant David Toutain
GASTRONOMY €€€

13 Ⓧ MAP P42, F2

Prepare to be wowed: David Toutain pushes the envelope at his eponymous Michelin-starred restaurant with some of the most creative high-end cooking in Paris. Mystery *dégustation* (tasting) courses include unlikely combinations such as smoked eel in green-apple-and-black-sesame mousse, cauliflower, white chocolate and coconut truffles, or candied celery and truffled rice pudding with artichoke praline. Stunning wine pairings are available. (01 45 50 11 10; http://davidtoutain.com; 29 rue Surcouf, 7e; 3-course lunch menu €55, tasting menus €80-140, wine pairings €70-100; 12.30-2pm & 8-10pm Mon, noon-2pm & 8-10pm Tue-Fri; Invalides)

Le Fontaine de Mars BISTRO €€

14 MAP P42, E3

For traditional French cooking look no further than this 1930s-styled neighbourhood bistro with signature lace curtains, checked tablecloths and – best of all – a fishmonger in front shucking oysters at his stall beneath the bistro arches. Snails, *boudin* (black pudding), *andouillette* (Lyonnais tripe sausage) and homemade *confit de canard* (preserved duck breast) are among the traditional mainstays, alongside sensational seafood platters. (01 47 05 46 44; www.fontainedemars.com; 129 rue St-Dominique, 7e; seafood platters from €49, mains €17-35; noon-3pm & 7.30-11pm; École Militaire)

Plume BISTRO €€€

15 MAP P42, H6

A minimalist, 1950s ambience co-coons discerning diners at Plume ('Feather'), the stylish neobistro of talented young Tunisian chef

Café Constant (p47)

GILLES TARGAT/PHOTO12/ALAMY ©

Youssef Gastli. His modern French cuisine translates as scallops with celeriac and horseradish perhaps, or fish of the day with wild rice, saffron, wild herbs and *poutargue* (cured fish roe), complemented by a fantastic wine list featuring wholly organic, biodynamic or natural wines. (☏ 01 43 06 79 85; www.restaurantplume.com; 24 rue Pierre Leroux, 7e; 2-/3-course lunch menu €27/37, 3-/5-course dinner menu €45/65, mains €29-32; ⏲ noon-2.15pm & 7.30-10.15pm Tue-Sat; Ⓜ Vaneau, Duroc)

Drinking

Coutume Café COFFEE

16 Ⓟ MAP P42, H5

The Parisian coffee revolution is thanks in no small part to Coutume, artisanal roaster of premium beans for scores of establishments around town. Its flagship cafe – a bright, light-filled, postindustrial space – is ground zero for innovative preparation methods including cold extraction and siphon brews. Couple some of Paris' finest coffee with a tasty, seasonal cuisine and the place is always packed out. (☏ 01 45 51 50 47; www.coutume cafe.com; 47 rue de Babylone, 7e; ⏲ 8.30am-5.30pm Mon-Fri, 9am-6pm Sat & Sun; 🛜; Ⓜ St-François Xavier)

Fitzgerald COCKTAIL BAR

17 Ⓟ MAP P42, F3

Smoked Bloody Mary, Like a Porn Star, Diamond, Rich Boy and Zelda

Gourmet Rue Cler

Pick up fresh bread, sandwich fillings, pastries and wine for a picnic along the typically Parisian commercial street rue Cler, 7e, which buzzes with local shoppers, especially on weekends.

Interspersed between the *boulangeries* (bakeries), *fromageries* (cheese shops), grocers, butchers, delis and other food shops (many with pavement stalls), lively cafe terraces overflow with locals.

Negroni (named after American writer F Scott Fitzgerald's wife) are among the evocatively named cocktails (€13 to €15) on the menu at chic Fitzgerald. Posh snacks to accompany include a truffle-laced croque monsieur and 22 month-aged Iberian ham, and there's a fully fledged restaurant should hard-on hunger strike. (☏ 01 45 50 38 63; http://fitzgerald.paris; 54 bd de la Tour Maubourg, 7e; ⏲ noon-3pm & 6pm-2am Mon-Sat; Ⓜ La Tour Maubourd)

Terres de Café COFFEE

18 Ⓟ MAP P42, D3

'Roasted with goodness' is the strapline of this specialist coffee roaster whose pocket-sized coffee shop on ave de la Bourdonnais is the perfect bolthole after scaling the Eiffel Tower or picnicking on neighbouring Champs de Mars.

Grab a pew at one of five tables inside or admire the barista's latte art over a cappuccino on the pavement terrace in front. (☎01 45 50 37 39; www.terresdecafe.com; 67 av de la Bourdonnais, 7e; ◷9am-6.30pm Mon-Sat, to 6pm Sun; ⓜÉcole Militaire)

The Club
COCKTAIL BAR

19 ⓔ MAP P42, F2

At street level The Club has New York–warehouse brickwork and big timber cabinets, but the lounge-like basement, strewn with red and black sofas, is even cooler. Cocktails include the house-speciality Club (lime, fresh ginger and Jack Daniels honey liqueur) and seasonally changing creations, or ask for the bar staff to surprise you with their own concoctions.

(☎01 45 50 31 54; www.the-club.fr; 24 rue Surcouf, 7e; ◷4pm-1.30am Mon-Sat; ⓜLa Tour-Maubourg)

Shopping

Cantin
CHEESE

20 🔒 MAP P42, E3

Opened in 1950 and still run by the same family today, this exceptional shop stocks cheeses only made in limited quantities on small rural farms. They're then painstakingly ripened in Cantin's own cellars (from two weeks up to two years) before being displayed for sale. Should you want to know how to concoct the perfect cheeseboard, Cantin runs informative tasting workshops. (☎01 45 5043 94; www.cantin.fr; 12 rue du Champs de Mars,

Fromagerie (cheese shop), rue Cler (p49)

BORIS KARPINSKI/ALAMY ©

Understand:
Charles de Gaulle & WWII

The WWII battle for France began in earnest in May 1940 and by 14 June France had capitulated. Paris was occupied, and almost half the population evacuated. General Charles de Gaulle, France's undersecretary of war, fled to London. In a radio broadcast on 18 June 1940, he appealed to French patriots to continue resisting the Germans. He set up a French government-in-exile and established the Forces Françaises Libres (Free French Forces), fighting alongside the Allies. Paris was liberated on 25 August 1944 by an Allied force spearheaded by Free French units.

De Gaulle returned to Paris and set up a provisional government, but in January 1946 he resigned, wrongly believing that the move would provoke a popular outcry for his return. De Gaulle formed his own party (Rassemblement du Peuple Français) and remained in opposition until 1958, when he was brought back to power to prevent a military coup over the uprising in Algeria. He resigned as president in 1969, succeeded by Gaullist prime minister Georges Pompidou.

7e; ⏱2-7.30pm Mon, 8.30am-7.30pm Tue-Sat, 8.30am-1pm Sun; Ⓜ École Militaire)

Maison Chaudun   CHOCOLATE

21 🅐 MAP P42, E2

Ganache *pavés* ('cobblestones' torn up and thrown during Paris' May 1968 student uprisings) are the stand-outs at Michel Chaudun's entrancing chocolate shop, which resembles a toy shop thanks to creations such as chocolate horses and chess pieces. (📞01 47 53 74 40; www.chaudun.com; 149 rue de l'Université, 7e; ⏱10am-7pm Mon-Sat, 10am-5pm Sun; Ⓜ La Tour Maubourg)

Chercheminippes   VINTAGE

22 🅐 MAP P42, H6

Shop for second-hand designer pieces of women's casual wear at this beautifully presented boutique. It has several other shops scattered along the same street, each specialsiing in a different genre: accessories at No 104, homewares at No 109, kids' fashion at No 110, men's fashion at No 111 and women's *haute couture* at No 114. (www.chercheminippes.com; 102 rue du Cherche Midi, 6e; ⏱11am-7pm Mon-Sat; Ⓜ Vaneau)

Explore ◈

Arc de Triomphe & the Champs-Élysées

Pomp and grandeur reign: Baron Haussmann famously reshaped the Parisian cityscape around the Arc de Triomphe, from which a dozen avenues radiate like the spokes of a wheel. The most celebrated is the luxury-shop-lined av des Champs-Élysées. The neighbourhood's splendour extends to its haute cuisine restaurants and haute couture (high fashion) houses.

Climb above the Champs-Élysées to the top of the Arc de Triomphe (p54), then stroll along this famous avenue named for the Elysian Fields. After visiting the Musée Jacquemart-André (p58), wander among the fashion houses of the Triangle d'Or, and admire ornate artefacts at the Musée Guimet des Arts Asiatiques (p58) or catch an exhibition at the Grand Palais (p59). Next, snap a postcard-perfect photo of the Eiffel Tower from the terrace of the Palais de Chaillot (p60) and visit its exceptional museum, the Cité de l'Architecture et du Patrimoine (p58).

Getting There & Around

Ⓜ Charles de Gaulle–Étoile (lines 1, 2, 6 and RER A) is adjacent to the Arc de Triomphe.

Ⓜ The Champs-Élysées' other metro stops are George V (line 1), Franklin D Roosevelt (lines 1 and 9) and Champs-Élysées–Clemenceau (1 and 13).

🚤 The hop-on, hop-off Batobus stops near the Champs-Élysées by Pont Alexandre III.

Neighbourhood Map on p56

The Champs-Élysées BENNY MARTY/SHUTTERSTOCK ©

Top Sight 📷
Arc de Triomphe

Napoléon's armies never did march through the Arc de Triomphe showered in honour, but the monument has nonetheless come to stand as the very symbol of French patriotism. It's not for nationalistic sentiments, however, that so many visitors huff up the narrow, spiralling staircase. Rather it's the sublime panoramas from the top that make the arch such a notable attraction.

◉ MAP P56, C2

www.paris-arc-de-triomphe.fr

place Charles de Gaulle, 8e

🕙 10am–11pm Apr–Sep, to 10.30pm Oct–Mar

Ⓜ Charles de Gaulle–Étoile

Beneath the Arch

Beneath the arch at ground level lies the **Tomb of the Unknown Soldier**. Honouring the 1.3 million French soldiers who lost their lives in WWI, the Unknown Soldier was laid to rest in 1921, beneath an eternal flame that is rekindled daily at 6.30pm.

Bronze plaques laid into the ground mark significant moments in modern French history, such as the proclamation of the Third French Republic (4 September 1870) and the text from Charles de Gaulle's famous London broadcast on 18 June 1940, which sparked the French Resistance to life.

Sculptures

The arch is adorned with four main sculptures, six panels in relief, and a frieze running beneath the top. The most famous sculpture is the one to the right as you approach from the Champs-Élysées: *La Marseillaise* (Departure of the Volunteers of 1792). Sculpted by François Rude, it depicts soldiers of all ages gathering beneath the wings of victory, en route to drive back the invading armies of Prussia and Austria.

Viewing Platform

Climb the 284 steps to the **viewing platform** (adult/child €12/free) at the top of the 50m-high arch and you'll be suitably rewarded with magnificent panoramas over western Paris. The Arc de Triomphe is the highest point in the line of monuments known as the *axe historique* (historic axis, also called the grand axis); it offers views that swoop east down the Champs-Élysées to the gold-tipped obelisk at place de la Concorde (and beyond to the Louvre's glass pyramid), and west to the skyscraper district of La Défense, where the colossal Grande Arche marks the axis' western terminus.

★ Top Tips

o Don't try to cross the traffic-choked roundabout above ground! Stairs on the Champs-Élysées' northeastern side lead beneath the Étoile to pedestrian tunnels that bring you out safely beneath the arch.

o Don't risk getting skittled by traffic by taking photos while crossing the Champs-Élysées.

o There is a lift (elevator) at the arch, but it's only for visitors with limited mobility or those travelling with young children, and there are still some unavoidable steps.

✗ Take a Break

o Right near the arch, **Publicis Drugstore** (☎01 44 43 75 07; www.publicisdrug store.com; 133 av des Champs-Élysées, 8e; ◷8am-2am Mon-Fri, 10am-2pm Sat & Sun; Ⓜ Charles de Gaulle-Étoile) is handy for a meal, drink or snack.

o Pair an evening visit with a traditional French dinner at Le Hide (p62).

Arc de Triomphe & the Champs-Élysées

E Parc Monceau **F** **G** **H**

R de Courcelles

R Murillo

R de Monceau

R de Lisbonne

Bd Malesherbes

R du Général Foy

R du Rocher

R de Rome

1

R du Docteur Lancereaux

Av de Messine

Musée Jacquemart-André **2**

Bd Haussmann

R de Courcelles

Av Percier

R de Miromesnil

Bd Haussmann **23**

Sq M Pagnol

St-Augustin

Pl St-Augustin

Bd Malesherbes

2

R de Berri

R d'Artois

St-Philippe du Roule

R de la Boétie

R du Faubourg St-Honoré

R de la Boétie

R de Penthièvre

R de la Boétie

R Cambacérès

R Roquépine

R de Surène

R d'Anjou

3

Galerie du Claridge **24**

R de Ponthieu

25

R du Colisée

8E

R Jean Mermoz

Miromesnil

Le Grand Musée du Parfum **6**

Pl Beauvau

R d'Aguesseau

20

R du Faubourg St-Honoré

R Boissy d'Anglas

3

R Marbeuf

21

Franklin D Roosevelt

R de Marignan

16

Rond Point Champs-Élysées Marcel Dassault

Av Matignon

Av de Marigny

R de l'Élysée

4

R François 1er

Av Montaigne

Av Franklin D Roosevelt

Champs-Élysées Clemenceau

Av du Général Eisenhower

Pl Clemenceau

Av Gabriel

Av des Champs-Élysées

Concorde

4

Pl François 1er

R Jean Goujon

14

Grand Palais **5**

Av Winston Churchill

Petit Palais **7**

Av Dutuit

Cours Albert 1er

Pl de la Concorde

5

Cours la Reine

Porte de la Conférence

Seine

Pont des Invalides

Pl de Finlande

Pont Alexandre III

Pont de la Concorde

Q d'Orsay

Q d'Orsay

R de l'Université

7E

Bd de la Tour Maubourg

R Fabert

Av du Maréchal Galliéni

Invalides

Assemblée Nationale

6

Esplanade des Invalides

E R St-Dominique **F** **G** **H**

For reviews see	
⊙ Top Sights	p54
⊙ Sights	p58
⊗ Eating	p61
⊖ Drinking	p64
⊖ Shopping	p65

Sights

Cité de l'Architecture et du Patrimoine

MUSEUM

1 ◉ MAP P56, A5

This mammoth 23,000-sq-metre space is an ode on three floors to French architecture. The highlight is the light-filled ground floor with a beautiful collection of plaster and wood *moulages* (casts) of cathedral portals, columns and gargoyles. Replicas of murals and stained glass originally created for the 1878 Exposition Univer-selle are on display on the upper floors. Views of the Eiffel Tower are equally monumental. (www.citechaillot.fr; 1 place du Trocadéro et du 11 Novembre, 16e; adult/child €8/free; ⏰11am-7pm Wed & Fri-Sun, to 9pm Thu; Ⓜ Trocadéro)

Musée Jacquemart-André

MUSEUM

2 ◉ MAP P56, F2

The home of art collectors Nélie Jacquemart and Édouard André, this opulent late-19th-century residence combined elements from different eras – seen here in the presence of Greek and Roman antiquities, Egyptian artefacts, period furnishings and portraits by Dutch masters. Its 16 rooms offers an absorbing glimpse of the lifestyle of Parisian high society: from the library, hung with canvases by Rembrandt and Van Dyck, to the marvellous Jardin d'Hiver – a glass-paned garden room backed by a magnificent double-helix staircase. (☎01 45 62 11 59; www.musee-jacquemart-andre.com; 158 bd Haussmann, 8e; adult/child €13.50/10.50; ⏰10am-6pm, to 8.30pm Mon during temporary exhibitions; Ⓜ Miromesnil)

Musée Guimet des Arts Asiatiques

GALLERY

3 ◉ MAP P56, B5

Connoisseurs of Japanese ink paintings and Tibetan thangkas won't want to miss the Musée Guimet, the largest Asian art museum in France. Observe the gradual transmission of both Buddhism and artistic styles along the Silk Road in pieces ranging from 1st-century Gandhara Buddhas from Afghanistan and Pakistan to later Central Asian, Chinese and Japanese Buddhist sculptures and art. (☎01 56 52 53 00; www.guimet.fr; 6 place d'Iéna, 16e; adult/child €8.50/free; ⏰10am-6pm Wed-Mon; Ⓜ Iéna)

Musée Yves Saint Laurent Paris

MUSEUM

4 ◉ MAP P56, C5

Housed in the legendary designer's studios (1974–2002), this museum holds retrospectives of YSL's avant-garde designs, from early sketches to finished pieces. Temporary exhibitions give an insight into the creative process of designing a *haute couture* collection and the history of fashion throughout the 20th century. The building can only accommodate a small number of visitors at a time, so buy tickets online or expect to queue outside. (☎01 44 31 64 00; www.museeyslparis.com; 5 av Marceau, 16e; adult/child €10/7; ⊙11am-6pm Tue-Thu, Sat & Sun, to 9pm Fri; Ⓜ Alma-Marceau)

Grand Palais GALLERY

5 ◉ MAP P56, F4

Erected for the 1900 Exposition Universelle (World's Fair), the Grand Palais today houses several exhibition spaces beneath its huge 8.5-tonne art nouveau glass roof. Some of Paris' biggest shows (Renoir, Chagall, Turner) are held in the **Galeries Nationales**, lasting three to four months. Hours, prices and exhibition dates vary significantly for all galleries. Reserving a ticket online for any show is strongly advised. Note that the Grand Palais

will close for renovations from late 2020 to mid-2024. (☎01 44 13 17 17; www.grandpalais.fr; 3 av du Général Eisenhower, 8e; adult/child €14/free; ⊙10am-8pm Thu-Mon, to 10pm Wed; Ⓜ Champs-Élysées–Clemenceau)

Le Grand Musée du Parfum MUSEUM

6 ◉ MAP P56, G3

There are several perfume museums in Paris, but this is the only one that's not run by a major brand. Opened in 2016, it starts with history exhibits (ancient perfume bottles, interpretive French/English panels) in the basement, but the most engaging sections are upstairs. The 1st floor is a heady sensory guide, revealing the chemical processes while you identify

Musée Yves Saint Laurent Paris

Fondation Louis Vuitton

Designed by Frank Gehry, the striking glass-panelled **Fondation Louis Vuitton** (01 40 69 96 00; www.fondationlouisvuitton.fr; 8 av du Mahatma Gandhi, 16e; adult/child €16/5; hours vary with exhibit; Les Sablons) in the Bois de Bologne hosts major temporary contemporary art exhibitions: check online for the latest show. A **shuttle** (Map p56, C2; 44 ave Friedland, 8e; round trip €2) runs from the Arc de Triomphe to the museum and back during opening hours.

scents. The 2nd floor showcases the art of fragrance creation and the instruments with which professional perfumers work. (01 42 65 25 44; www.grandmuseeduparfum.fr; 73 rue du Faubourg St-Honoré, 8e; adult/child €14.50/5; 10.30am-7pm Tue-Sun; Miromesnil)

Petit Palais
GALLERY

 7 MAP P56, G5

This architectural stunner was built for the 1900 Exposition Universelle, and is home to the **Musée des Beaux-Arts de la Ville de Paris** (City of Paris Museum of Fine Arts). It specialises in medieval and Renaissance objets d'art, such as porcelain and clocks, tapestries, drawings, and 19th-century French paintings and sculpture; there are also paintings by such artists as Rembrandt, Colbert, Cézanne, Monet, Gauguin and Delacroix. (Musée des Beaux-Arts de la Ville de Paris; 01 53 43 40 00; www.petitpalais.paris.fr; av Winston Churchill, 8e; suggested donation €2; 10am-6pm Tue-Sun, to 9pm Fri; Champs-Élysées–Clemenceau)

Palais de Chaillot
HISTORIC BUILDING

8 MAP P56, A6

The two curved, colonnaded wings of this building (built for the 1937 International Expo) and central terrace afford an exceptional panorama of the **Jardins du Trocadéro**, Seine and Eiffel Tower. The eastern wing houses the standout Cité de l'Architecture et du Patrimoine (p58), devoted to French architecture and heritage, as well as the **Théâtre National de Chaillot** (01 53 65 30 00; http://theatre-chaillot.fr), staging dance and theatre. The Musée de la Marine, closed for renovations until 2021, and the **Musée de l'Homme** (Museum of Humankind; 01 44 05 72 72; www.museedelhomme.fr; adult/child €10/free; 10am-6pm Wed-Mon) are housed in the western wing. (place du Trocadéro et du 11 Novembre, 16e; Trocadéro)

Palais de Tokyo
GALLERY

 9 MAP P56, C5

The Tokyo Palace, created for the 1937 Exposition Internationale des Arts et Techniques dans la Vie Moderne (International Exposition of Art and Technology in Modern Life), has no permanent collection. Instead, its shell-like interior of concrete and steel is a stark backdrop to interactive contemporary-art exhibitions and installations. Its bookshop is fabulous for art and design magazines, and its eating and drinking options are magic. (01 81 97 35 88; www.palaisdetokyo.com; 13 av du Président Wilson, 16e; adult/child €12/free; noon-midnight Wed-Mon; Ména)

Palais Galliera MUSEUM

10 MAP P56, C5

Paris' Fashion Museum warehouses some 100,000 outfits and accessories – from canes and umbrellas to fans and gloves – from the 18th century to the present day. The permanent collection will go on display beginning in 2019. The sumptuous Italianate palace and gardens dating from the mid-19th century are worth a visit in themselves. It is closed until 2019 for renovations. (01 56 52 86 00; www.palaisgalliera.paris.fr; 10 av Pierre 1er de Serbie, 16e; adult/child €10/free; 10am-6pm Tue-Sun, to 9pm Thu; Ména)

Musée d'Art Moderne de la Ville de Paris GALLERY

11 MAP P56, C5

The permanent collection at Paris' modern-art museum displays works representative of just about every major artistic movement of the 20th and (nascent) 21st centuries, with works by Modigliani, Matisse, Braque and Soutine. The real jewel, though, is the room hung with canvases by Dufy and Bonnard. Look out for cutting-edge temporary exhibitions (not free). (01 53 67 40 00; www.mam. paris.fr; 11 av du Président Wilson, 16e; admission free; 10am-6pm Tue, Wed, Fri-Sun, 10am-10pm Thu; Ména)

Eating

Ladurée PASTRIES €€

12 MAP P56, D3

One of Paris' oldest patisseries, Ladurée has been around since 1862 and first created the lighter-than-air, ganache-filled macaron in the 1930s. Its tearoom is the classiest spot to indulge on the

Grande Arche

La Défense's landmark edifice is the marble **Grande Arche** (01 40 90 52 20; www.lagrande arche.fr; 1 Parvis de la Défense; adult/child €15/7; 10am-7pm; Méla Défense), a cube-like arch built in the 1980s to house government and business offices. The arch marks the western end of the *axe historique* (historic axis), though Danish architect Johan-Otto von Sprekelsen deliberately placed the Grande Arche fractionally out of alignment. Spectacular views extend from the rooftop. Temporary photojournalism exhibits are held in the museum.

Moveable Feast

A true moveable feast, **Bustronome** (Map p56, B3; 📱09 54 44 45 55; www.bustronome.com; 2 av Kléber, 16e; 4-course lunch €65, 6-course dinner €100; ⏱by reservation 12.15pm, 12.45pm, 7.45pm & 8.45pm; 📱🚹; MKléber, Charles de Gaulle–Étoile) is a voyage into French gastronomy aboard a glass-roofed bus, with Paris' famous monuments – the Arc de Triomphe, Grand Palais, Palais Garnier, Notre Dame and Eiffel Tower – gliding by as you dine on seasonal creations prepared in the purpose-built vehicle's lower-deck galley. Children's menus for lunch/dinner cost €40/50; vegetarian, vegan and gluten-free menus are available.

Champs. Alternatively, pick up some pastries to go – from croissants to its trademark macarons, it's all quite heavenly. A three-course children's menu costs €19. (📱01 40 75 08 75; www.laduree.com; 75 av des Champs-Élysées, 8e; pastries from €2.60, mains €18-47, 2-/3-course menu €35/42; ⏱7.30am-11pm Sun-Thu, 7.30am-midnight Fri & Sat; 🚹; MGeorge V)

Le Hide   FRENCH €€

13 🍴 MAP P56, B1

A perpetual favourite, Le Hide is a tiny neighbourhood bistro serving scrumptious traditional

French fare: snails, seared duck breast with celery puree and truffle oil, baked shoulder of lamb, and monkfish with *beurre blanc* (white sauce). Unsurprisingly, this place fills up faster than you can scamper down the steps of the nearby Arc de Triomphe (p54) – reserve well in advance. (📱01 45 74 15 81; www.lehide.fr; 10 rue du Général Lanrezac, 17e; 2-/3-course menus €36/48; ⏱6-10.30pm Mon-Sat; MCharles de Gaulle–Étoile)

Lasserre   GASTRONOMY €€€

14 🍴 MAP P56, F4

Since 1942, this exceedingly elegant restaurant in the Triangle d'Or has hosted style icons, including Audrey Hepburn, and is still a superlative choice for a Michelin-starred meal to remember. A bellhop-attended lift (elevator), white-and-gold chandeliered decor, extraordinary retractable roof and flawless service set the stage for inspired creations such as roast blue lobster *à la Parisienne* with tarragon sauce. Observe the dress code. (📱01 43 59 02 13; www.restaurant-lasserre.com; 17 av Franklin D Roosevelt, 8e; 3-course lunch menu €60, tasting menu €190, mains €85-130; ⏱noon-2pm Thu & Fri, 7-10pm Tue-Sat; MFranklin D Roosevelt)

86 Champs   PASTRIES €€

15 🍴 MAP P56, D3

A swirling fantasy of floral aromas – vervain, rose, lavender – lures visitors into this opulent shrine to French pastries.

It's half Pierre Hermé (of macaron fame), half L'Occitane (Provençe-themed beauty products); after you're done browsing the boutique, head to the horseshoe-shaped dessert bar in the back, where you can dine on whimsical creations prepared in front of you. (☎01 70 38 77 38; www.86champs.com; 86 av Champs-Élysées, 8e; ⏰8.30am-11.30pm Sun-Thu, to 12.30am Fri & Sat; Ⓜ George V)

Framboise

CRÊPES €

16 MAP P56, F3

Tucked in among a string of Asian takeaways is this delightful, contemporary crêperie. With an emphasis on quality (eg organic buckwheat flour), this is a top pick for an inexpensive meal off the Champs-Élysées. (☎01 74 64 02 79; www.creperieframboise.fr; 7 rue de Ponthieu, 8e; 2-course lunch €13.90, crêpes from €8.70; ⏰noon-2.30pm & 7-10pm; Ⓜ Franklin D Roosevelt)

Philippe & Jean-Pierre

FRENCH €€€

17 MAP P56, D4

Philippe graciously oversees the elegant, white-tableclothed dining room, while co-owner Jean-Pierre helms the kitchen. Seasonal menus incorporate dishes such as cauliflower cream soup with mushrooms and truffles, sautéed scallops with leek and Granny Smith sauce, and melt-in-the-middle *moelleux au chocolat* cake. Given the service, quality and gilt-edged Triangle d'Or location, prices are almost a bargain. (☎01 47 23 57 80;

Macarons, Ladurée (p61)

7 rue du Boccador, 8e; 4-/5-course menu €44/54, mains €26-43; ⏰noon-2.15pm Mon-Fri, 7.15-10.45pm Mon-Sat; Ⓜ Alma Marceau)

Atelier Vivanda
FRENCH €€

18 ⊗ MAP P56, B3

A micro outpost of carnivore heaven, tucked away down an inconspicuous side street 10 minutes from the Arc de Triomphe. The Atelier focuses uniquely on high-quality meat and poultry; the three-course meal is a deal in this neighbourhood. You can also get frog legs, snails and fondue in season. Reserve. (☏01 40 67 10 00; www.ateliervivanda.com; 18 rue Lauriston, 16e; 2-/3-course meal €32/38, mains €28; ⏰noon-2.30pm & 7.30-10.30pm Mon-Fri; Ⓜ Charles de Gaulle–Étoile)

Drinking

St James Paris
BAR

19 ⏰ MAP P56, A3

Hidden behind a stone wall, this historic mansion-turned-hotel opens its bar nightly to nonguests – and the setting redefines extraordinary. Winter drinks are in the wood-panelled library; summer drinks are on the impossibly romantic 300-sq-metre garden terrace with giant balloon-shaped gazebos (the first hot-air balloons took flight here). It has over 70 cocktails and an adjoining Michelin-starred restaurant. (www.saint-james-paris.com; 43 av Bugeaud, 16e; ⏰7pm-1am; 📶; Ⓜ Porte Dauphine)

Honor
COFFEE

20 ⏰ MAP P56, H3

Hidden off ritzy rue du Faubourg St-Honoré in a courtyard adjoining fashion house Comme des Garçons is Paris' 'first and only outdoor independent coffee shop', an opaque-plastic-sheltered black-and-white timber kiosk brewing coffee from small-scale producers around the globe. It also serves luscious cakes, filled-to-bursting lunchtime sandwiches, quiches and salads (dishes €5 to €10.50), along with fresh juices, wine and beer. (www.honor-cafe.com; 54 rue du Faubourg St-Honoré, 8e; ⏰9am-6pm Mon-Sat; Ⓜ Madeleine)

Zig Zag Club
CLUB

21 ⏰ MAP P56, E4

With star DJs, a great sound and light system, and a spacious dance floor, Zig Zag has some of the hippest electro beats in western Paris. It can be pricey, but it still fills up quickly, so don't start the party too late. (http://zigzagclub.fr; 32 rue Marbeuf, 8e; ⏰11.30pm-7am Fri & Sat; Ⓜ Franklin D Roosevelt)

Upper Crèmerie
BAR

22 ⏰ MAP P56, C3

The sun-flooded tables at this hybrid cafe–cocktail bar in a quintessential Parisian pavement terrace heave at lunchtime and after work with a well-dressed crowd from surrounding offices. Inside, vivid colours and neon lighting reassure trendsetters that the place is anything but traditional. Cocktails and food (€11 to €13) hit the spot. (📞01 40 70 93 23; 71 av Marceau, 16e; 🕑9am-midnight Mon-Fri; 📶; Ⓜ Kléber, George V)

Shopping

Les Caves Augé   WINE

23 🔒 MAP P56, H2

Founded in 1850, this fantastic wine shop, with bottles stacked in every conceivable nook and cranny, should be your first choice if you trust the taste of Marcel Proust, who was a regular customer. The shop organises tastings every other Saturday (see website), where you can meet local winemakers from different regions. (📞01 45 22 16 97; www.cavesauge. com; 116 bd Haussmann, 8e; 🕑10am-7.30pm Mon-Sat; Ⓜ St-Augustin)

Guerlain   PERFUME

24 🔒 MAP P56, E3

Guerlain is Paris' most famous parfumerie, and its shop (dating from 1912) is one of the most beautiful in the city. With its shimmering mirror-and-marble art deco interior, it's a reminder of the former glory of the Champs-Élysées. For total indulgence, make an appointment

Golden Triangle

A stroll around the legendary **Triangle d'Or** (Golden Triangle; bordered by avs George V, Champs-Élysées and Montaigne, 8e) constitutes the walk of fame of top French fashion. Rubbing shoulders with the world's top international designers are Paris' most influential French fashion houses, such as Chanel, Chloé, Dior, Givenchy, Hermès, Lanvin, Louis Vuitton and Saint Laurent.

at its heavenly spa. (📞spa 01 45 62 11 21; www.guerlain.com; 68 av des Champs-Élysées, 8e; 🕑10.30am-8pm Mon-Sat, noon-8pm Sun; Ⓜ Franklin D Roosevelt)

Galeries Lafayette – Champs-Élysées   DEPARTMENT STORE

25 🔒 MAP P56, E3

The new Galeries Lafayette on the Champs-Élysées is located in one of the avenue's earliest art deco buildings. Although smaller than the main Haussmann store (p87), it will undoubtedly be more modern with a layout specifically tailored to today's shoppers. It's expected to open in early 2019. (www.galerieslafayette.com; 52 av Champs-Élysées; Ⓜ Franklin D Roosevelt)

Explore ◈

Louvre, Tuileries & Opéra

Carving its way through the city, Paris' axe historique (historic axis) passes through the Tuileries gardens before reaching IM Pei's glass pyramid at the entrance to Paris' mightiest museum, the Louvre. Gourmet shops garland the Église de la Madeleine, while further north are the splendid Palais Garnier opera house and art nouveau department stores of the Grands Boulevards.

Navigating the immense Louvre (p68) takes a while, so it's an ideal place to start your day. Other museums well worth a visit include the Musée de l'Orangerie (p78), showcasing Monet's enormous Water Lilies, and the Jeu de Paume (p78) photography museum, both enveloped by the elegant lawns, fountains and ponds of the Jardin des Tuileries (p78). Go behind the scenes of the Palais Garnier (p79), then shop at the beautiful Galeries Lafayette (p87) and Le Printemps (p88) department stores and take in the free panoramas from their rooftops.

Getting There & Around

Ⓜ The Louvre has two metro stations: Palais Royal– Musée du Louvre (lines 1 and 7), and Louvre–Rivoli (line 1).

Ⓜ Châtelet–Les Halles is Paris' main hub, with many metro and RER lines converging here.

🚢 The hop-on, hop-off Batobus stops outside the Louvre.

Neighbourhood Map on p76

Jardin des Tuileries (p78) MEANDERING TRAIL MEDIA/SHUTTERSTOCK ©

Top Sight 📷
Louvre

Few art galleries are as prized or as daunting as the Louvre, Paris' pièce de résistance that no first-time visitor to the city can resist. This is, after all, one of the world's largest and most diverse museums, showcasing 35,000 works of art. It would take nine months to glance at every piece, rendering advance planning essential.

◎ MAP P76, E6

www.louvre.fr

rue de Rivoli & quai des Tuileries, 1er

adult/child €15/free

🕑9am-6pm Mon, Thu, Sat & Sun, to 9.45pm Wed & Fri

Ⓜ Palais Royal–Musée du Louvre

Palais du Louvre

The Louvre today rambles over four floors and through three wings: the **Sully Wing** (pictured left) creates the four sides of the Cour Carrée (literally 'Square Courtyard') at the eastern end of the complex; the **Denon Wing** stretches 800m along the Seine to the south; and the northern **Richelieu Wing** skirts rue de Rivoli. The building started life as a fortress built by Philippe-Auguste in the 12th century – medieval remnants are still visible on the lower ground floor (Sully). In the 16th century it became a royal residence and after the Revolution, in 1793, it was turned it into a national museum. Its booty was no more than 2500 paintings and objets d'art.

Over the centuries French governments amassed the paintings, sculptures and artefacts displayed today. The 'Grand Louvre' project inaugurated by the late President Mitterrand in 1989 doubled the museum's exhibition space, and both new and renovated galleries have since opened, including the state-of-the-art **Islamic art galleries** (lower ground floor, Denon) in the stunningly restored Cour Visconti.

Priceless Antiquities

Whatever your plans are, don't rush by the Louvre's astonishing cache of treasures from antiquity: both **Mesopotamia** (ground floor, Richelieu) and **Egypt** (ground and 1st floors, Sully) are well represented, as seen in the *Code of Hammurabi* (Room 3, ground floor, Richelieu) and *The Seated Scribe* (Room 22, 1st floor, Sully). Room 12 (ground floor, Sully Wing) holds impressive friezes and an enormous **two-headed-bull column** from the Darius Palace in ancient Iran, while an enormous seated **statue of Pharaoh Ramesses II** highlights the temple room (Room 12, Sully).

★ Top Tips

○ You need to queue twice to get in: once for security and then again to buy tickets.

○ The longest queues are usually outside the Grande Pyramide; use the Carrousel du Louvre entrance (99 rue de Rivoli or direct from the metro) instead.

○ A Paris Museum Pass (http://en.paris museumpass. com) or Paris City Passport gives you priority; buying tickets online (€2 surcharge) will also help expedite the process.

✕ Take a Break

○ Tickets to the Louvre are valid for the whole day, meaning you can nip out for lunch. For a quick and easy meal, grab a sandwich in the Hall Napoléon for picnic in the Jardin des Tuileries (p78).

○ Alternatively, stroll five minutes to enjoy fine cuisine at Chez La Vieille (p82).

Also worth a look are the mosaics and figurines from the Byzantine empire (lower ground floor, Denon), and the Greek statuary collection, culminating with the world's most famous armless duo, the **Venus de Milo** (Room 16, ground floor, Sully) and the **Winged Victory of Samothrace** (top of Daru staircase, 1st floor, Denon).

Mona Lisa

Easily the Louvre's most admired work (and world's most famous painting) is Leonardo da Vinci's *La Joconde* (in French; *La Gioconda* in Italian), the lady with that enigmatic smile known as *Mona Lisa* (Room 6, 1st floor, Denon). For centuries admirers speculated on everything about the painting, from the possi-

bility that the subject was mourning the death of a loved one to the possibility that she might have been in love or in bed with her portraitist.

Mona (*monna* in Italian) is a contraction of *madonna,* and Gioconda is the feminine form of the surname Giocondo. Canadian scientists used infrared technology to peer through paint layers and confirm *Mona Lisa's* identity as Lisa Gherardini (1479–1542?), wife of Florentine merchant Francesco de Giocondo. Scientists also discovered that her dress was covered in a transparent gauze veil typically worn in early-16th-century Italy by pregnant women or new mothers; it's surmised that the work was painted to commemorate the birth of her second son around 1503, when she was aged about 24.

Winged Victory of Samothrace

French & Italian Masterpieces

The **1st floor of the Denon Wing**, where the *Mona Lisa* is found, is easily the most popular part of the Louvre – and with good reason. Rooms 75 through 77 are hung with monumental French paintings, many iconic: look for the *Consecration of the Emperor Napoléon I* (David), *The Raft of the Medusa* (Géricault) and *Grande Odalisque* (Ingres).

Rooms 1, 3, 5 and 8 are also must-visits. Filled with classic works by **Renaissance** masters (Raphael, Titian, Uccello, Botticini), this area culminates in the crowds around the *Mona Lisa*. But you'll find plenty else to contemplate, from Botticelli's graceful frescoes (Room 1) to the superbly detailed *Wedding Feast at Cana* (Room 6). On the ground floor of the Denon Wing, take time for the Italian sculptures, including Michelangelo's *The Dying Slave* and Canova's *Psyche and Cupid* (Room 4).

Northern European Paintings

The 2nd floor of the Richelieu Wing, directly above the gilt and crystal of the **Napoleon III Apartments** (1st floor), allows for a quieter meander through the Louvre's inspirational collection of Flemish and Dutch paintings spearheaded by the works of Peter Paul Rubens and Pieter Bruegel the Elder. Vermeer's *The Lacemaker* can be found in Room 38, while Room 31 is devoted chiefly to works by Rembrandt.

Glass Pyramid

Almost as stunning as the masterpieces inside is the 21m-high glass pyramid designed by Chinese-born American architect IM Pei that bedecks the main entrance to the Louvre. Beneath Pei's Grande Pyramide is the **Hall Napoléon**, the museum's main entrance area. To revel in another Pei pyramid of equally dramatic dimensions, head towards the **Carrousel du Louvre**, a busy shopping mall that loops underground from the Grande Pyramide to the **Arc de Triomphe du Carrousel** – its centrepiece is Pei's **Pyramide Inversée** (inverted glass pyramid).

Trails & Tours

Self-guided thematic trails range from Louvre masterpieces and the art of eating to family-friendly topics. Download trail brochures in advance from the website. Another good option is to rent a Nintendo 3DS multimedia guide (€5; ID required). More formal, English-language **guided tours** (☏01 40 20 52 63; adult/child €12/9; ⏰11am & 2pm except 1st Sun of month) depart from the Hall Napoléon. Reserve a spot by telephone up to 14 days in advance or sign up on arrival at the museum.

Louvre

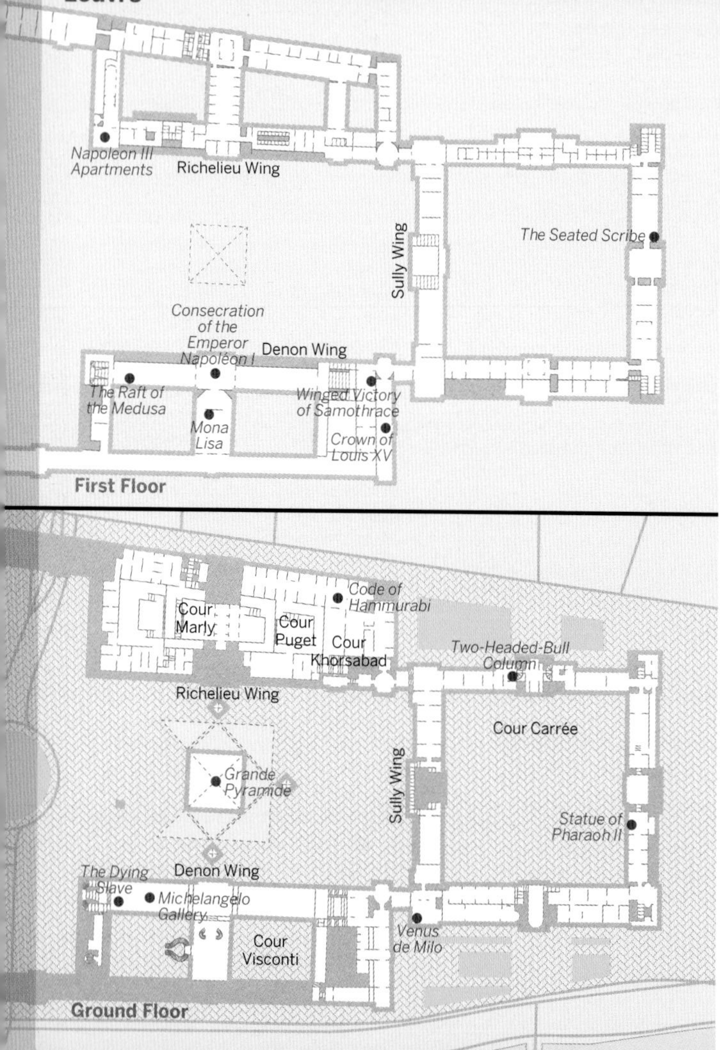

First Floor

Napoleon III Apartments

Richelieu Wing

The Seated Scribe

Sully Wing

Consecration of the Emperor Napoléon I

Denon Wing

The Raft of the Medusa

Mona Lisa

Winged Victory of Samothrace

Crown of Louis XV

Ground Floor

Cour Marly

Cour Puget

Cour Khorsabad

Code of Hammurabi

Two-Headed-Bull Column

Richelieu Wing

Cour Carrée

Grande Pyramide

Sully Wing

Statue of Pharaoh II

The Dying Slave

Denon Wing

Michelangelo Gallery

Cour Visconti

Venus de Milo

Other Louvre Museums

A trio of privately administered collections – Applied Arts & Design, Advertising & Graphic Design, and Fashion & Textiles – sit in the Rohan Wing of the vast Palais du Louvre. They are collectively known as the **Musée des Arts Décoratifs** (☏01 44 55 57 50; www.lesartsdecoratifs.fr; 107 rue de Rivoli, 1er; adult/child €11/free; ☉11am-6pm Tue-Sun, to 9pm Thu); admission includes entry to all three. For an extra €2, you can scoop up a combo ticket that also includes the Musée Nissim de Camondo in the 8e.

The **Applied Arts & Design** collection takes up the majority of the space and displays furniture, jewellery and such objets d'art as ceramics and glassware from the Middle Ages and the Renaissance through the art nouveau and art deco periods to modern times. Its collections span from Europe to East Asia.

On the other side of the building is the smaller **Advertising & Graphic Design** collection, which has some 100,000 posters in its collection dating as far back as the 13th century as well as innumerable promotional materials. Most of the space is given over to special exhibitions.

Haute couture creations by the likes of Chanel and Jean-Paul Gaultier can be ogled in the **Fashion & Textiles** collection, home to some 16,000 costumes from the 16th century to the present day. Items are only on display during regularly scheduled themed exhibitions.

Renovating the Louvre

In late 2014 the Louvre embarked on a 30-year renovation plan, with the aim of modernising the museum to make it more accessible. Phase 1 increased the number of main entrances to reduce security wait times (even still, buy tickets online or use the Paris Museum Pass; lines at the underground Carrousel du Louvre entrance are often shorter). It also revamped the central Hall Napoléon to vastly improve what was previously bewildering chaos. Important changes to come include increasing the number of English-language signs and artwork texts to aid navigation.

In 2018, two new rooms were opened to the public on the 2nd floor of the Richelieu Wing, displaying a handful of artworks stolen during the Nazi occupation of France. Many objects were recovered by the French government after the war, though some of them went unclaimed by their original owners.

Walking Tour 🥾

Right Bank Covered Passages

Stepping into the passages couverts (covered shopping arcades) of the Right Bank is the best way to get a feel for what life was like in early-19th-century Paris. Around half a century later, Paris had around 150 of these decorated arcades. This walking tour is tailor-made for a rainy day, but it's best avoided on a Sunday, when some arcades are shut.

Walk Facts

Start Galerie Véro Dodat; Ⓜ Palais Royal–Musée du Louvre

Finish Passage Verdeau; Ⓜ Le Peletier

Length 3km; two hours

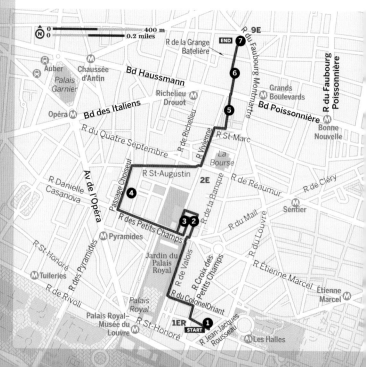

❶ Galerie Véro Dodat

At 19 rue Jean-Jacques Rousseau, **Galerie Véro Dodat** (btwn rue Jean-Jacques-Rousseau & 2 rue du Bouloi; ⏰7am-10pm Mon-Sat, shop hrs vary; Ⓜ Louvre Rivoli, Palais Royal–Musée du Louvre) retains its 19th-century skylights, ceiling murals, Corinthian columns, tiled floor, gas globe fittings (now electric) and shopfronts including furniture restorers.

❷ Galerie Vivienne

Built in 1826, Galerie Vivienne is decorated with floor mosaics and bas-reliefs on the walls. Don't miss wine shop **Legrand Filles & Fils** (📞01 42 60 07 12; www.caves-legrand. com; 1 rue de la Banque, 2e; ⏰11am-7pm Mon, 10am-7.30pm Tue-Sat; Ⓜ Bourse), **Wolff et Descourtis**, selling silk scarves, and **Emilio Robba**, one of the most beautiful flower shops in Paris.

❸ Galerie Colbert

Enter this 1826-built passage, featuring a huge glass dome and rotunda, from rue Vivienne. Exit on rue des Petits Champs (and check out the fresco above).

❹ Passage Choiseul

This 1824-built, 45m-long passage has scores of shops including many specialising in discount and vintage clothing, beads and costume jewellery as well as cheap eateries.Comedies are performed at the **Théâtre des Bouffes Parisiens**, which backs onto the passage's northern end.

❺ Passage des Panoramas

From 10 rue St-Marc, enter Paris' oldest covered arcade (1800) and the first to be lit by gas (1817). It was expanded in 1834 with four interconnecting passages – Feydeau, Montmartre, St-Marc and Variétés – and is full of eateries and unusual shops, such as autograph dealer **Arnaud Magistry**. Exit at 11 bd Montmartre.

❻ Passage Jouffroy

Enter at 10-12 bd Montmartre into passage Jouffroy, Paris' last major passage (1847). There's a wax museum, the **Musée Grévin** (📞01 47 70 85 05; www.grevin.com; 10 bd Montmartre, 9e; adult/child €22.50/17.50; ⏰9.30am-7pm, shorter hours winter; Ⓜ Grands Boulevards), and wonderful boutiques including bookshops, silversmiths and **M&G Segas**, where Toulouse- Lautrec bought his walking sticks. Exit at 9 rue de la Grange Batelière.

❼ Passage Verdeau

Cross the road to 6 rue de la Grange Batelière to the last of this stretch of covered arcades. There's lots to explore: vintage comic books, antiques, old postcards and more. The northern exit is at 31bis rue du Faubourg Montmartre.

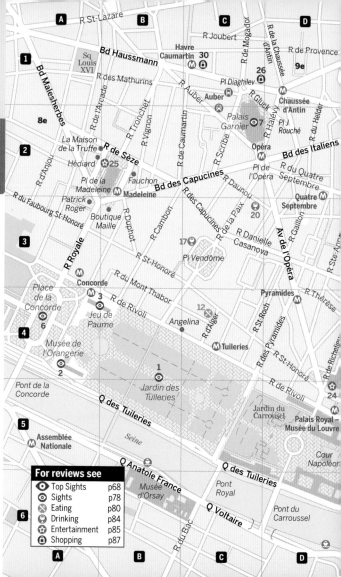

Louvre, Tuileries & Opéra

A R St-Lazare **B** **C** R Joubert R de Mogador R de la Chaussée d'Antin R de Provence **D**

1 Bd Maleherbes Sq Louis XVI Bd Haussmann Havre Caumartin **30** Pl Diaghilev **26** **9e**

R des Mathurins R de l'Arcade R Auber R de la Chaussée d'Antin R Halévy R Gluck Chaussée d'Antin Pl J. Rouché R du Helder

8e R Tronchet R Vignon R de Caumartin Auber Palais Garnier **7**

2 La Maison de la Truffe R de Sèze Scribe Opéra Bd des Italiens
Hédiard **25** Fauchon R du Quatre Septembre
R d'Anjou Pl de la Madeleine Madeleine Bd des Capucines Pl de l'Opéra R Danou Quatre Septembre

Patrick Roger R Duphot R des Capucines R de la Paix **20** Av de l'Opéra R Galilon

3 R du Faubourg St-Honoré Boutique Maille R Cambon R St-Honoré **17** Pl Vendôme R Danielle Casanova R Ste-Anne

R Royale R du Mont Thabor Pyramides R Thérèse

Place de la Concorde **3** R de Rivoli **12** R St-Roch R des Pyramides R de Richelieu

4 **6** Jeu de Paume Angelina R d'Alger **Tuileries** R St-Honoré **24**

Musée de l'Orangerie **2** **1** R de Rivoli

Pont de la Concorde Jardin des Tuileries Jardin du Carrousel Palais Royal – Musée du Louvre

5 Assemblée Nationale Seine Cour Napoléon

Q des Tuileries Q des Tuileries

Q Anatole France Musée d'Orsay Pont Royal

Q Voltaire Pont du Carroussel

R du Bac

For reviews see

◉	Top Sights	p68
◎	Sights	p78
✪	Eating	p80
◉	Drinking	p84
✪	Entertainment	p85
🔒	Shopping	p87

6

A **B** **C** **D**

Sights

Jardin des Tuileries PARK

1 ⊙ MAP P76, B4

Filled with fountains, ponds and sculptures, the formal 28-hectare Tuileries Garden, which begins just west of the Jardin du Carrousel, was laid out in its present form in 1664 by André Le Nôtre, architect of the gardens at Versailles. The Tuileries soon became the most fashionable spot in Paris for parading about in one's finery. It now forms part of the Banks of the Seine Unesco World Heritage site. (rue de Rivoli, 1er; ⏱7am-9pm Apr-late Sep, 7.30am-7.30pm late Sep-Mar; MTuileries, Concorde)

Musée de l'Orangerie MUSEUM

2 ⊙ MAP P76, A4

Monet's extraordinary cycle of eight enormous *Decorations des Nymphéas* (Water Lilies) occupies two huge oval rooms purpose-built in 1927 on the artist's instructions. The lower level houses more of Monet's impressionist works and many by Sisley, Renoir, Cézanne, Gauguin, Picasso, Matisse and Modigliani, as well as Derain's *Arlequin et Pierrot*. The orangery, along with photography gallery Jeu de Paume, is all that remains of the former Palais des Tuileries, which was razed during the Paris Commune in 1871. Audioguides cost €5. (☎01 44 77 80 07; www.musee-orangerie.fr; place de la Concorde, 1er; adult/child €9/free; ⏱9am-6pm Wed-Mon; MConcorde)

Jeu de Paume GALLERY

3 ⊙ MAP P76, A4

The Galerie du Jeu de Paume, which stages innovative photography exhibitions, is housed in an erstwhile *jeu de paume* (royal tennis court) of the former Palais des Tuileries in the northwestern corner of the Jardin des Tuileries. Cinema screenings and concert performances also take place – check the agenda online. (☎01 47 03 12 50; www.jeudepaume.org; 1 place de la Concorde, 1er; adult/child €10/free; ⏱11am-9pm Tue, to 7pm Wed-Sun; MConcorde)

Église St-Eustache CHURCH

4 ⊙ MAP P76, G5

Just north of the gardens adjoining the city's old marketplace, now the Forum des Halles (p80), is one of the most beautiful churches in Paris. Majestic, architecturally magnificent and musically outstanding, St-Eustache was constructed between 1532 and 1632 and is primarily Gothic. Artistic highlights include a work by Rubens, Raymond Mason's colourful bas-relief of market vendors (1969) and Keith Haring's bronze triptych (1990) in the side chapels. (www.st-eustache.org; 2 impasse St-Eustache, 1er; ⏱9.30am-7pm Mon-Fri, 9am-7.15pm Sat & Sun; MLes Halles or RER Châtelet–Les Halles)

Jardin du Palais Royal

GARDENS

5 MAP P76, E4

The Jardin du Palais Royal is a perfect spot to sit, contemplate and picnic between boxed hedges, or shop in the trio of beautiful arcades that frame the garden: the **Galerie de Valois** (east), **Galerie de Montpensier** (west) and **Galerie Beaujolais** (north). However, it's the southern end of the complex, polka-dotted with sculptor Daniel Buren's 260 black-and-white striped columns, that has become the garden's signature feature. (www.domaine-palais-royal.fr; 2 place Colette, 1er; 8am-10.30pm Apr-Sep, to 8.30pm Oct-Mar; M Palais Royal–Musée du Louvre)

Place de la Concorde

SQUARE

6 MAP P76, A4

Paris spreads around you, with views of the Eiffel Tower, the Seine and along the Champs-Élysées, when you stand in the city's largest square. Its 3300-year-old pink granite obelisk was a gift from Egypt in 1831. The square was first laid out in 1755 and originally named after King Louis XV, but its royal associations meant that it took centre stage during the Revolution – Louis XVI was the first to be guillotined here in 1793. (8e; M Concorde)

Palais Garnier

HISTORIC BUILDING

7 MAP P76, C2

The fabled 'phantom of the opera' lurked in this opulent opera house

Louvre, Tuileries & Opéra Sights

Place de la Concorde

CYNTHIA LIANG/SHUTTERSTOCK ©

Collection Pinault Paris

Paris' newest art museum is housed in the eye-catching **Bourse de Commerce** (Map p76, F5; www.collectionpinault paris.com; 2 rue de Viarmes, 1er; MLes Halles or RER Châtelet–Les Halles) – an 18th-century rotunda that once held the city's grain market and stock exchange. Japanese architect Tadao Ando designed the ambitious new interior, where three floors of galleries will display contemporary art from the \$1.4 billion collection of François Pinault, who previously teamed up with Ando to open the Palazzo Grassi and Punta della Dogana in Venice. It's slated to open in early 2019.

designed in 1860 by Charles Garnier (then an unknown 35-year-old architect). Reserve a spot on a 90-minute English-language guided tour, or visit on your own (audioguides available; €5). Don't miss the Grand Staircase and gilded auditorium with red velvet seats, a massive chandelier and Chagall's ceiling mural. Also worth a peek is the museum, with posters, costumes, backdrops, original scores and other memorabilia. (☑08 92 89 90 90; www.operade paris.fr; cnr rues Scribe & Auber, 9e; self-guided tours adult/child €12/8, guided tours adult/child €15.50/8.50;

⊙self-guided tours 10am-5pm, guided tours 11am & 2.30pm; MOpéra)

Forum des Halles NOTABLE BUILDING

8 MAP P76, G5

Paris' main wholesale food market stood here for nearly 800 years before being replaced by this underground shopping mall in 1971. Long considered an eyesore by many Parisians, the mall's exterior was finally demolished in 2011 to make way for its golden-hued translucent canopy, unveiled in 2016. Below, four floors of stores (more than 100), some 20 eateries and entertainment venues including cinemas and a swimming pool extend down to the city's busiest metro hub. (www.forumdeshalles.com; 1 rue Pierre Lescot, 1er; ⊙shops 10am-8pm Mon-Sat, 11am-7pm Sun; MLes Halles or RER Châtelet–Les Halles)

Eating

Maison Maison MEDITERRANEAN €€

9 MAP P76, F6

Halfway down the stairs by Pont Neuf is this wonderfully secret space beneath the *bouquinistes*, where you can watch the bateaux-mouches float by as you dine on artful creations such as beetroot and pink-grapefruit-cured bonito or gnocchi with white asparagus and broccoli pesto. In nice weather, cocktails at the glorious riverside terrace are not to be missed. (☑09 67 82 07 32; www.facebook.

com/maisonmaisonparis; opposite 16 quai du Louvre, 1er; 2-/3-course lunch menu €20/25, small plates €7-16; ☺10am-2am Wed-Sun, 6pm-2am Tue; M Pont Neuf)

Richer BISTRO €

10 🍴 MAP P76, G1

Richer's pared-back, exposed-brick decor is a smart setting for genius creations including smoked-duck-breast ravioli in miso broth, and quince-and-lime cheesecake for dessert. It doesn't take reservations, but it serves snacks and Chinese tea, and has a full bar (open until midnight). Fantastic value. (www.lericher.com; 2 rue Richer, 9e; mains €17-21; ☺noon-2.30pm & 7.30-10.30pm; M Poissonière, Bonne Nouvelle)

Frenchie BISTRO €€€

11 🍴 MAP P76, G3

Tucked down an inconspicuous alley, this tiny bistro with wooden tables and old stone walls is always packed and for good reason: excellent-value dishes are modern, market-driven and prepared with unpretentious flair by French chef Gregory Marchand. Reserve well in advance or arrive early and pray for a cancellation (it does happen). Alternatively, head to **Frenchie Bar à Vins** (dishes €9-23; ☺6.30-11pm), located just next door. (📞01 40 39 96 19; www.frenchie-restaurant.com; 5 rue du Nil, 2e; 4-course lunch menu €45, 5-course dinner menu €74, with wine €175; ☺6.30-11pm Mon-Fri, noon-2.30pm Thu & Fri in summer; M Sentier)

Rue Montorgueil 🍽️

A splinter of the historic Les Halles, rue Montorgueil was once the oyster market and the final stop for seafood merchants hailing from the coast. Immortalised by Balzac in *La Comédie humaine*, this compelling strip still draws Parisians to eat and shop – it's lined with *fromageries* (cheese shops), cafes, and street stalls selling fruit, veg and other foodstuffs.

Highlights include 1730-opened patisserie **Stohrer** (Map p76; www. stohrer.fr; 51 rue Montorgueil, 2e; ☺7.30am-8.30pm; M Étienne Marcel, Sentier), with pastel murals added in 1864 by Paul-Jacques-Aimé Baudry, who also decorated the Palais Garnier's Grand Foyer; a greatest-hits range of pastries from Paris' finest pastry chefs at **Fou de Pâtisserie** (Map p76; 45 rue Montorgueil, 2e; ☺11am-8pm Mon-Fri, 10am-8pm Sat, 10am-6pm Sun; M Les Halles, Sentier, or RER Châtelet–Les Halles); and **Au Rocher de Cancale** (Map p76; 📞01 42 33 50 29; 78 rue Montorgueil, 2e; dozen oysters €20, seafood platter €30; ☺8am-2am; M Sentier, Les Halles, or RER Châtelet–Les Halles), which still serves oysters today.

Living Wall

On the corner of rue des Petits Carreaux (the northern extension of foodie street rue Montorgueil, p81), the extraordinary *mur végétal* ('vertical garden') **L'Oasis d'Aboukir** (Map p76, G3; 83 rue d'Aboukir, 2e; M Sentier) was installed on a 25m-high blank building façade by the modern innovator of the genre, French botanist Patrick Blanc. Since 2013 it's flourished to cover a total surface area of 250 sq metre in greenery. Subtitled Hymne à la Biodiversité (Ode to Biodiversity), the 'living wall' incorporates some 7600 different plants from 237 different species.

Balagan   ISRAELI €€

12 🍽 MAP P76, C4

Cool navy blues and creamy diamond tiling contrast with the chic vibe at this Israeli hot spot. Come here to sample delectable small plates: deconstructed kebabs, crispy halloumi cheese with dates, onion confit Ashkenazi chicken liver, or, our favourite, a spicy, succulent tuna tartare with fennel, cilantro, capers and pistachios. Mains, such as the seabream black pasta, are just as praiseworthy. (📞01 40 20 72 14; www.balagan-paris.com; 9 rue d'Alger, 1er; lunch menus from €24,

mains €23-28; ⊙noon-2pm Mon-Sat, 7-10pm daily; M Tuileries)

Chez La Vieille   FRENCH €€

13 🍽 MAP P76, F5

In salvaging this history-steeped eatery within a 16th-century building, star chef Daniel Rose pays homage to the former wholesale markets, the erstwhile legendary owner Adrienne Biasin (many of her timeless dishes have been updated, from terrines and rillettes to veal blanquette), and the soul of Parisian bistro cooking itself. Dine at the street-level bar or upstairs in the peacock-blue dining room. (📞01 42 60 15 78; www.chezlavieille.fr; 1 rue Bailleul, 1er; mains €24-26; ⊙noon-2.30pm Fri & Sat, 6-10.30pm Tue-Sat; M Louvre–Rivoli)

Le Grand Véfour   GASTRONOMY €€€

14 🍽 MAP P76, E4

Holding two Michelin stars, this 18th-century jewel on the northern edge of the Jardin du Palais Royal has been a dining favourite since 1784; the names ascribed to each table span Napoléon and Victor Hugo to Colette (who lived next door). Expect a voyage of discovery from chef Guy Martin in one of the most beautiful restaurants in the world. (📞01 42 96 56 27; www.grand-vefour.com; 17 rue de Beaujolais, 1er; lunch/dinner menu €115/315, mains €99-126; ⊙noon-2.30pm & 7.30-10.30pm Mon-Fri; M Pyramides)

La Tour de Montlhéry – Chez Denise   FRENCH €€

15 MAP P76, F5

The most traditional eatery near the former Les Halles marketplace, this boisterous old half-timbered bistro with red-chequered tablecloths stays open until dawn and has been run by the same family since 1966. If you're ready to feast on all the French classics – snails in garlic sauce, veal liver, steak tartare, braised beef cheeks and house-made pâté – reservations are in order. (☏01 42 36 21 82; 5 rue des Prouvaires, 1er; mains €23-28; ☉noon-3pm & 7.30pm-5am Mon-Fri mid-Aug–mid-Jun; ⓂLes Halles or RER Châtelet–Les Halles)

Le Cochon à l'Oreille   FRENCH €€

16 MAP P76, F4

A Parisian jewel and listed monument, the hole-in-the-wall Le Cochon à l'Oreille retains 1890-laid tiles depicting vibrant market scenes of the old *halles*, while an iron staircase leads to a second dining room upstairs. Bistro-style dishes are traditional French (the steak tartare is excellent), and are accompanied by well-chosen wines. Hours can vary. Cash only. (☏01 40 15 98 24; 15 rue Montmartre, 1er; lunch/dinner menus from €16/19.50; ☉10am-2am Tue-Sat; ⓂLes Halles or RER Châtelet–Les Halles)

Louvre, Tuileries & Opéra Eating

Forum des Halles (p80)

KIEVVICTOR/SHUTTERSTOCK ©

Drinking

Bar Hemingway
COCKTAIL BAR

17 🔢 MAP P76, C3

Black-and-white photos and memorabilia (hunting trophies, old typewriters and framed handwritten letters by the great writer) fill this snug bar inside the **Ritz**. Head bartender Colin Field mixes monumental cocktails, including three different Bloody Marys made with juice from freshly squeezed seasonal tomatoes. Legend has it that Hemingway himself, wielding a machine gun, helped liberate the bar during WWII. (www.ritz paris.com; Hôtel Ritz Paris, 15 place Vendôme, 1er; ⏰6pm-2am; 📶; Ⓜ️Opéra)

Le Garde Robe
WINE BAR

18 🔢 MAP P76, F5

Le Garde Robe is possibly the world's only bar to serve alcohol alongside a detox menu. While you probably shouldn't come here for the full-on cleansing experience, you can definitely expect excellent, affordable natural wines, a casual atmosphere and a good selection of food, ranging from cheese and charcuterie plates to adventurous options (tuna gravlax with black quinoa and guacamole). (📞01 49 26 90 60; 41 rue de l'Arbre Sec, 1er; ⏰12.30-2.30pm & 6.30pm-midnight Tue-Fri, 4.30pm-midnight Mon-Sat; Ⓜ️Louvre Rivoli)

Danico
COCKTAIL BAR

19 🔢 MAP P76, E3

While not exactly a secret, Danico still feels like one – first you'll need to find the hidden, candlelit backroom in **Daroco** (📞01 42 21 93 71; www.daroco.fr; mains €14-40; ⏰noon-2.30pm & 7-11.30pm; 🍴) before you get to treat yourself to one of Nico de Soto's extravagant cocktails. Chia seeds, kombucha tea, ghost peppers and pomegranate Champagne are some of the more unusual ingredients you'll find on the drink list. (www.facebook.com/danicoparis; 6 rue Vivienne, 2e; ⏰6pm-2am; Ⓜ️Bourse)

Harry's New York Bar
COCKTAIL BAR

20 🔢 MAP P76, C3

One of the most popular American-style bars in the prewar years, Harry's once welcomed writers including F Scott Fitzgerald and Ernest Hemingway, who no doubt sampled the bar's unique cocktail and creation: the Bloody Mary. The Cuban mahogany interior dates from the mid-19th century and was brought over from a Manhattan bar in 1911. (📞01 42 61 71 14; http://harrysbar.fr; 5 rue Daunou, 2e; ⏰noon-2am Mon-Sat, 4pm-1am Sun; Ⓜ️Opéra)

Matamata
COFFEE

21 🔢 MAP P76, F4

Beans from Parisian roastery Café Lomi are expertly brewed at this small, two-level space with tables and light fittings made from recycled timber and repurposed metal, and subtropical fern wallpaper. Homemade cakes, such as carrot or banana, go with its exceptional coffee, sandwiches, salads and house-toasted granola. In summer, cool down with a cold-drip coffee over ice. (📞 01 71 39 44 58; www. matamatacoffee.com; 58 rue d'Argout, 2e; 🕐 8am-5pm Mon-Fri, 9am-5.30pm Sat & Sun; 📶; Ⓜ Sentier)

Le Tambour   BAR

22 🍴 MAP P76, F4

Insomniacs head to local landmark 'the Drummer' for its rowdy, good-natured atmosphere and filling, inexpensive French fare (including legendary desserts such as its tarte Tatin – traditional upside-down caramelised-apple tart) served until 3.30am or 4am. But what makes this place truly magical is its salvaged decor, such as an old Stalingrad metro map and Parisian street furniture. (📞 01 42 33 06 90; 41 rue Montmartre, 2e; 🕐 8.30am-6am; Ⓜ Étienne Marcel, Sentier)

Le Rex Club   CLUB

Attached to the art deco Grand Rex cinema (see 23 ⭐ Map p76, G2), this is Paris' premier house and techno venue where some of the world's hottest DJs strut their stuff on a 70-speaker, multidiffusion sound system. (📞 01 42 36 10 96; www. rexclub.com; 5 bd Poissonnière, 2e; 🕐 midnight-7am Wed-Sat; Ⓜ Bonne Nouvelle)

Paris' Best Hot Chocolate

Clink china with lunching ladies, their posturing poodles and half the students from Tokyo University at **Angelina** (Map p76, C4; 📞 01 42 60 82 00; www.angelina-paris.fr; 226 rue de Rivoli, 1er; 🕐 7.30am-7pm Mon-Fri, 8.30am-7.30pm Sat & Sun; Ⓜ Tuileries), a grande-dame tearoom dating from 1903. Decadent pastries are served here, but it's the super-thick 'African' hot chocolate (€8.20), which comes with a pot of whipped cream and a carafe of water, that prompts the constant queue for a table.

Entertainment

Palais Garnier   OPERA, BALLET

The city's original opera house (see 7 ⓞ Map p76, C2) is smaller than its Bastille counterpart, but has perfect acoustics. Due to its odd shape, some seats have limited or no visibility – book carefully. Ticket prices and conditions (including last-minute discounts) are available from the **box office** (📞 international calls 01 71 25 24 23, within France 08 92 89 90 90; www. operadeparis.fr; cnr rues Scribe & Auber; 🕐 10am-6.30pm Mon-Sat; Ⓜ Opéra). Online flash sales are held from noon on Wednesdays. (place de l'Opéra, 9e; Ⓜ Opéra)

Rue des Lombards

Rue des Lombards is the street to swing by for live jazz. **Le Baiser Salé** (Map p76; 01 42 33 37 71; www.lebaisersale.com; 58 rue des Lombards, 1er; daily, hours vary; Châtelet), meaning the Salty Kiss, is known for its Afro and Latin jazz, jazz fusion concerts, and combining big names and unknown artists. The place has a relaxed vibe, with sets usually starting at 7.30pm or 9.30pm. You'll find two venues in one at trendy, well-respected **Sunset & Sunside** (Map p76; 01 40 26 46 60; www.sunset-sunside.com; 60 rue des Lombards, 1er; daily, hours vary; Châtelet): electric jazz, fusion and occasional salsa downstairs; acoustics and concerts upstairs.

Le Grand Rex   CINEMA

23 ⭐ MAP P76, G2

Blockbuster screenings and concerts aside, this 1932 art deco cinematic icon runs 50-minute behind-the-scenes tours (English soundtracks available) during which visitors – tracked by a sensor slung around their neck – are whisked up (via a lift) behind the giant screen, tour a soundstage and experiment in a recording studio. Whizz-bang special effects along the way will stun adults and kids alike. (01 45 08 93 89; www. legrandrex.com; 1 bd Poissonnière, 2e; tours adult/child €11/9, cinema tickets adult/child €11/4.50; tours 10am-6pm Wed, Sat & Sun, extended hours during school holidays; Bonne Nouvelle)

Forum des Images   CINEMA

A five-screen cinema showing films set in Paris is the centrepiece of the city's film archive (see 8 ⊙ Map p76, G5). Created in 1988 to establish an audiovisual archive of the city, and renovated in dramatic shades of pink, grey and black, the complex has a library and research centre with newsreels, documentaries and advertising. Its online program lists thematic series, festivals and events. (01 44 76 63 00; www. forumdesimages.fr; Forum des Halles, 2 rue du Cinéma, Porte St-Eustache, 1er; cinema tickets adult/child €6/4; 12.30-9pm Tue-Fri, 2-9pm Sat & Sun; Les Halles or RER Châtelet–Les Halles)

Comédie Française   THEATRE

24 ⭐ MAP P76, D5

Founded in 1680 under Louis XIV, this state-run theatre bases its repertoire on the works of classic French playwrights. The theatre has its roots in an earlier company directed by Molière at the Palais Royal. (01 44 58 15 15; www. comedie-francaise.fr; place Colette, 1er; Palais Royal–Musée du Louvre)

Klosque Théâtre
Madeleine
BOOKING SERVICE

25 ⭐ MAP P76, B2

Pick up half-price tickets for same-day performances of ballet, opera and music at this freestanding kiosk. (www.kiosqueculture.com; opposite 15 place de la Madeleine, 8e; ⏱12.30-7.30pm Tue-Sat, to 3.45pm Sun; Ⓜ Madeleine)

Shopping

Galeries
Lafayette
DEPARTMENT STORE

26 Ⓐ MAP P76, C1

Grande-dame department store Galeries Lafayette is spread across the main store (its magnificent stained-glass dome is over a century old), men's store, and homewares store with a gourmet emporium. Catch modern art in the 1st-floor **gallery** (☎01 42 82 81 98; www.galeriedesgaleries.com; admission free; ⏱11am-7pm Tue-Sun), take in a **fashion show** (☎bookings 01 42 82 81 98; ⏱3pm Fri Mar-Jun & Sep-Dec by reservation), ascend to a free, windswept rooftop panorama, or take a break at one of its 24 restaurants and cafes. (☎01 42 82 34 56; http://haussmann.galerieslafayette.com; 40 bd Haussmann, 9e; ⏱9.30am-8.30pm Mon-Sat, 11am-7pm Sun; 📶; Ⓜ Chaussée d'Antin or RER Auber)

L'Exception
DESIGN

27 Ⓐ MAP P76, G5

Over 400 different French designers come together under one roof at this light-filled concept

Galeries Lafayette

THANAKRIT SATHAVORNMANEE/SHUTTERSTOCK ©

store, which showcases rotating collections of men's and women's fashion along with accessories including lingerie and swimwear, shoes, eyewear, gloves, hats, scarves, belts, bags, watches and jewellery. It also sells design books, cosmetics, candles, vases and other gorgeous homewares, and has a small in-house coffee bar. (☎01 40 39 92 34; www.lexception. com; 24 rue Berger, 1er; ⏰10am-8pm Mon-Sat, 11am-7pm Sun; Ⓜ Les Halles or RER Châtelet–Les Halles)

Didier Ludot   FASHION & ACCESSORIES

28 Ⓐ MAP P76, E4

In the rag trade since 1975, collector Didier Ludot sells the city's finest couture creations of yesteryear, hosts exhibitions and has published a book portraying the evolution of the little black dress. (☎01 42 96 06 56; www.didierludot. fr; 24 Galerie de Montpensier, 1er; ⏰10.30am-7pm Mon-Sat; Ⓜ Palais Royal–Musée du Louvre)

La Samaritaine   DEPARTMENT STORE

29 Ⓐ MAP P76, F6

One of Paris' four big department stores, the 10-storey La Samaritaine is finally emerging from its much contested and drawn-out 14-year overhaul. Pritzker Prize–winning Japanese firm Sanaa has preserved much of the gorgeous art nouveau and art deco exterior, in addition to the glass ceiling topping the central Hall Jourdain. It's slated to open in 2019. (☎01 56 81

28 40; www.lasamaritaine.com; 19 rue de la Monnaie, 1er; Ⓜ Pont Neuf)

Le Printemps   DEPARTMENT STORE

30 Ⓐ MAP P76, C1

Famous department store Le Printemps encompasses Le Printemps de la Mode, for women's fashion, and Le Printemps de l'Homme, for men's fashion, both with established and up-and-coming designer wear. Le Printemps de la Beauté et Maison, for beauty and homewares, offers a staggering display of perfume, cosmetics and accessories. (☎01 42 82 50 00; www.printemps.com; 64 bd Haussmann, 9e; ⏰9.35am-8pm Mon-Sat, to 8.45pm Thu, 11am-7pm Sun; 🛜; Ⓜ Havre Caumartin)

Champagne cocktail, Bar Hemingway (p84)

CHAMPAGNE/ALAMY ©

Place de la Madeleine

Ultragourmet food shops garland **place de la Madeleine** (Ⓜ Madeleine); many have in-house dining options. Notable names include the following:

La Maison de la Truffe (Map p76, A2; 🖉 01 42 65 53 22; www.maison-de-la-truffe.com; 19 place de la Madeleine, 8e; ⏱10am-10pm Mon-Sat) Truffle dealers.

Hédiard (Map p76, A2; 🖉 01 43 12 88 88; www.hediard.fr; 21 place de la Madeleine, 8e) Luxury food shop which reopens in 2019 after head-to-toe renovations.

Boutique Maille (Map p76, B3; www.maille.com; 6 place de la Madeleine, 8e; ⏱10am-7pm Mon-Sat) Mustard specialist.

Fauchon (Map p76, B2; 🖉 01 70 39 38 00; www.fauchon.fr; 26 & 30 place de la Madeleine, 8e; ⏱10am-8.30pm Mon-Sat) Paris' most famous caterer has mouthwatering delicacies from foie gras to jams, chocolates and pastries.

Patrick Roger (Map p76, A3; 🖉 09 67 08 24 47; www.patrickroger.com; 3 place de la Madeleine, 8e; ⏱10.30am-7.30pm) Extravagant chocolate sculptures.

E Dehillerin

HOMEWARES

31 🅐 MAP P76, F4

Founded in 1820, this extraordinary two-level store – more like an old-fashioned warehouse than a shiny, chic boutique – carries an incredible selection of professional-quality *matériel de cuisine* (kitchenware). Poultry scissors, turbot poacher, professional copper cookware or an Eiffel Tower–shaped cake tin – it's all here. (🖉01 42 36 53 13; www.edehillerin.fr; 18-20 rue Coquillière, 1er; ⏱9am-12.30pm & 2-6pm Mon, 9am-6pm Tue-Sat; Ⓜ Les Halles)

À la Mère de Famille

FOOD & DRINKS

32 🅐 MAP P76, F1

Founded in 1761, this is the original location of Paris' oldest chocolatier. Its beautiful belle époque façade is as enchanting as the rainbow of sweets, caramels and chocolates inside. (🖉01 47 70 83 69; www.lameredefamille.com; 35 rue du Faubourg Montmartre, 9e; ⏱9.30am-8pm Mon-Sat, 10am-7.30pm Sun; Ⓜ Le Peletier)

Walking Tour 🥾

Seine-Side Romantic Meander

The world's most romantic city has no shortage of beguiling spots, but the Seine and its surrounds are Paris at its most seductive. On this walk you'll pass graceful gardens, palaces, intimate parks, a flower market and an enchanting bookshop. Descend the steps along the quays wherever possible to stroll along the water's edge.

Walk Facts

Start Place de la Concorde; M Concorde

Finish Jardin des Plantes; M Gare d'Austerlitz

Length 7km; three hours

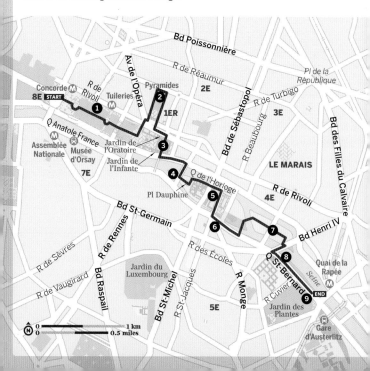

❶ Jardin des Tuileries

After taking in the panorama from place de la Concorde (p79), stroll through the Jardin des Tuileries (p78).

❷ Jardin du Palais Royal

Browse the arcades flanking the Jardin du Palais Royal (p79), adjoining the 17th-century palace where Louis XIV once lived.

❸ Cour Carrée

Walk through the Jardin de l'Oratoire to the Cour Carrée courtyard of the Louvre (p68) and exit at the Jardin de l'Infante (Garden of the Princess).

❹ Square du Vert Galant

From the Pont Neuf (p144), take the steps to the park at Île de la Cité's tip, Square du Vert Galant, before ascending to place du Pont Neuf to cross place Dauphine.

❺ Marché aux Fleurs Reine Elizabeth II

Parisians have been buying bouquets at the Marché aux Fleurs Reine Elizabeth II (p150), newly renamed in honour of Britain's Queen Elizabeth II, for centuries. Choose carefully: tradition has it that chrysanthemums are only for cemeteries, carnations bring bad luck, and yellow roses imply adultery.

❻ Shakespeare & Company

Amid handpainted quotations, make a wish in the wishing well, leave a message on the 'mirror of love' or curl up with a volume of poetry in the reading library of the magical bookshop Shakespeare & Company (p169).

❼ Berthillon

Cross Pont de l'Archevêché to Île de la Cité, then take Pont St-Louis to Île St-Louis and share an ice cream from *glacier* (ice-cream maker) Berthillon (p145).

❽ Musée de la Sculpture en Plein Air

Along quai St-Bernard, wander among more than 50 late-20th century unfenced sculptures by artists such as César and Brancusi at the open-air sculpture museum (p161).

❾ Jardin des Plantes

End your romantic meander at the tranquil Jardin des Plantes (p159). For the ultimate denouement, cruise back along the Seine by Batobus (p210).

Explore

Sacré-Cœur & Montmartre

Montmartre's slinking streets, lined with crooked ivy-clad buildings, retain a fairy-tale charm, despite the area's popularity. Crowned by the Sacré-Cœur basilica, Montmartre is the city's steepest quarter (mont means hill; the martyr was St Denis, beheaded here in about AD 250). The lofty views, wine-producing vines and hidden village squares have lured painters since the 19th century.

Montmartre makes for an enchanting stroll, especially early morning when tourists are few. Start at the top of the Butte de Montmartre at Sacré-Cœur (p94) for exceptional views (particularly from inside its dome), then drop by the Espace Dalí (p99). Wander through the peaceful Cimetière de Montmartre (p100), before visiting one of Paris' loveliest small museums, the Musée de la Vie Romantique (p99), dedicated to author George Sand. Downhill, Montmartre's southern neighbour, Pigalle is a (tame) red-light district fast becoming better known for its food and cocktails.

Getting There & Around

Ⓜ Anvers (line 2) is the most convenient for Sacré-Cœur and its funicular.

Ⓜ Abbesses and Lamarck–Caulaincourt (line 12) are in Montmartre's heart.

Ⓜ Blanche and Pigalle (line 2) are your best bet for the restaurants and nightlife around Pigalle.

Neighbourhood Map on p98

Place du Tertre (p97) TAKASHI IMAGES/SHUTTERSTOCK ©

Top Sight 📷
Sacré-Cœur

More than just a place of worship, the distinctive dove-white domed Basilique du Sacré-Cœur (Sacred Heart Basilica) is a veritable experience. Reached by 270 steps, the parvis (forecourt) in front of the basilica provides a postcard-perfect city panorama. Buskers and street artists perform on the steps, while picnickers spread out on the hillside park.

◎ MAP P98, D2

📞 01 53 41 89 00

www.sacre-coeur-montmartre.com

Parvis du Sacré-Cœur

admission free

🕑 basilica 6am-10.30pm

Ⓜ Anvers, Abbesses

History

Initiated in 1873 to atone for the bloodshed and controversy during the Franco-Prussian War (1870–71), designed by architect Paul Abadie and begun in 1875, the Roman-Byzantine basilica was funded largely by private, often small, donations. It was completed in 1914 but wasn't consecrated until after WWI in 1919.

In 1944, 13 Allied bombs were dropped on Montmartre. Although Sacré-Cœur's stained-glass windows were shattered, miraculously no one died and the basilica sustained no other damage.

Blessed Sacrament

In a sense, atonement here has never stopped: a prayer 'cycle' that began in 1835 continues around the clock, with perpetual adoration of the Blessed Sacrament that's on display above the high altar.

The Dome

Outside, to the west of the main entrance, 300 spiralling steps lead you to the basilica's **dome** (adult/child €6/4, cash only; ⏱8.30am-8pm May-Sep, 9am-5pm Oct-Apr), which affords one of Paris' most spectacular panoramas; it's said you can see for 30km on a clear day.

France's Largest Bell

La Savoyarde, in the basilica's huge square bell tower, is the largest bell in France, weighing in at 19 tonnes. It can be heard ringing out across the neighbourhood and beyond.

The Christ in Majesty Mosaic

The magnificent apse mosaic *Christ in Majesty*, designed by Luc-Olivier Merson in 1922, is one of the largest of its kind in the world. Its golden hues lighten Sacré-Cœur's otherwise dark interior.

★ Top Tips

o Skip most of the climb up to the basilica with the short but useful **Funicular de Montmartre** (www.ratp.fr; place St-Pierre, 18e; ⏱6am-12.45am; Ⓜ Anvers, Abbesses); use a regular metro ticket.

o For the best views, pick a blue-sky day to visit; don't climb to the top of the dome in bad weather.

o Download a free audioguide online.

✗ Take a Break

In fine weather head to **L'Été en Pente Douce** (☎ 01 42 64 02 67; http://lete-en-pente-douce.business.site; 8 rue Paul Albert, 18e; mains €10.50-17; ⏱noon-midnight; Ⓜ Château Rouge) for classic French fare and jumbo salads on a dreamy pavement terrace with green-lawn view.

Stop in for brunch or an expertly brewed coffee at **Hardware Société** (☎ 01 42 51 69 03; 10 rue Lamarck, 18e; ⏱9am-4pm Mon-Fri, 9.30am-4.30pm Sat & Sun; 📶; Ⓜ Château Rouge).

Walking Tour 🥾

Art in Montmartre

For centuries Montmartre was a bucolic country village filled with moulins (mills) that supplied Paris with flour. Incorporated into the capital in 1860, its picturesque – and affordable – charm attracted painters including Manet, Degas, Renoir, Van Gogh, Toulouse-Lautrec, Dufy, Picasso, Utrillo, Modigliani and Dalí in its late 19th- and early 20th-century heyday. Although much frequented by tourists, its local village atmosphere endures.

Walk Facts

Start Café des Deux Moulins; Ⓜ Blanche

Finish Ⓜ Abbesses

Length 1.65 km, 1.5 hours

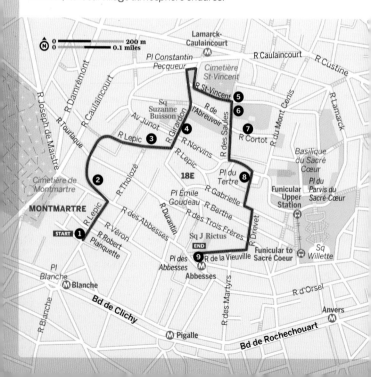

❶ Amélie's Cafe

Start with a coffee at this arty cafe, where Amélie worked as a waitress in the quirky film of the same name. **Café des Deux Moulins** (www.cafedesdeuxmoulins.fr; 15 rue Lepic, 18e; ⏱7.30am-2am Mon-Fri, from 8am Sat & Sun; 📶; Ⓜ Blanche) hangs on as a down-to-earth local.

❷ Van Gogh's House

Théo Van Gogh owned the house at **54 rue Lepic**; his brother, the artist Vincent, stayed with him on the 3rd floor for two years from 1886.

❸ Renoir's Dance Hall

Montmartre's two surviving windmills are the **Moulin Blute-Fin** and, 100m east, the **Moulin Radet** (83 rue Lepic, 18e; Ⓜ Abbesses), now a restaurant. In the 19th century, the windmills were turned into an open-air dance hall, immortalised by Renoir in his 1876 tableau *Le Bal du Moulin de la Galette* (now displayed in the Musée d'Orsay).

❹ Walker Through Walls

Crossing place Marcel Aymé you'll see a man emerging from a stone wall. The **Passe-Muraille statue** portrays Dutilleul, the hero of Marcel Aymé's short story *Le Passe-Muraille* (The Walker Through Walls). Aymé lived in the adjacent building from 1902 to 1967.

❺ Gill's Rabbit

Look for caricaturist André Gill's mural *Le Lapin à Gill*. It shows a rabbit jumping out of a cooking pot on the façade of long-running local cabaret **Au Lapin Agile**.

❻ Montmartre's Vineyard

The only vineyard in central Paris, **Clos Montmartre** (18 rue des Saules, 18e; Ⓜ Lamarck–Caulaincourt) dates from 1933. Its 2000 vines produce on average 800 bottles of wine each October, celebrated by the five-day Fête des Vendanges de Montmartre, with festivities including a parade.

❼ Local History Lessons

Local history comes to life at the Musée de Montmartre (p99), housed in Montmartre's oldest building – a 17th-century garden-set manor where Renoir, Utrillo and Dufy once lived. The manor also houses Suzanne Valadon's restored studio, open to the public.

❽ Artists at Work

The main square of the original village, **place du Tertre** (18e; Ⓜ Abbesses) has drawn countless painters in its time. While it's awash with visitors, local, often very talented, artists paint, sketch and sell their creations here, and the portraitists, buskers and crowds create an unmissable carnival-like atmosphere.

❾ The Art of Travel

With its original glass canopy and twin wrought-iron lamp posts still intact, **Abbesses** has the finest remaining example of art nouveau designer Hector Guimard's metro entrances.

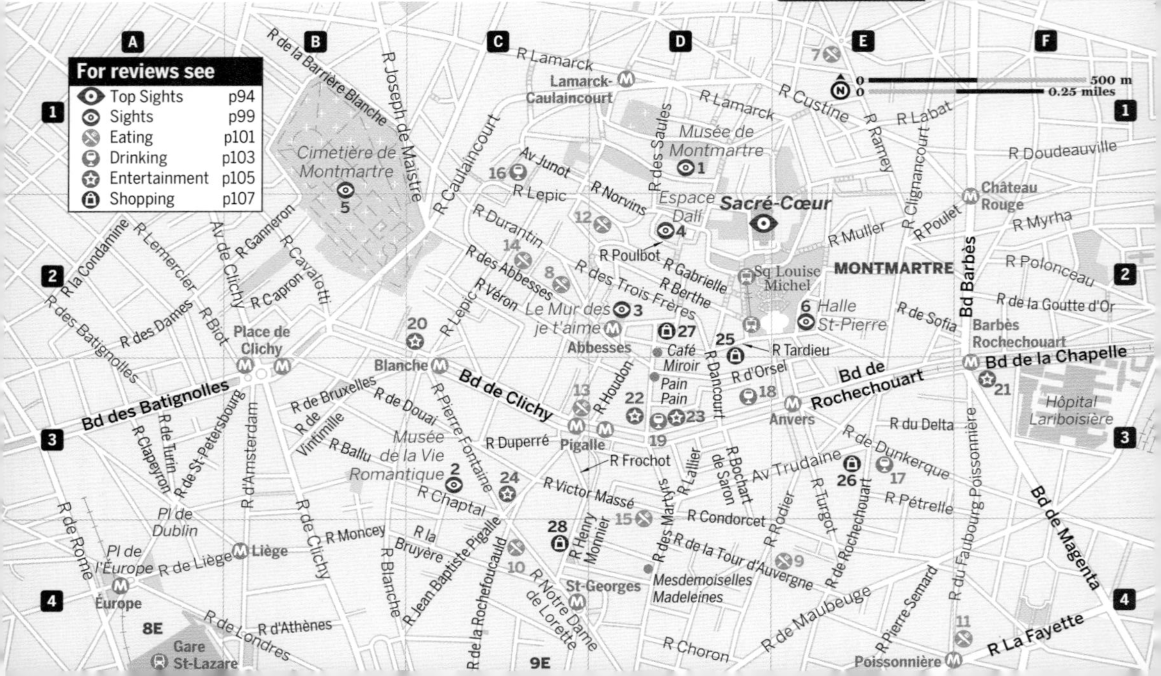
For reviews see
Top Sights p94
Sights p99
Eating p101
Drinking p103
Entertainment p105
Shopping p107
A
B
C
D
E
F
1
2
3
4
0 500 m
0 0.25 miles
N
Sacré-Cœur
MONTMARTRE
Cimetière de Montmartre
Musée de Montmartre
Espace Dalí
Sq Louise Michel
Halle St-Pierre
Le Mur des je t'aime
Café Miroir
Pain Pain
Musée de la Vie Romantique
Hôpital Lariboisière
Mesdemoiselles Madeleines
Place de Clichy
Pl de Dublin
Pl de l'Europe
Lamarck-Caulaincourt
Abbesses
Blanche
Pigalle
Anvers
Château Rouge
Barbès Rochechouart
Liège
Europe
St-Georges
Poissonnière
Gare St-Lazare
8E
9E
R Lamarck
R Custine
R Ramey
R Labat
R Clignancourt
R Doudeauville
R Myrha
R Poulet
R Muller
R Polonceau
R de la Goutte d'Or
R de Sofia
Bd Barbès
Bd de la Chapelle
Bd de Rochechouart
R Tardieu
R d'Orsel
R du Delta
R de Dunkerque
R Pétrelle
R du Faubourg Poissonnière
Bd de Magenta
R La Fayette
R Pierre Semard
R de Maubeuge
R de Rochechouart
R Turgot
R Rodier
Av Trudaine
R Bochart de Saron
R Condorcet
R de la Tour d'Auvergne
R des Martyrs
R Lallier
R Dancourt
R Choron
R Notre Dame de Lorette
R Henry Monnier
R Victor Massé
R Frochot
R Houdon
R des Saules
R Norvins
R Poulbot
R Gabrielle
R Berthe
R des Trois Frères
R des Abbesses
R Véron
R Durantin
R Lepic
Av Junot
R Caulaincourt
R Joseph de Maistre
R de la Barrière Blanche
R Ganneron
R Cavalotti
R Capron
Av de Clichy
R Biot
R des Dames
R Lemercier
R la Condamine
R des Batignolles
Bd des Batignolles
Bd de Clichy
R de St-Petersbourg
R de Turin
R Clapeyron
R d'Amsterdam
R de Bruxelles
R de Vintimille
R Ballu
R de Douai
R Pierre Fontaine
R Duperré
R Chaptal
R de Clichy
R Moncey
R la Bruyère
R Blanche
R Jean Baptiste Pigalle
R de la Rochefoucauld
R de Liège
R de Rome
R de Londres
R d'Athènes

Sights

Musée de Montmartre MUSEUM

1 ◎ MAP P98, D1

This delightful 'village' museum showcases paintings, lithographs and documents illustrating Montmartre's bohemian, artistic and hedonistic past – one room is dedicated entirely to the French cancan. It's housed in a 17th-century manor where several artists, including Renoir and Raoul Dufy, had their studios in the 19th century. You can also visit the studio of painter Suzanne Valadon, who lived and worked here with her son Maurice Utrillo and partner André Utter between 1912 and 1926. (🖉 01 49 25 89 39; www.museedemontmartre.fr; 12 rue Cortot, 18e; adult/child €9.50/5.50, garden only €4; ⏰10am-7pm Apr-Sep, to 6pm Oct-Mar; M Lamarck–Caulaincourt)

Musée de la Vie Romantique MUSEUM

2 ◎ MAP P98, C3

Framed by green shutters, this mansion where George Sand (Amantine Lucile Aurore Dupin) and painter Ary Scheffer once lived sits in a cobbled courtyard at the end of a tree-shaded alley. The objects exhibited create a wonderful flashback to Romantic-era Paris when Chopin (Sand's lover), Delacroix et al attended salons here. Admission is free except when there's a temporary exhibition. End your visit with tea and cake in the museum's cafe, open spring to autumn, in the enchanting garden. (🖉 01 55 31 95 67; www.vie-romantique.paris.fr; 16 rue Chaptal, 9e; ⏰10am-6pm Tue-Sun; M Blanche, St-Georges)

Le Mur des je t'aime PUBLIC ART

3 ◎ MAP P98, D2

Few visitors can resist a selfie in front of Montmartre's 'I Love You' wall, a public artwork created in a small park by artists Frédéric Baron and Claire Kito in the year 2000. Made from 511 dark-blue enamel tiles, the striking mural features the immortal phrase 'I love you' 311 times in nearly 250 different languages (the red fragments, if joined together, would form a heart). Find a bench beneath a maple tree and brush up your language skills romantic-Paris-style. (www.lesjetaime.com; Sq Jehan Rictus, place des Abbesses ,18e; ⏰8am-9.30pm Mon-Fri, from 9am Sat & Sun mid-May–Aug, shorter hours Sep–mid-May; M Abbesses)

Espace Dalí GALLERY

4 ◎ MAP P98, D2

More than 300 works by Salvador Dalí (1904–89), the flamboyant Catalan surrealist printmaker, painter, sculptor and self-promoter, are on display at this basement museum located just west of place du Tertre. The collection includes Dalí's strange sculptures, lithographs, and many of his illustrations and furniture, including the famous *Mae West Lips Sofa*. (🖉 01 42 64 40 21; www.daliparis.com;

Belle Époque Paris

The belle époque saw creativity flourish from the advent of France's Third Republic in 1870.

This 'beautiful era' launched art nouveau architecture, a whole field of artistic 'isms' from impressionism onwards, and advances in science and engineering, including the first metro line (1900). World Exhibitions were held in the capital in 1889 (showcased by the Eiffel Tower) and again in 1900 (by the Grand Palais and Petit Palais).

The Paris of nightclubs and artistic cafes made its first appearance around this time, and Montmartre became a magnet for artists, writers, pimps and prostitutes, with artists such as Toulouse-Lautrec creating cabaret posters of the Moulin Rouge's cancan dancers.

Other glamorous hot spots still operating include the restaurant Maxim's, now with an art nouveau museum upstairs, and the newly renovated Ritz Paris. The Musée d'Orsay contains a wealth of artistic expression from this era, from paintings through to exquisite furniture.

This inspired time lasted until the onset of WWI in 1914 – it was named in retrospect, recalling a peaceful 'golden age'.

11 rue Poulbot, 18e; adult/child €12/9; ◷10am-6pm Sep-Jun, to 8pm Jul & Aug; Ⓜ Abbesses)

Cimetière de Montmartre
CEMETERY

5 ◉ MAP P98, B1

This 11-hectare cemetery opened in 1825. It contains the graves of writers Émile Zola (whose ashes are now in the Panthéon), Alexandre Dumas *fils* and Stendhal, composers Jacques Offenbach and Hector Berlioz, artists Edgar Degas and Gustave Moreau, film director François Truffaut and dancer Vaslav Nijinsky, among others. Steps from the rue Caulaincourt road bridge, built in 1888, lead down to the entrance on av Rachel, just off bd de Clichy. (20 av Rachel, 18e; ◷8am-6pm Mon-Sat, from 9am Sun May-Sep, 8am-5.30pm Mon-Sat, 9am-5pm Sun Oct-Apr; Ⓜ Place de Clichy)

Halle St-Pierre
GALLERY

6 ◉ MAP P98, E2

Founded in 1986, this museum and gallery is in a lovely former covered market. It focuses on the primitive and Art Brut schools; there is no permanent collection, but the museum stages several temporary exhibitions a year. It also has an auditorium, a cafe and a bookshop. (☎01 42 58 72 89; www.hallesaintpierre.org; 2 rue Ronsard, 18e; adult/child €9/6; ◷11am-6pm Mon-Fri, to 7pm Sat, noon-6pm Sun; Ⓜ Anvers)

Eating

Abattoir Végétal
VEGAN €

7 MAP P98, E1

Mint-green wrought-iron chairs and tables line the pavement outside the 'plant slaughterhouse' (it occupies a former butcher shop), while the light, bright interior has bare-bulb downlights, distempered walls and greenery-filled hanging baskets. Each day there's a choice of three raw and cooked organic dishes per course, cold-pressed juices and craft beers from Parisian brewery BapBap. (61 rue Ramey, 18e; 3-course lunch menu €18, mains €13-16, Sunday brunch adult/child €25/5; 9am-6pm Tue & Wed, 9am-11.45pm Thu & Fri, 10am-11.45pm Sat, 10.30am-4.30pm Sun; M Jules Joffrin)

Le Grenier à Pain
BAKERY €

8 MAP P98, C2

A past winner of Paris' annual 'best baguette' prize, this enchanting bakery with a semi-open kitchen is an ideal place to pick up picnic fare. Join the queue for a crusty baguette sandwich, Provence-style *fougasse* bread and alluring mini breads topped with fig and goat's cheese or bacon and olives. End on a sweet high with a fruit-bejewelled loaf cake. (www.legrenierapain.com; 38 rue des Abbesses, 18e; 7.30am-8pm Thu-Mon; M Abbesses)

Aspic
BISTRO €€€

9 MAP P98, E4

Chef Quentin Giroud ditched the high-flying world of finance for the stoves, and this small vintage-style space with a semi-open kitchen is testament to his conviction. Weekly changing, no-choice tasting menus feature inspired creations such as peppercorn pancetta with kaffir lime butter, warm octopus with cashew purée, and celeriac with mustard shoots and grated raw cauliflower. (09 82 49 30 98; 24 rue de la Tour d'Auvergne, 9e; 7-course tasting menu €65, with wine €100; 7.30-9.30pm Tue-Sat; M Anvers)

L'affineur Affiné
CHEESE €

10 MAP P98, C4

With 120 French cheeses, this *fromagerie* (cheese shop) is a fabulous place to stock up and taste them at its on-site *bar à fromages* (cheese bar). Let the staff know your preferences and they'll prepare platters of two to 15 varieties, with charcuterie available as well as paired wines. Weekend brunch is a multi-course feast. (09 66 94 22 15; www.laffineuraffine.com; 51 rue Notre Dame de Lorette, 9e; cheese platters €6.50-39, weekend brunch €20; kitchen noon-2.30pm Mon, noon-2.30pm & 5.30-9pm Wed-Sat, 11.30am-2pm & 5.30-7pm Sun, shop 10.30am-2.30pm Mon, to 9pm Wed-Sat, to 7pm Sun; M St-Georges)

Abri
BISTRO €€

11 MAP P98, F4

It's no bigger than a shoebox and the decor is borderline nonexistent, but that's all part of the charm. Katsuaki Okiyama is a seriously talented chef with an artistic flair, and his surprise tasting menus (three courses at lunch, six at dinner) are exceptional. On Saturdays, a giant gourmet sandwich is all that's served for lunch. Reserve months in advance. (☏01 83 97 00 00; 92 rue du Faubourg Poissonnière, 9e; lunch/dinner menus €26/49; ◷12.30-2pm Mon, 12.30-2pm & 7.30-10pm Tue-Fri, 12.30-3pm & 7.30-10pm Sat; Ⓜ Poissonnière)

Le Bistrot de la Galette

BISTRO €€

🔟2 ⊗ MAP P98, D2

In the shadow of Montmartre windmill Moulin de la Galette, this vintage-fitted bistro is the creation of pastry chef Gilles Mar chal, who uses locally hand-milled flour in *feuilletés* (delicately laminated pastry puffs) that accompany most dishes, such as *galette parisienne* (roast ham, sautéed mushrooms and Comté) and *galette provençale* (shredded roast lamb, aubergine, garlic and sun-dried tomatoes). (☏01 46 06 19 65; www.bistrotdelagalette.fr; 102ter rue Lepic, 18e; mains €14-17; ◷11am-10pm Tue-Sun; Ⓜ Abbesses, Lamarck–Caulaincourt)

Bouillon Pigalle

BRASSERIE €

🔟3 ⊗ MAP P98, C3

Brilliant prices, all-day service and quality ingredients used in unapologetically traditional dishes – snails with garlic and parsley butter, welks with sorrel aioli, *pot-au-feu* (hotpot) and *tête de veau* (boiled calf's head) – are the keys to the success of this new-generation *bouillon* (workers' canteen-style 'soup kitchen'). It doesn't take reservations, so arrive outside peak times or expect to queue. (www.bouillonpigalle.com; 22 bd de Clichy, 18e; mains €8.50-11.50; ◷noon-midnight; Ⓜ Pigalle)

La Mascotte

SEAFOOD €€

🔟4 ⊗ MAP P98, C2

Founded in 1889, this cavernous bar with green-and-white-striped awnings is as authentic as it gets in Montmartre. It specialises in quality seafood (lobster, langoustine, scallops and more); you can just pull up a seat at the bar for a glass of wine and plate of oysters in season. The children's *menu* is €22. (☏01 46 06 28 15; www.la-mascotte-montmartre.com; 52 rue des Abbesses, 18e; 2-course lunch menus €32, 3-course dinner menus €49, mains €26-36; ◷noon-11.30pm; 🚼; Ⓜ Abbesses)

Bouillon Pigalle

Rue des Martyrs

Stretching 960m from the 18e (metro Abbesses) to the 9e (metro Notre Dame de Lorette), sloping rue des Martyrs is a foodie's fantasyland, lined with gourmet shops, award-winning *boulangeries* (bakeries) such as **Pain Pain** (Map p98, D3; www.pain-pain.fr; 88 rue des Martyrs, 18e; sandwiches & pastries €2.20-5.25; 🕑7am-8pm Tue-Sat, 7.30am-7.30pm Sun; **M** Abbesses), and patisseries (pastry shops), including specialists such as **Mesdemoiselles Madeleines** (Map p98, D4; www.mllesmadeleines.com; 37 rue des Martyrs, 9e; madeleines small €0.70, large €2.50-4.50; 🕑10.30am-7pm Tue-Sat, 10.30am-2pm & 3.30-6.30pm Sun; **M** St-Georges), solely devoted to madeleine cakes.

Interspersed between them are Parisian cafes and bistros, such as locals' favourite **Café Miroir** (Map p98, D2; 📞01 46 06 50 73; www.cafemiroir.com; 94 rue des Martyrs, 18e; 3-course midweek lunch menu €19.50, mains €23-37; 🕑8am-10pm Tue-Sat; **M** Abbesses), and regional and international restaurants (Corsican, Portuguese, Spanish, Greek...). Down the southern end, grocers, fishmongers and butchers set up pavement stalls. From late 2018, 300m between rue de Navarin and rue St-Lazare will prioritise pedestrians.

Le Pantruche
FRENCH €€

15 🍴 MAP P98, D3

Oak-furnished Pantruche woos foodies in the dining hot spot of south Pigalle with its intimate setting, reasonable prices and seasonal neobistro fare. Daring creations might include oysters with green lettuce foam, lamb ravioli with mimolette and mint, wild hare with beetroot jus, or red mullet and bacon-wrapped polenta. Some mains incur a supplement. Reserve well in advance. (📞01 48 78 55 60; 3 rue Victor Massé, 9e; 2-/3-course lunch menus €19/36, mains €22; 🕑12.30-2.30pm & 7.30-10.30pm Mon-Fri; **M** Pigalle)

Drinking

Le Très Particulier
COCKTAIL BAR

16 🍸 MAP P98, C1

The clandestine cocktail bar of boutique Hôtel Particulier Montmartre is an entrancing spot for a summertime alfresco cocktail. Ring the buzzer at the unmarked black gated entrance and make a beeline for the 1871 mansion's flowery walled garden (or the adjacent conservatory-style interior). DJs spin tunes from 9.30pm Wednesday to Saturday and from 7pm on Sunday. (📞01 53 41 81 40; www.hotel-particulier-montmartre.com; Pavillon D, 23 av Junot, 18e; 🕑6pm-2am; **M** Lamarck–Caulaincourt)

Chez Bouboule SPORTS BAR

17 MAP P98, E3

Pétanque game washed out? Head to Chez Bouboule, which has a packed-sand indoor *boulodrome* (pitch for playing the bowls-like sport) right inside the buzzing bar (equipment is free). Craft beer, wine and cider is available alongside cocktails such as its signature Bouboule, made with gin, mint, cinnamon, pepper and juniper berries. It also has table football and shows big-screen sporting fixtures. (www.chezbouboule.fr; 79 rue de Dunkerque, 9e; 5pm-2am Tue-Sat; M Anvers)

Le Petit Trianon CAFE

18 MAP P98, D3

With its large windows and a few carefully chosen antiques, this belle époque cafe at the foot of Montmartre seems as timeless as the Butte itself. Dating back to 1894 and attached to the venerable Le Trianon theatre, it's no stretch to imagine artists like Toulouse-Lautrec and crowds of show-goers once filling the place in the evening. All-day food too. (01 44 92 78 08; 80 bd de Rochechouart, 18e; 8am-2am; M Anvers)

La Fourmi BAR

19 MAP P98, D3

A Pigalle institution, sociable La Fourmi hits the mark with its high ceilings, long zinc bar, timber-panelled walls and unpretentious vibe. It's a great place to find out about live music and club nights or grab a drink before heading out to a show. Bonus: table football.

Moulin Rouge

©MOULIN ROUGE® S.BERTRAND

SoPi
Cocktails

Old girlie bars in rapidly gentrifying red-light district south Pigalle (SoPi) have morphed into some of the city's most exciting cocktail bars: start a bar crawl on rue Frochot (Map p98, C3) at **Lipstick** (www.lipstickparis.com; 5 rue Frochot, 9e; ⏱6pm-5am Tue-Sat; Ⓜ Pigalle), with bordello-style decor; Prohibition-era New Orleans–styled **Lulu White** (www.luluwhite.bar; 12 rue Frochot, 9e; ⏱7pm-2am Mon, Wed, Thu & Sun, to 4am Fri & Sat; Ⓜ Pigalle); Parisian-brewed Paname beers and spectacular cocktails such as Ticket de Metro at **Glass** (www.quixotic-projects.com/venue/glass; 7 rue Frochot, 9e; ⏱7pm-4am Sun-Thu, to 5am Fri & Sat; Ⓜ Pigalle); or tiki bar **Dirty Dick** (10 rue Frochot, 9e; ⏱6pm-2am; Ⓜ Pigalle).

(74 rue des Martyrs, 18e; ⏱8am-2am Mon-Thu, to 4am Fri 9am-4am Sat, 10am-2am Sun; Ⓜ Pigalle)

La Machine du Moulin Rouge

CLUB

Part of the original Moulin Rouge (see 20 ⭐ Map p98, C2) – well, the boiler room, anyway – this club packs 'em in on weekends with a dance floor, a concert hall, a Champagne bar and an outdoor terrace. Check the agenda online for weekday soirées and happenings. (www.lamachinedumoulinrouge.com; 90 bd de Clichy, 18e; admission €9-16; ⏱midnight-6am Fri & Sat, variable Sun-Thu; Ⓜ Blanche)

Entertainment

Moulin Rouge

CABARET

20 ⭐ MAP P98, C2

Immortalised in Toulouse-Lautrec's posters and later in Baz Luhrmann's film, Paris' legendary cabaret twinkles beneath a 1925 replica of its original red windmill. Yes, it's packed with bus-tour crowds. But from the opening bars of music to the last high cancan kick, it's a whirl of fantastical costumes, sets, choreography and Champagne. Book in advance and dress smartly (no trainers or sneakers). (☎01 53 09 82 82; www.moulinrouge.fr; 82 bd de Clichy, 18e; show only from €87, lunch & show from €165, dinner & show from €190; ⏱show only 2.45pm, 9pm & 11pm, lunch & show 1.45pm, dinner & show 7pm; Ⓜ Blanche)

Le Louxor

CINEMA

21 ⭐ MAP P98, F3

Built in neo-Egyptian art-deco style in 1921 and saved from demolition by a neighbourhood association seven decades later, this historical monument is a palatial place to catch a new release, classic, piano-accompanied 'ciné-concert', short-film festival, special

Flea Markets

Spanning 9 hectares, the vast flea market **Marché aux Puces de St-Ouen** (www.marcheauxpuces-saintouen.com; rue des Rosiers, St-Ouen; ☺Sat-Mon; Ⓜ Porte de Clignancourt) was founded in 1870 and is said to be Europe's largest. Over 2000 stalls are grouped into 15 *marchés* (markets) selling everything from 17th-century furniture to 21st-century clothing. Each market has different opening hours – check the website for details. There are miles upon miles of 'freelance' stalls; come prepared to spend some time. Dining options here include the legendary **Chez Louisette** (☏ 01 40 12 10 14; Marché Vernaison, 130 av Michelet, St-Ouen, Marché aux Puces de St-Ouen; mains €14-17; ☺11am-7pm Sat-Mon; Ⓜ Porte de Clignancourt), where singers perform rousing *chansons*.

Nearby, an abandoned station of the Petite Ceinture (the steam-train line that once encircled Paris) has been repurposed as **La REcyclerie** (www.larecyclerie.com; 83 bd Ornano, 18e; ☺8am-midnight Mon-Thu, to 2am Fri & Sat, to 10pm Sun early Jan–mid-Dec; Ⓜ Porte de Clignancourt), an eco-hub with an urban farm along the old railway line, featuring community vegetable and herb gardens and chickens, a mostly vegetarian cafe-canteen, workshops and events including its own flea markets.

workshop (such as singalongs) or live-music performance. Don't miss a drink at its bar, which opens onto an elevated terrace overlooking Sacré-Cœur. (☏ 01 44 63 96 98; www.cinemalouxor.fr; 170 bd de Magenta, 10e; tickets adult/child €9.70/5; Ⓜ Barbès-Rochechouart)

Le Divan du Monde
LIVE MUSIC

22 ⭐ MAP P98, D3

Take some cinematographic events and *nouvelles chansons françaises* (new French songs). Add in soul/funk fiestas, air-guitar face-offs and rock parties of the Arctic Monkeys/Killers/Libertines persuasion... You may now be

getting some idea of the inventive, open-minded approach at this excellent cross-cultural venue in Pigalle. (☏ 01 40 05 08 10; www.divandumonde.com; 75 rue des Martyrs, 18e; Ⓜ Pigalle)

La Cigale
LIVE MUSIC

23 ⭐ MAP P98, D3

Now classed as a historical monument, this music hall dates from 1887 but was redecorated a century later by Philippe Starck. Artists who have performed here include Ryan Adams, Ibrahim Maalouf and the Dandy Warhols. (☏ 01 49 25 89 99; www.lacigale.fr; 120 bd de Rochechouart, 18e; Ⓜ Pigalle)

Bus Palladium

LIVE MUSIC

24 ⊛ MAP P98, C3

The place to be in the 1960s (Dalí, Hallyday and Jagger all hung out here), the Bus is back in business half-a-century later, with a mixed bag of performances by DJs and indie and pop groups. (📞01 45 26 80 35; www.buspalladium.com; 6 rue Pierre Fontaine, 9e; ⊙Tue-Sat; Ⓜ Pigalle, Blanche)

Shopping

Belle du Jour

FASHION & ACCESSORIES

25 🔒 MAP P98, D2

Be whisked back in time to the elegance of belle époque Paris at this Montmartre shop specialising in perfume bottles. Gorgeous 19th-century atomisers, smelling salts and powder boxes in engraved or enamelled Bohemian, Baccarat and Saint-Louis crystal share shelf space with more contemporary designs. Whether you're after art deco or art nouveau, pink-frosted or painted glass, it's here. (www.belle-de-jour.fr; 7 rue Tardieu, 18e; ⊙11am-1pm & 2-7pm Tue-Fri, 11am-1pm & 2-6pm Sat; Ⓜ Anvers, Abbesses)

Balades Sonores

MUSIC

26 🔒 MAP P98, E3

One of Paris' best vinyl shops, Balades Sonores sprawls over two adjacent buildings. The ground floor of 1 av Trudaine stocks con-

temporary pop, rock metal, garage and all genres of French music. Its basement holds secondhand blues, country, new wave and punk from the '60s to '90s. Next door, No 3 has soul, jazz, funk, hip-hop, electronica and world music. (www.baladessonores.com; 1-3 av Trudaine, 9e; ⊙noon-8pm Mon-Sat; Ⓜ Anvers)

Spree

FASHION & ACCESSORIES

27 🔒 MAP P98, D2

Allow plenty of time to browse this super-stylish boutique-gallery, with a carefully selected collection of designer fashion put together by stylist Roberta Oprandi and artist Bruni Hadjadj. What makes shopping here fun is that all the furniture – vintage 1950s to 1980s pieces by Eames and other midcentury designers – is also for sale, as is the contemporary artwork on the walls. (📞01 42 23 41 40; www.spree.fr; 16 rue de la Vieuville, 18e; ⊙11am-7.30pm Tue-Sat, 3-7pm Sun & Mon; Ⓜ Abbesses)

Pigalle

FASHION & ACCESSORIES

28 🔒 MAP P98, C4

Pick up a hoodie emblazoned with the black-and-white Pigalle logo from this leading Parisian mens-wear brand, created by designer and basketball player Stéphane Ashpool, who grew up in the 'hood. (www.pigalle-paris.com; 7 rue Henry Monnier, 9e; ⊙noon-8pm Mon-Sat, from 2pm Sun; Ⓜ St-Georges)

Walking Tour 🚶

Exploring the Canal St-Martin

Bordered by shaded towpaths and criss-crossed with iron footbridges, Canal St-Martin (about 4km north of Notre Dame) wends through the city's northern quartiers (quarters). You can float past on a canal cruise, but strolling among the cool cafes, offbeat boutiques and hip bars and clubs lets you see why it's beloved by Parisian bobos (bourgeois bohemians).

Getting There

Ⓜ République (lines 3, 5, 8, 9 and 11) is centrally located.

Ⓜ Château d'Eau, Jacques Bonsergent, Gare de l'Est and Parmentier are useful stations.

❶ Coffee with the Locals

Kick off with coffee at **52 Faubourg St-Denis** (www.faubourgstdenis.com; 52 rue du Faubourg St-Denis, 10e; mains €17-20; ☉kitchen noon-2.30pm & 7-11pm, bar 8am-midnight, closed Aug; ☎), a contemporary neighbourhood restaurant-cafe.

❷ Retro Clothes Shopping

Flip through colour-coded racks of vintage cast-offs at **Frivoli** (26 rue Beaurepaire, 10e; ☉1-7pm Mon, from 11am Tue-Sat, from 2pm Sun).

❸ Pizza Picnic

Order a pizza from **Pink Flamingo** (☎01 42 02 31 70; www.pinkflamingopizza.com; 67 rue Bichat, 10e; pizzas €11.50-17.50; ☉7-11.30pm Mon-Thu, noon-2.30pm & 7-11.30pm Fri & Sat, noon-11.30pm Sun) and receive a pink helium balloon; it's used to locate you at your picnic spot when the pizza is delivered.

❹ Cultural Cool

Within a converted warehouse, alternative cultural centre **Point Éphémère** (☎01 40 34 02 48; www.pointephemere.org; 200 quai de Valmy, 10e; ☉12.30pm-2am Mon-Sat, to 11pm Sun; ☎) has resident artists and musicians, exhibitions and a chilled bar-restaurant.

❺ Cafe Culture

Watch the boats from spirited **L'Atmosphère** (49 rue Lucien Sampaix, 10e; ☉9am-2am Mon-Sat, to midnight Sun), hit barista-run **Holybelly** (www.holybellycafe.com; 5 rue Lucien Sampaix, 10e; dishes €6.50-16.50; ☉9am-5pm; ☎) or head to original *bobo* hang-out **Chez Prune** (36 rue Beaurepaire, 10e; cnr quai de Valmy; ☉8am-2am Mon-Sat, 10am-2am Sun).

❻ Hilltop Heaven

A far cry from its former incarnation as a rubbish tip and quarry for Baron Haussmann's 19th-century reformation, hilly **Parc des Buttes Chaumont** (rue Manin & rue Botzaris, 19e; ☉7am-10pm May-Sep, to 8pm Oct-Apr) conceals grottoes, artificial waterfalls and a temple-topped island, plus dance hall/cafe **Rosa Bonheur** (www.rosabonheur.fr; 2 allée de la Cascade, Parc des Buttes Chaumont, 19e; ☉noon-midnight Thu & Fri, from 10am Sat & Sun).

❼ Wine-bar Dining

Animated wine bar **Le Baratin** (☎01 43 49 39 70; 3 rue Jouye-Rouve, 20e; lunch menus €19, mains €22-34; ☉noon-2.30pm Tue-Fri, plus 7.30-11.15pm Tue-Sat) offers some of the best French food in the 20e with its ever-changing blackboard options.

❽ Nightcap, Nightlife

Finish with a drink at the belle époque **Café Charbon** (www.lecafecharbon.fr; 109 rue Oberkampf, 11e; ☉8am-2am Mon-Wed, to 5am Thu, to 6am Fri & Sat; ☎) or kick on at its live music and DJ venue, **Nouveau Casino** (www.nouveaucasino.net).

Explore ⊚
Centre Pompidou & Le Marais

Paris' marais (marsh) was cleared in the 12th century but Haussmann's reformations left its tangle of medieval laneways largely intact. Hip bars and restaurants, emerging designers' boutiques and the city's thriving gay and Jewish communities all squeeze into this vibrant neighbourhood and its equally buzzing eastern neighbour, Bastille.

The twice-weekly Marché Bastille (p121) is one of the largest, liveliest street markets in Paris – catch it if you can before visiting the Musée National Picasso (p118) and the Maison de Victor Hugo (p118), the author's former home on elegant place des Vosges (p121). Stroll along the leafy Promenade Plantée (p120) walkway above an old railway viaduct, or simply spend the afternoon browsing Le Marais' trove of independent shops. The Centre Pompidou (p112) keeps extended hours, so head here in the late afternoon to see its amazing collection of modern and contemporary art and the awesome views from its roof.

Getting There & Around

Ⓜ Rambuteau (line 11) is the most convenient for the Centre Pompidou.

Ⓜ Other central metro stations include Hôtel de Ville (lines 1 and 11), St-Paul (line 1) and Bastille (lines 1, 5 and 8).

🚤 The hop-on, hop-off Batobus stops outside the Hôtel de Ville.

Neighbourhood Map on p116

Top Sight 📷

Centre Pompidou

The Centre Pompidou has amazed and delighted visitors ever since it opened in 1977, not just for its outstanding collection of modern art but also for its radical architectural statement. The dynamic and vibrant arts centre delights and enthrals with its irresistible cocktail of galleries, exhibitions, workshops, dance performances, bookshop, design boutique, cinemas and a research library.

◉ MAP P116, A2

☎ 01 44 78 12 33

www.centrepompidou.fr

place Georges Pompidou, 4e

museum, exhibitions & panorama adult/child €14/free

🕙 11am-9pm Wed-Mon, temporary exhibits to 11pm Thu

Ⓜ Rambuteau

The Architecture

Former French president Georges Pompidou wanted an ultra-contemporary artistic hub and he got it: competition-winning architects Renzo Piano and Richard Rogers effectively designed the building inside out, with utilitarian features such as plumbing, pipes, air vents and electrical cables forming part of the external façade, freeing up the interior space for exhibitions and events.

The then controversial, now much-loved centre opened in 1977. Viewed from a distance (such as from Sacré-Cœur) its primary-coloured, box-like form amid a sea of muted-grey Parisian rooftops makes it look like a child's Meccano set abandoned on someone's elegant living-room rug.

Musée National d'Art Moderne

Europe's largest collection of modern art fills the airy, well-lit galleries of the National Museum of Modern Art. On a par with the permanent collection are the two temporary exhibition halls (on the ground floor/basement and the top floor) which host memorable block-buster exhibits. There's a wonderful children's gallery on the 1st floor.

The permanent collection changes every two years, but incorporates artists such as Picasso, Matisse, Chagall, Kandinsky, Kahlo, Warhol, Pollock and many more. The 5th floor showcases artists active between 1905 and 1970 (give or take a decade); the 4th floor focuses on more contemporary art, architecture and design.

The Rooftop

Although the Centre Pompidou is just six storeys high, Paris' low-rise cityscape means sweeping views (panorama only ticket €5/free) extend from its rooftop, reached by external escalators enclosed in tubes.

★ Top Tips

o The Centre Pompidou opens late every night (except Tuesday, when it's closed), so head here around 5pm to avoid the daytime crowds.

o You'll still have to queue to get through security, but the entry process will go faster if you buy museum and events tickets online.

o Rooftop entry is included in museum and exhibition admission; alternatively, buy a panorama ticket (€5) just for the roof.

✕ Take a Break

Georges' outdoor terrace on the 6th floor is a fabulous spot for a drink with a view.

For a meal or casual drink, head to nearby **Café La Fusée** (☏ 01 42 76 93 99; 168 rue St-Martin, 3e; ◷ 9am-2am Mon-Fri, 10am-2am Sat & Sun; M Rambuteau, Étienne Marcel) or **Dame Tartine** (☏ 01 42 77 32 22; 2 rue Brisemiche, 4e; tartines €9.90-14; ◷ 9am-11.30pm; ☎; M Hôtel de Ville).

Walking Tour 🥾

A Heads-Up on the Haut Marais

The lower Marais has long been fashionable but the real buzz these days is in the haut Marais (upper, ie northern Marais). Its warren of narrow streets is a hub for up-and-coming fashion designers, art galleries, and vintage, accessories and homewares boutiques, alongside long-established enterprises enjoying a renaissance.

Walk Facts

Start Merci,
Ⓜ St-Sébastien Froissart

Finish Le Mary Céleste,
Ⓜ Filles du Calvaire

Length 1.3km, one hour

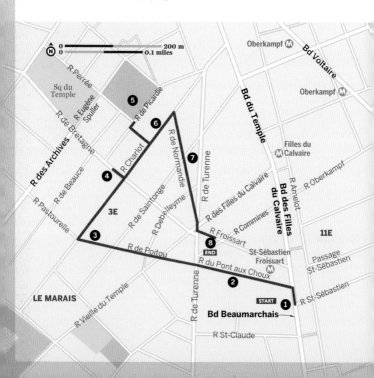

❶ Charitable Fashion

Fronted by a Fiat Cinquecento, unique concept store Merci (p130) donates all profits from its cutting-edge fashions, homewares, gifts, cafe and canteen to a children's charity in Madagascar.

❷ Coffee Fix

Reboot with a Parisian-roasted coffee at Boot Café (p128). Set inside an old cobbler's shop, which has a beautifully preserved original washed-blue façade and 'Cordon-nerie' lettering.

❸ Discounted Fashion

Savvy Parisians grab last season's designer wear (for both men and women) at up to 70% off original prices at **L'Habilleur** (www.habilleur. fr; 44 rue de Poitou, 3e; ⏰noon-7pm Mon-Sat; Ⓜ St-Sébastien–Froissart).

❹ Market Lunch

Hidden behind an inconspicuous green metal gate, Marché des Enfants Rouges (p125) has produce stalls and dishes that range from bento boxes to crêpes, which you can eat at communal tables.

❺ Cultural Happenings

The quarter's old covered market with magnificent art nouveau ironwork, **Le Carreau du Temple** (☎01 83 81 93 30; www.carreaudu temple.eu; 2 rue Perrée, 3e; ⏰box office 10am-9pm Mon-Fri, to 7pm Sat; Ⓜ Temple) is now a vast stage for exhibitions, concerts, sports classes and theatre.

❻ Fibre Fashion

Clothing and textile artworks crafted from natural and rare animal fibres are exhibited and sold at **La Boutique Extraordinaire** (www.laboutiqueextraordinaire.com; 67 rue Charlot, 3e; ⏰11am-8pm Tue-Sat, 3-7pm Sun; Ⓜ Filles du Calvaire).

❼ Children's Fashion

Homegrown Le Marais label **Finger in the Nose** (www.fingerinthe nose.com; 60 rue de Saintonge, 3e; ⏰11am-7pm Tue-Sat; Ⓜ Filles du Calvaire) creates edgy, urban clothing for kids at its nearby workshop and showcases its collections here at its flagship boutique. Look out for limited-edition lines, house-designed graphic prints and a great range of jeans.

❽ Cocktail Hour

Snag a stool at the central circular bar of ubercool **Le Mary Céleste** (www.quixotic-projects. com/venue/mary-celeste; 1 rue Commines, 3e; ⏰6pm-2am, kitchen 7-11.30pm; Ⓜ Filles du Calvaire) for creative cocktails and tapas-style 'small plates'.

Centre Pompidou & Le Marais

3E

LE MARAIS

4E

For reviews see

◉	Top Sights	p112
◎	Sights	p118
✗	Eating	p121
◎	Drinking	p127
★	Entertainment	p129
🅐	Shopping	p130

Musée des Arts et Métiers ◉ 4

R de Turbigo
R Réaumur
R de Turbigo
R St-Martin
R Beaubourg
R au Maire
Le Tango
R des Gravilliers
R Chapon
R aux Ours
R Michel le Comte
R du Temple
Musée d'Art et d'Histoire du Judaïsme
Rambuteau Ⓜ
R Rambuteau
◉ Centre Pompidou
Lafayette ◎ 7 Anticipations
Open Café
R du Renard
Hôtel de Ville Ⓜ BHV
Quetzal 40 33
🅐 39
R de Rivoli
35
Hôtel de Ville ◎ 8
R François Miron
Mémorial de la Shoah
2 ◎ 32
6 ◎
Pont Louis-Philippe
Île de la Cité
Parc Rives de Seine
Seine
Q de l'Hôtel de Ville
Pont St-Louis
Île St-Louis
Pont Marie
Q des Célestins
Q d'Anjou
R St-Louis en l'Île
Pont de Sully

R de Turbigo
R du Temple
R Dupetit Thouars
R Béranger
Bd du Temple
Bd Voltaire
Sq du Temple
19 R de Bretagne
38
30
Filles du Calvaire
R de Saintonge
23
28
R des Filles du Calvaire
R Oberkampf
R de Poitou
St-Sébastien Froissart
31
Bd Beaumarchais
R Charlot
R de Turenne
14 R des Coutures St-Gervais
Musée National Picasso ◉ 1
R de Thorigny
R St-Claude
36 🅐
37 🅐
13
Bd Amelot
LE MARAIS
R des Quatre-Fils
R des Blancs Manteaux
R des Archives
R Barbette
10 Musée Cognacq-Jay
R du Parc Royal
R Elzévir
Vieille du Temple
R des Francs Bourgeois
20
R des Rosiers
Art Nouveau Synagogue
3w Kafé
R Pavée
R Malher
R de Sévigné
R du Roi de Sicile
R des Écouffes
R St-Gilles
R de Béarn
R du Pas de la Mule
Pl des Vosges
R des Tournelles
Chemin Vert Ⓜ
St-Paul Ⓜ
25
R François Miron
R St-Paul
R Charlemagne
R Charles V
R du Petit Musc
Maison de Victor Hugo ◎ 3
22
R St-Antoine
Bastille Ⓜ
Pont Marie
R des Nonnains d'Hyères
Sully-Morland Ⓜ
Bd Henri IV
Bd Morland
Bd Bourdon
R de l'Arsenal
R Mornay
Bd de la Bastille

▲ N
0 ——— 400 m
0 ——— 0.2 miles

E R Jean-Pierre Timbaud
F
G
H Bd de Ménilmontant

Bd Richard Lenoir

R Oberkampf

R Crespin du Gast

Le Perchoir

1

R des Bluets

Oberkampf

Av de la République

R Ternaux
16

Av Parmentier

St-Maur

R de la Folie Méricourt

R Pasteur

R St-Ambroise

L'Atelier des Lumières
5

2

R du Chemin Vert

R Merlin

Passage St-Pierre Amelot
Passage St-Sébastien
21
R-St-Sébastien

St-Ambroise

R Lacharrière

Sq Maurice Gardette
29

R St-Maur

15

R Duranti

Richard Lenoir

Bd Voltaire

Av Parmentier

R Sevran

Sq de la Roquette

3

Bd Richard Lenoir

R Pelée
Allée Verte

R Mouffe

R du Chemin Vert

R Pétion

R St-Sabin

R Froment

R Bréguet

R Popincourt

Pl Léon Blum

R de la Roquette

R Léon Frot

R de Belfort

Bd Voltaire

4

Bréguet–Sabin

R St-Sabin

Cadet Larry

R du

R Sedaine

Voltaire

12

R Daval

R de la Roquette

Passage Charles Dallery

Av Ledru-Rollin

R Godefroy Cavaignac

Charonne

Place de la Bastille
11

41
Le Balajo

La Chapelle des Lombards

R des Taillandiers

R Keller

R Bastrot

R de Charonne

24

R Jules Vallès

R Jean Mace
27

5

18

Bastille

R de Lappe
26

R de Charonne

R Charles Delescluze

R St-Bernard

R Faidherbe

R Paul Bert

34
Bastille

R du Faubourg St-Antoine

Ledru–Rollin

R Trousseau

R de Montreuil

Faidherbe-Chaligny

6

R de Lyon

R de Charenton

Ledru–Rollin

R Théophile Roussel

R de Cotte

Marché d'Aligre

R de Cîteaux

R de Reuilly

Promenade Plantée
9

12E

Av Ledru-Rollin

R de Prague

R d'Aligre

R Crozatier

St-Antoine

R Jules César

Av Daumesnil

R Émilio Castelar
Marché Beauvau

Pl d'Aligre

Marché aux Puces d'Aligre

E
F
G
H

Sights

Musée National Picasso
MUSEUM

1 MAP P116, C3

One of Paris' most treasured art collections is showcased inside the mid-17th-century Hôtel Salé, an exquisite private mansion owned by the city since 1964. The Musée National Picasso is a staggering art museum devoted to Spanish artist Pablo Picasso (1881–1973), who spent much of his life living and working in Paris. The collection includes more than 5000 drawings, engravings, paintings, ceramic works and sculptures by the *grand maître* (great master), although they're not all displayed at the same time. (01 85 56 00 36; www.museepicassoparis.fr; 5 rue de Thorigny, 3e; adult/child €12.50/free; 10.30am-6pm Tue-Fri, from 9.30am Sat & Sun; Chemin Vert, St-Paul)

Mémorial de la Shoah
MUSEUM

2 MAP P116, B4

Established in 1956, the Memorial to the Unknown Jewish Martyr has metamorphosed into the Memorial of the Shoah – 'Shoah' is a Hebrew word meaning 'catastrophe' and it's synonymous in France with the Holocaust. Museum exhibitions relate to the Holocaust and German occupation of parts of France and Paris during WWII. The actual memorial to the victims stands at the entrance. The wall is inscribed with the names of 76,000 men, women and children deported from France to Nazi extermination camps. (www.memorialdelashoah.org; 17 rue Geoffroy l'Asnier, 4e; admission free; 10am-6pm Sun-Wed & Fri, to 10pm Thu; Pont Marie, St-Paul)

Maison de Victor Hugo
MUSEUM

3 MAP P116, D4

Between 1832 and 1848 the celebrated novelist and poet Victor Hugo lived in an apartment in Hôtel de Rohan-Guéménée, a townhouse overlooking one of Paris' most elegant squares. Hugo moved here a year after the publication of *Notre Dame de Paris* (The Hunchback of Notre Dame), completing *Ruy Blas* during his stay. It's now a museum devoted to his life and works, with an impressive collection of his personal drawings and portraits. Temporary exhibitions command an admission fee. (01 42 72 10 16; www.maisonsvictorhugo.paris.fr; 6 place des Vosges, 4e; admission free; 10am-6pm Tue-Sun; Bastille)

Musée des Arts et Métiers
MUSEUM

4 MAP P116, B1

The Arts and Crafts Museum, dating to 1794 and Europe's oldest science and technology museum, is a must for families – or anyone with an interest in how things tick or work. Housed inside the sublime 18th-century priory of St-Martin des Champs, some 2400 instruments, machines and working models from the 18th to 20th centuries are displayed across three floors. In the priory's attached church is Foucault's original pendulum, introduced to the world at the Universal Exhibition in Paris in 1855. (www.arts-et-metiers.net; 60 rue de Réaumur, 3e; adult/child €8/free, 6-9.30pm Thu & 1st Sun of month free; ⏰10am-6pm Tue, Wed & Fri-Sun, to 9.30pm Thu; Ⓜ Arts et Métiers)

L'Atelier des Lumières   MUSEUM

5 ◉ MAP P116, G2

A former foundry dating from 1835 that supplied iron for the French navy and railroads now houses Paris' first digital art museum, opened in 2018. The 1500-sq-metre La Halle mounts dazzling light projections that take over the bare walls. Long programs lasting around 30 minutes are based on historic artists' works; there's also a shorter contemporary program. Screenings are continuous. In the separate Le Studio space, you can discover emerging and established digital artists. (www.atelier-lumieres.com; 38-40 rue St-Maur, 11e; adult/child €14.50/9.50; ⏰10am-6pm Sun-Thu, to 10pm Fri & Sat; Ⓜ Voltaire)

Parc Rives de Seine   PARK

6 ◉ MAP P116, B5

Following the success of the former expressway turned park on the Left Bank (p185), this 3.3km stretch of Unesco-listed Right Bank is now also a car-free Parisian playground. Opened in 2017, the park has cycle and walking paths, *pétanque* (similar to lawn bowls)

Maison de Victor Hugo

and other sporting facilities, along with kids' play areas, and year-round bars, plus hammocks, sunloungers and umbrella-shaded tables in summer. Free 'timescope' binoculars at various intervals provide cool audiovisual history lessons. (btwn Bassin de l'Arsenal, 4e & quai des Tuileries, 1er; Ⓜ Quai de la Rapéé, Pont Marie or Pont Neuf)

Lafayette Anticipations
MUSEUM

7 ◉ MAP P116, A3

In 2018 the corporate foundation of French retailer Galeries Lafayette opened this unique multi-disciplinary space for producing, experimenting with and exhibiting new works of contemporary art, design and fashion. Transformed by Dutch architect Rem Koolhaas, the 1891 building now has 2500 sq metres of exhibition space and a striking 18m-high glass tower. Three to four exhibitions take place annually alongside performances and workshops. (Fondation d'entreprise Galeries Lafayette; 📞 01 57 40 64 17; www.lafayetteanticipations.com; 9 rue du Plâtre, 4e; adult/child €8/free; ⏱ 11am-8pm Mon, Wed & Sun, to 10pm Thu-Sat; Ⓜ Rambuteau)

Hôtel de Ville
ARCHITECTURE

8 ◉ MAP P116, A4

Paris' beautiful town hall was gutted during the Paris Commune of 1871 and rebuilt in luxurious neo-Renaissance style between 1874 and 1882. The ornate façade is decorated with 108 statues of illustrious Parisians, and the outstanding temporary exhibitions (admission free; enter at 29 rue de Rivoli, 4e) have a Parisian theme. (www.paris.fr; place de l'Hôtel de Ville, 4e; admission free; Ⓜ Hôtel de Ville)

Promenade Plantée
PARK

9 ◉ MAP P116, E6

The disused 19th-century Vincennes railway viaduct was reborn as the world's first elevated park, planted with a fragrant profusion of cherry trees, maples, rose trellises, bamboo corridors and lavender. Three storeys above ground, it provides a unique aerial vantage point on the city. Along the first, northwestern section, above av Daumesnil, art-gallery workshops beneath the arches form the **Viaduc des Arts** (www.leviaducdesarts.com). Staircases provide access (lifts/elevators here invariably don't work). (La Coulée Verte René-Dumont; cnr rue de Lyon & av Daumesnil, 12e; ⏱ 8am-9.30pm Mon-Fri, from 9am Sat & Sun Mar-Oct, 8am-5.30pm Mon-Fri, from 9am Sat & Sun Nov-Feb; Ⓜ Bastille, Gare de Lyon, Daumesnil)

Musée Cognacq-Jay
MUSEUM

10 ◉ MAP P116, C3

This museum inside the Hôtel de Donon displays oil paintings, pastels, sculpture, objets d'art, jewellery, porcelain and furniture from the 18th century assembled by Ernest Cognacq (1839–1928), founder of La Samaritaine department store, and his wife Louise

Jay. Although Cognacq appreciated little of his collection, boasting that he had never visited the Louvre and was only acquiring collections for the status, the artwork and objets d'art give a good idea of upper-class tastes during the Age of Enlightenment. (www.cognacq-jay.paris.fr; 8 rue Elzévir, 3e; admission free; ☉10am-6pm Tue-Sun; M St-Paul, Chemin Vert)

Place de la Bastille
SQUARE

11 ◉ MAP P116, E5

A 14th-century fortress built to protect the city gates, the Bastille became a prison under Cardinal Richelieu, which was mobbed on 14 July 1789, igniting the French Revolution. At the centre of the square is the 52m-high **Colonne de Juillet** (www.colonne-de-juillet.fr) a green-bronze column topped by a gilded, winged Liberty. Revolutionaries from the uprising of 1830 are buried beneath; the crypt will open to the public as part of a major redevelopment that will link the square to Bassin de l'Arsenal. (12e; M Bastille)

Eating

Marché Bastille
MARKET €

12 ✖ MAP P116, E4

If you only get to one open-air street market in Paris, this one – stretching between the Bastille and Richard Lenoir metro stations – is among the very best. Its 150-plus stalls are piled high with

Place des Vosges

Inaugurated in 1612 as place Royale and thus Paris' oldest square, **place des Vosges** (4e; M Bastille, Chemin Vert) is a strikingly elegant ensemble of 36 symmetrical houses with ground-floor arcades, steep slate roofs and large dormer windows arranged around a leafy square with four symmetrical fountains and an 1829 copy of a mounted statue of Louis XIII. The square received its present name in 1800 to honour the Vosges *département* (administrative division) for being the first in France to pay its taxes.

fruit and vegetables, meats, fish, shellfish, cheeses and seasonal specialities such as truffles. You'll also find clothing, leather handbags and wallets, and a smattering of antiques. (bd Richard Lenoir, 11e; ☉7am-2.30pm Thu, to 3pm Sun; M Bastille, Bréguet–Sabin)

La Maison Plisson
CAFE, DELI €

13 ✖ MAP P116, D3

Framed by glass-canopied wrought-iron girders, this gourmand's dream incorporates a covered-market-style, terrazzo-floored food hall filled with exquisite, mostly French produce: meat, vegetables, cheese, wine, chocolate, jams, freshly baked breads and much more. If your appetite's

Pre-Revolutionary Architecture

Le Marais largely escaped Baron Haussmann's large-scale renovations, and today it's one of the few neighbourhoods of Paris that still has much of its pre-revolutionary architecture intact. This includes the house at **3 rue Volta**, **3e**, parts of which date to 1292; Paris' oldest building still standing (now a restaurant) at **51 rue de Montmorency**, **3e**, built in 1407 and once the residence of celebrated alchemist and writer Flamel (1330–1417); and the half-timbered 16th-century building at **11 & 13 rue François Miron**, **4e**.

whet, its cafe, opening to twin terraces, serves charcuterie, foie gras and cheese planks, bountiful salads and delicacies such as olive-oil-marinated, Noilly Prat–flambéed sardines. (www.lamaisonplisson.com; 93 bd Beaumarchais, 3e; mains €8-15; ⏱9.30am-9pm Mon, from 8.30am Tue-Sat, 9.30am-8pm Sun; Ⓜ St-Sébastien–Froissart)

Breizh Café

CRÊPES €

 MAP P116, C2

Everything at the Breizh ('Breton' in Breton) is 100% authentic, including its organic-flour crêpes and *galettes* that top many Parisians' lists for the best in the city. Other specialities include Cancale oysters and 20 types of cider.

Tables are limited and there's often a wait; book ahead or try its deli, **L'Épicerie** (crêpes & galettes €6.80-18.80; ⏱11.30am-10pm), next door. (☎01 42 72 13 77; www.breizhcafe.com; 109 rue Vieille du Temple, 3e; crêpes & galettes €6.80-18.80; ⏱11.30am-11pm Mon-Sat, to 10pm Sun; Ⓜ St-Sébastien–Froissart)

Le Servan

BISTRO €€

 MAP P116, H2

Ornate cream-coloured ceilings with moulded cornices and pastel murals, huge windows and wooden floors give this neighbourhood neobistro near Père Lachaise a light, airy feel on even the greyest Parisian day. Sweetbread wontons, cockles with chilli and sweet basil, and roast pigeon with tamarind *jus* are among the inventive creations on the daily changing menu. Reserve to avoid missing out. (☎01 55 28 51 82; http://leservan.com; 32 rue St-Maur, 11e; 3-course lunch menu €27, mains €25-38; ⏱7.30-10.30pm Mon, noon-2.30pm & 7.30-10.30pm Tue-Fri; Ⓜ Voltaire, Rue St-Maur, Père Lachaise)

Chambelland

BAKERY €

16 MAP P116, F1

Using rice and buckwheat flour from its own mill in southern France, this pioneering 100% gluten-free bakery creates exquisite cakes and pastries as well as sourdough loaves and brioches peppered with nuts, seeds, chocolate and fruit. Stop for lunch at one of the handful of formica tables in this relaxed space, strewn with sacks of flour and books. (☎01 43 55 07 30; www.chambelland.com; 14 rue Ternaux, 11e; lunch menus €10-12, pastries €2.50-5.50; ⏱9am-8pm Tue-Sat, to 6pm Sun; Ⓜ Parmentier)

Pastelli
GELATO €

17 ❌ MAP P116, B2

The youngest winner of Milan's prestigious Cone d'Oro (Golden Cone), artisan gelato maker Mary Quarta has more than 100 different flavours in her all-natural repertoire, and serves around a dozen different freshly made small batches each day at her light, white-painted Haut Marais shop. Standouts include avocado, black sesame, peach Champagne bellini and coffee-laced tiramisu. (Mary; 60 rue du Temple, 3e; gelato 1/2/3/4 scoops €3.50/5/6.50/7.50; ⏱11am-10pm; Ⓜ Rambuteau)

Le Bistrot Paul Bert
BISTRO €€

18 ❌ MAP P116, H5

When food writers list Paris' best bistros, Paul Bert's name consistently pops up. The timeless vintage decor and classic dishes such as *steak-frites* and hazelnut-cream Paris-Brest pastry reward those booking ahead. Look for its siblings in the same street: **L'Écailler du Bistrot** (☎01 43 72 76 77; 22 rue Paul Bert, 11e; oysters per half-dozen €9-20, mains €32-46, seafood platters per person from €40; ⏱noon-2.30pm & 7.30-11pm Tue-Sat) for seafood; **La Cave Paul Bert** (☎01 58 53 50 92; 16 rue Paul Bert, 11e; ⏱noon-midnight, kitchen noon-2pm & 7.30-11.30pm), a wine bar with small plates; and **Le**

Marché Bastille (p121)

CÉCILE MARION/ALAMY ©

Pletzl's Jewish Community

Cacher (kosher) grocery shops, butchers, restaurants, delis and takeaway felafel joints cram the narrow streets of Pletzl (from the Yiddish for 'little square'), home to Le Marais' long-established Jewish community. It starts in rue des Rosiers and continues along rue Ste-Croix de la Bretonnerie to rue du Temple. Don't miss the **art nouveau synagogue** (Agoudas Hakehilos Synagogue; Map p116, C4; 10 rue Pavée, 4e; M St-Paul) designed in 1913 by Hector Guimard, who was also responsible for the city's famous metro entrances.

For an in-depth look at Jewish history, visit the **Musée d'Art et d'Histoire du Judaïsme** (Map p116, B2; 01 53 01 86 62; www.mahj. org; 71 rue du Temple, 3e; adult/child €9/free; 11am-6pm Tue-Fri, from 10am Sat & Sun; M Rambuteau), housed in Pletzl's sumptuous Hôtel de St-Aignan, dating from 1650.

6 Paul Bert (01 43 79 14 32; www. le6paulbert.com; 6 rue Paul Bert, 12e; 6-course menu €60, mains €24-35; noon-2pm & 7.30-11pm Tue-Sat) for modern cuisine. (01 43 72 24 01; 18 rue Paul Bert, 11e; 2-/3-course lunch/dinner menu €19/41; noon-2pm & 7.30-11pm Tue-Sat, closed Aug; M Faidherbe-Chaligny)

Bontemps Pâtisserie PASTRIES €

19 MAP P116, C1

Buttery *sablés* (shortbread biscuits), rich chocolate fondant and light-as-air *tarte au citron* (lemon tart) are among the exquisite treats at this jewel-box-like *pâtisserie* (cake shop) on foodie rue de Bretagne. If you can't wait to tuck in, there's a handful of aqua-painted metallic tables and chairs outside the stone shopfront. (01 42 74 10 68; 57 rue de Bretagne, 3e; pastries from €4; 11am-2pm & 3-7.30pm Wed-Fri, 10am-2pm & 2.30-7.30pm Sat, 10am-2pm & 3-6pm Sun; M Temple)

L'As du Fallafel FELAFEL €

20 MAP P116, B3

The lunchtime queue stretching halfway down the street from this place says it all. This Parisian favourite, 100% worth the inevitable wait, is the address for kosher, perfectly deep-fried falafel (chickpea balls) and turkey or lamb shawarma sandwiches. Do as every Parisian does and get them to take away. (34 rue des Rosiers, 4e; takeaway €5.50-8.50, mains €12-18; noon-midnight Sun-Thu, to 4pm Fri; ; M St-Paul)

Au Passage BISTRO €€

21 MAP P116, E2

Rising-star chefs continue to make their name at this *petit bar de quartier* (little neighbourhood bar). Choose from a good-value, uncomplicated selection *of petites assiettes* (small tapas-style plates) of cold meats, raw or cooked fish, vegetables and so on, and larger meat dishes such as slow-roasted lamb shoulder or *côte de bœuf* (rib steak) to share. Reservations are essential. (📞01 43 55 07 52; www. restaurant-aupassage.fr; 1bis passage St-Sébastien, 11e; small plates €9-18, meats to share €25-70; ⏱7-10.30pm Tue-Sat; Ⓜ︎St-Sébastien-Froissart)

Brasserie Bofinger BRASSERIE €€

22 🍴 MAP P116, D5

Founded in 1864, Bofinger is reputedly Paris' oldest brasserie, though its polished art-nouveau brass, glass and mirrors indicate redecoration a few decades later. Alsatian-inspired specialities include six kinds of *choucroute* (sauerkraut), along with oysters (€11 to €35 per half-dozen) and magnificent seafood platters (€30 to €140). Ask for a seat downstairs beneath the *coupole* (stained-glass dome). (📞01 42 72 87 82; www.bofingerparis.com; 5-7 rue de la Bastille, 4e; 2-/3-course menus €26/32, mains €19.50-29.50; ⏱noon-3pm & 6.30pm-midnight Mon-Fri, noon-3.30pm & 6.30pm-midnight Sat, noon-11pm Sun; 🛜👶; Ⓜ︎Bastille)

Marché des Enfants Rouges MARKET €

23 🍴 MAP P116, C2

Built in 1615, Paris' oldest covered market is secreted behind an inconspicuous green-metal gate.

A glorious maze of 20-odd food stalls selling ready-to-eat dishes from around the globe (Moroccan couscous, Japanese bento boxes, and more), as well as produce, cheese and flower stalls, it's a great place to meander and to dine with locals at communal tables. (39 rue de Bretagne & 33bis rue Charlot, 3e; ⏱8.30am-1pm & 4-7.30pm Tue-Sat, 8.30am-2pm Sun, individual stall hours vary; Ⓜ︎Filles du Calvaire)

Septime GASTRONOMY €€€

24 🍴 MAP P116, G5

The alchemists in Bertrand Grébaut's Michelin-starred kitchen

Marché d'Aligre

A favourite with chefs and locals, the **Marché d'Aligre** (Map p116, G6; rue d'Aligre, 12e; ⏱8am-1pm Tue-Sun; Ⓜ︎Ledru-Rollin) has market stalls are piled with fruit, vegetables and seasonal delicacies such as truffles. Behind them, specialist shops stock cheeses, coffee, chocolates, meat, seafood and wine. More are located in the adjoining covered market hall, **Marché Beauvau** (Map p116, G6; place d'Aligre, 12e; ⏱9am-2pm & 4-7.30pm Tue-Sat, 9am-2pm Sun). The small but bargain-filled flea market **Marché aux Puces d'Aligre** (Map p116, G6; place d'Aligre, 12e; ⏱8am-1pm Tue-Sun) takes place on the square.

produce truly beautiful creations, served by blue-aproned waitstaff. The menu reads like an obscure shopping list: each dish is a mere listing of three ingredients, while the mystery *carte blanche* dinner *menu* puts you in the hands of the innovative chef. Reservations require planning and perseverance – book at least three weeks in advance. (☏01 43 67 38 29; www.septime-charonne.fr; 80 rue de Charonne, 11e; 4-course lunch menu with/without wine €70/€42, 7-course dinner menu with/without wine €135/€80; ⏰7.30-10pm Mon, 12.15-2pm & 7.30-10pm Tue-Fri; Ⓜ Charonne)

Rainettes

FRENCH €€

25 ✕ MAP P116, C4

Bar à grenouilles (frog legs bar) Rainettes serves five types of frog legs platters, including Normandes (with apples, calvados and crème fraîche), Alsaciennes (Riesling, shallots and parsley) and Provençales (aubergine and garlic), as well as a daily vegetarian and meat dish. The street-level dining room has a *mur végétal* (vertical garden); there are another 30 tables in the cellar. (☏09 70 38 61 61; www.rainettes.com; 5 rue Caron, 4e; 2-/3-course lunch menus €16/20, mains €17-25; ⏰7-11.45pm Tue & Wed, from 6pm Thu, from noon Fri-Sun; Ⓜ St-Paul)

Chez Paul

BISTRO €€

26 ✕ MAP P116, F5

This is Paris as your grandmother knew it: chequered red-and-white napkins, faded photographs on the walls, old red banquettes and

Chez Paul

GARDEN PHOTO WORLD/ALAMY ©

traditional French dishes such as pig trotters, *andouillette* (a feisty tripe sausage) and *tête de veau et cervelle* (calf head and brains). If offal isn't for you, alternatives include a steaming bowl of *pot au feu* (beef stew). (☏01 47 00 34 57; www.chezpaul.com; 13 rue de Charonne, 11e; 2-/3-course weekday lunch menu €18/21, mains €17-27; ☺noon-12.30am; Ⓜ Ledru-Rollin)

Le Chardenoux BISTRO €€€

27 🍴 MAP P116, H5

Dating from 1908, this picture-perfect Parisian bistro with a polished-timber façade, patterned tiled floors, marble-topped tables, mirrored walls, bevelled frosted-glass screens and a centrepiece zinc bar is a listed historic monument. Star chef Cyril Lignac recreates classical French dishes: Aubrac beef tartare and *frites*, chicken in white wine, and brioche toast with poached pears and hazelnut caramel. (☏01 43 71 49 52; www.restaurantlechardenoux.com; 1 rue Jules Vallès, 11e; 2-/3-course lunch menus €25/30, 3-course dinner menu €41; ☺noon-2.30pm & 7-11pm; Ⓜ Charonne)

Drinking

Candelaria COCKTAIL BAR

28 🍸 MAP P116, C2

A lime-green *taqueria* serving homemade tacos, quesadillas and tostadas conceals one of Paris' coolest cocktail bars through an

---

---

unmarked internal door. Phenomenal cocktails made from agave spirits, including mezcal, are inspired by Central and South America, such as a Guatemalan El Sombrerón (tequila, vermouth, bitters, hibiscus syrup, pink-pepper-infused tonic and lime). Weekend evenings kick off with DJ sets. (www.quixotic-projects.com; 52 rue de Saintonge, 3e; ☺bar 6pm-2am, taqueria noon-10.30pm Sun-Wed, to 11.30pm Thu-Sat; Ⓜ Filles du Calvaire)

Beans on Fire COFFEE

29 ☕ MAP P116, G2

Outstanding coffee is guaranteed at this innovative space. Not only a welcoming local cafe, it's also a collaborative roastery, where movers and shakers on Paris' reignited coffee scene come to roast their beans (ask about two-hour roasting workshops, available in English, if you're keen to roast your own). Overlooking a park, the terrace is a neighbourhood hot spot on sunny days. (www.thebeansonfire.com; 7 rue du Général Blaise, 11e; ⊙8.30am-5pm Mon-Fri, 9.30am-6pm Sat & Sun; 🛜; Ⓜ St-Ambroise)

Little Red Door

COCKTAIL BAR

 30 MAP P116, C1

Behind an inconspicuous timber façade, a tiny crimson doorway is the illusionary portal to this low-lit, bare-brick drinking den filled with flickering candles. Ranked among the World's 50 Best Bars, it's a must for serious mixology fans. Its annual collection of 11 cocktails, in themes from 'art' to 'architecture', are intricately crafted from ingredients such as glacier ice and paper syrup. (📞01 42 71 19 32; www.lrdparis.com; 60 rue Charlot, 3e; ⊙6pm-2am Sun-Thu, to 3am Fri & Sat; Ⓜ Filles du Calvaires)

Boot Café

COFFEE

31 MAP P116, D2

The charm of this three-table cafe is its façade. An old cobbler's shop, its original washed-blue exterior, 'Cordonnerie' lettering and fantastic red-boot sign above are beautifully preserved. The excellent coffee is roasted in Paris, to boot. (19 rue du Pont aux Choux, 3e; ⊙10am-6pm; 🛜; Ⓜ St-Sébastien–Froissart)

La Caféothèque

COFFEE

32 MAP P116, B4

From the industrial grinder to elaborate tasting notes, this coffee house and roastery is serious. Grab a seat, and pick your bean, filtration method (Aeropress, V60 filter, piston or drip) and preparation style. The in-house coffee school has tastings of different *crus* and various courses including two-hour Saturday-morning tasting initiations (five *terroirs*, five extraction methods) for €60

Gay & Lesbian Marais

Guys' favourite venues in Le Marais include sociable **Open Café** (Map p116, A3; www.opencafe.fr; 17 rue des Archives, 4e; ⊙11am-2am Sun-Thu, to 3am Fri & Sat; Ⓜ Hôtel de Ville) and cruisy **Quetzal** (Map p116, A3; 10 rue de la Verrerie, 4e; ⊙5pm-4am; Ⓜ Hôtel de Ville).

Girls will want to head to **3w Kafé** (Map p116, B4; www.facebook.com/3wkafe; 8 rue des Écouffes, 4e; ⊙7pm-3am Wed & Sun, to 4am Thu, to 6.30am Fri & Sat; Ⓜ St-Paul), which stands for 'women with women'.

A mixed gay and lesbian crowd loves **Le Tango** (Map p116, B1; www.boite-a-frissons.fr; 13 rue au Maire, 3e; admission Fri & Sat €9, Sun €6; ⊙10pm-5am Fri & Sat, 6-11pm Sun; Ⓜ Arts et Métiers), especially during Sunday's legendary gay tea dance.

(English available). (☎01 53 01 83 84; www.lacafeotheque.com; 52 rue de l'Hôtel de Ville, 4e; ⏰8.30am-7.30pm Mon-Fri, from noon Sat & Sun; 📶; MPont Marie, St-Paul)

La Belle Hortense BAR

33 🍴 MAP P116, B3

Behind its charming chambray-blue façade, this creative wine bar named after a Jacques Roubaud novel fuses shelf after shelf of literary novels with an excellent wine list, rare varieties of armagnac, cognac, calvados and pastis, and an enriching weekly agenda of book readings, signings and art events. (www.cafeine.com/belle-hortense; 31 rue Vieille du Temple, 4e; ⏰5pm-2am; MHôtel de Ville)

Entertainment

Opéra Bastille OPERA

34 ⭐ MAP P116, E5

Paris' premier opera hall, Opéra Bastille's 2745-seat main auditorium also stages ballet and classical concerts. Online tickets go on sale up to three weeks before telephone or box-office sales (from noon on Wednesdays; online flash sales offer significant discounts). Standing-only tickets (*places debouts;* €5) are available 90 minutes before performances. French-language 90-minute **guided tours** take you backstage. (☎international calls 01 71 25 24 23, within France 08 92 89 90 90; www.operadeparis.fr; 2-6 place de la Bastille, 12e; ⏰box office

Rue de Lappe

Quiet during the day, little rue de Lappe comes alive at night when its string of bars are in full swing. Catch music at the 1936-opened dance hall **Le Balajo** (Map p116, E5; ☎01 47 00 07 87; www.balajo.fr; 9 rue de Lappe, 11e; ⏰hours vary; MBastille), with everything from salsa to R&B, plus old-time tea dancing during *musettes* (accordion gigs) from 2pm to 7pm on Sundays and Mondays. Or try **La Chapelle des Lombards** (Map p116, E5; ☎01 43 57 24 24; www.la-chapelle-des-lombards.com; 19 rue de Lappe, 11e; ⏰11pm-5am Wed, Thu & Sun, to 6am Fri & Sat; MBastille), which has regular live concerts.

11.30am-6.30pm Mon-Sat, 1hr prior to performances Sun; MBastille)

Cave du 38 Riv' JAZZ

35 ⭐ MAP P116, B4

In the heart of Le Marais on busy rue de Rivoli, a tiny street frontage gives way to a fantastically atmospheric vaulted stone cellar with jazz concerts most nights; check the agenda online. Jam sessions with free admission typically take place on Mondays, Thursdays and Fridays. (☎01 48 87 56 30; www.38riv.com; 38 rue de Rivoli, 4e; concerts €15-30; ⏰concerts from 8.30pm Mon-Sat, from 5pm Sun; MHôtel de Ville)

Shopping

Merci

GIFTS & SOUVENIRS

36 🔒 MAP P116, D2

A Fiat Cinquecento marks the entrance to this unique concept store, which donates all its profits to a children's charity in Madagascar. Shop for fashion, accessories, linens, lamps and nifty designs for the home. Complete the experience with a coffee in its hybrid used-bookshop-cafe, a juice at its **Cinéma Café** (⏱11am-2pm Mon-Sat) or lunch in its stylish **La Cantine de Merci** (mains €16-21; ⏱10am-7.30pm). (🕿01 42 77 00 33; www.merci-merci.com; 111 bd Beaumarchais, 3e; ⏱10am-7.30pm; Ⓜ St-Sébastien–Froissart)

Kerzon

HOMEWARES, COSMETICS

37 🔒 MAP P116, D3

Candles made from natural, biodegradable wax in Parisian scents such as Jardin du Luxembourg (with lilac and honey), Place des Vosges (rose and jasmine) and Parc des Buttes-Chaumont (cedar and sandalwood) make aromatic souvenirs of the city. The pretty white and sage-green boutique also stocks room fragrances, scented laundry liquids, and perfumes, soaps, bath oils and other toiletries. (www.kerzon.paris; 68 rue de Turenne, 3e; ⏱11.30am-8pm Tue-Sat; Ⓜ St-Sébastien–Froissart)

Le Marais

Empreintes

DESIGN

38 MAP P116, C1

Spanning more than 600 sq metres over four floors, this design emporium has over 1000 items for sale at any one time from more than 6000 emerging and established French artists and designers. Handcrafted jewellery, fashion and art are displayed alongside striking homewares (ceramics, cushions, furniture, lighting and more). Upstairs there's a cafe and a reference library. (www.empreintes-paris.com; 5 rue de Picardie, 3e; ⊙11am-7pm Mon-Sat; Ⓜ Temple)

Paris Rendez-Vous

GIFTS & SOUVENIRS

39 MAP P116, A4

This chic city has its own designer line of souvenirs, sold in its own ubercool concept store inside the Hôtel de Ville (town hall). Shop here for everything from clothing and homewares to Paris-themed books, wooden toy sailing boats and signature Jardin du Luxembourg Fermob chairs. *Quel style!* (www.rendezvous.paris.fr; 29 rue de Rivoli, 4e; ⊙10am-7pm Mon-Sat; Ⓜ Hôtel de Ville)

Mariage Frères

DRINKS

40 MAP P116, B3

Founded in 1854, Paris' first and arguably finest tea shop has more than 500 varieties of tea sourced from some 35 countries. On the same street there's a **tearoom** (kitchen noon to 7pm), where you can sample its teas along with light dishes, and a tiny **tea museum** (admission free, 10.30am to noon and 3pm to 5pm Thursday to Saturday). (www.mariagefreres.com; 30, 32 & 35 rue du Bourg Tibourg, 4e; ⊙10am-8pm; Ⓜ Hôtel de Ville)

La Manufacture de Chocolat

FOOD

41 MAP P116, E5

If you dine at superstar chef Alain Ducasse's restaurants, the chocolate will have been made here at Ducasse's own chocolate factory (the first in Paris to produce 'bean-to-bar' chocolate), which he set up with his former executive pastry chef Nicolas Berger. Deliberate over ganaches, pralines and truffles and no fewer than 44 flavours of chocolate bar. (www.lechocolat-alainducasse.com; 40 rue de la Roquette, 11e; ⊙9.30am-6pm Mon-Fri; Ⓜ Bastille)

Worth a Trip 🔭
Père Lachaise

The world's most visited cemetery opened in 1804. Its 44 hectares hold more than 70,000 ornate tombs and a stroll here is akin to exploring a verdant sculpture garden. Père Lachaise was intended as a response to local neighbourhood graveyards being full – at the time, it was groundbreaking for Parisians to be buried outside the quartier in which they'd lived.

📞 01 55 25 82 10

www.pere-lachaise.com

16 rue du Repos & 8 bd de Ménilmontant, 20e

🕙 8am-6pm Mon-Fri, from 8.30am Sat, from 9am Sun mid-Mar–Oct, shorter hours Nov–mid-Mar

Ⓜ Père Lachaise, Gambetta

A Perfect City Stroll

For those visiting Paris to experience its exceptional art and architecture, this vast cemetery – the city's largest – is not a bad starting point. It's one of central Paris' biggest green spaces, with 5300 trees and shrubs, and a trove of magnificent 19th-century sculptures by artists such as David d'Angers, Hector Guimard, Visconti and Chapu. Consider the walking tour detailed in the photographic book *Meet Me At Père Lachaise* by Anna Erikssön and Mason Bendewald, or simply begin with architect Étienne-Hippolyte Godde's neoclassical chapel and portal at the main entrance.

Famous Occupants

Paris residency was the only criterion needed to be buried in Père Lachaise, hence the cemetery's cosmopolitan population. Among the 800,000-odd buried here are composer Chopin; playwright Molière; poet Apollinaire; writers Balzac, Proust, Gertrude Stein and Colette; actors Simone Signoret, Sarah Bernhardt and Yves Montand; painters Pissarro, Seurat, Modigliani and Delacroix; *chanteuse* Édith Piaf alongside her two-year-old daughter; and dancer Isadora Duncan.

The grave of Irish playwright and humorist Oscar Wilde (1854–1900), division 89, is among the most visited (as attested by the glass barrier erected around his sculpted tomb, designed to prevent fans impregnating the stone with red lipstick imprints). The other big hitter, likewise barricaded from overzealous fans, is 1960s rock star Jim Morrison (1943–71), division 6.

Commemorative memorials to victims of almost every war in modern history form a poignant alley alongside the Mur des Fédérés, a plain brick wall against which Communard insurgents were lined up, shot and buried in a mass grave in 1871.

ⓘ Getting There

Take metro line 3 or 3bis to Gambetta; line 2 or 3 to Père Lachaise; or line 2 to Philippe Auguste or Alexandre Dumas.

★ Top Tips

○ Get a free map of the graves from the Conservation Office (16 rue du Repos, 20e) in the cemetery's southwestern corner.

○ From the Gambetta metro stop, it's a downhill walk through the cemetery.

✕ Take a Break

During the week, prebook a table at superb neobistro Le Servan (p122), a short walk from the cemetery.

For creative grilled sandwiches, salads, cakes and coffee – to eat in or go – duck into **Broken Biscuits** (10 Passage Rochebrune, 11e; pastries €2-5.50, sandwiches €6.50-7.50; ⊙8.30am-6pm Wed-Fri, from 10am Sat & Sun; Ⓜ Rue St-Maur, St-Ambroise).

Explore ◉

Notre Dame & the Islands

Paris' geographic and spiritual heart is situated here in the Seine. The Île de la Cité is the larger of the two inner-city islands. To its east, linked by the Pont St-Louis, the serene Île St-Louis is graced with elegant, exclusive apartments, along with a handful of intimate hotels and charming cafes, restaurants and boutiques.

Landmark cathedral Notre Dame (p136) dominates the Île de la Cité, so where better to start your explorations? (Heading here first also means you'll beat the crowds.) In addition to viewing its stained-glass interior, allow around an hour to visit the top and another to explore the archaeological crypt (p141). For more beautiful stained-glass, don't miss nearby Sainte-Chapelle (p144). From here it's a few footsteps to the French Revolution prison, the Conciergerie (p144). Cross the Pont St-Louis – where you're likely to catch buskers and street performers – to browse the Île St Louis' boutiques and buy a sublime Berthillon (p145) ice cream.

Getting There & Around

Ⓜ Cité (line 4) on the Île de la Cité is the islands' only metro station, and the most convenient for Notre Dame.

Ⓜ Pont Marie (line 7), on the Right Bank, is the Île St-Louis' closest station.

🚤 The hop-on, hop-off Batobus stops opposite Notre Dame on the Left Bank.

Neighbourhood Map on p142

Notre Dame (p136) from the Seine ©MATT MUNRO/LONELY PLANET

Top Sight
Notre Dame

Paris' most visited unticketed site, with upwards of 14 million visitors per year, is a masterpiece of French Gothic architecture. Highlights include its three spectacular rose windows, treasury and bell towers which can be climbed. From the North Tower, 400-odd steps spiral to the top of the western facade, where you'll find yourself face-to-face with frightening gargoyles and a spectacular view of Paris.

◎ MAP P142, E4

☏ 01 42 34 56 10

www.notredamedeparis.fr

6 Parvis Notre Dame –
place Jean-Paul-II, 4e

cathedral free,

🕑 7.45am-6.45pm Mon-Fri, to 7.15pm Sat & Sun

Ⓜ Cité

Architecture

Built on a site occupied by earlier churches and, a millennium prior, a Gallo-Roman temple, Notre Dame was begun in 1163 and largely completed by the early 14th century. The cathedral was badly damaged during the Revolution, prompting architect Eugène Emmanuel Viollet-le-Duc to oversee extensive renovations between 1845 and 1864. Enter the magnificent forest of ornate **flying buttresses** that encircle the cathedral chancel and support its walls and roof.

Notre Dame is known for its sublime balance, though if you look closely you'll see all sorts of minor asymmetrical elements introduced to avoid monotony, in accordance with standard Gothic practice. These include the slightly different shapes of each of the three main **portals**, whose statues were once brightly coloured to make them more effective as a *Biblia pauperum* – a 'Bible of the poor' to help the illiterate faithful understand Old Testament stories, the Passion of the Christ and the lives of the saints.

Rose Windows

A cathedral highlight, the three rose windows colouring its vast 127m-long, 48m-wide interior are its most spectacular feature. Admire a 10m-wide window over the western façade above the organ – one of the largest in the world, with 7800 pipes (900 of which have historical classification), 111 stops, five 56-key manuals and a 32-key pedalboard – and the window on the northern side of the transept (virtually unchanged since the 13th century).

Towers

A constant queue marks the entrance to the **Tours de Notre Dame** (☏01 53 10 07 00; www.tours-notre-dame-de-paris.fr; adult/child towers €10/free; ☉10am-6.30pm Sun-Thu, 10am-11pm Fri & Sat Jul & Aug, 10am-6.30pm Apr-Jun & Sep,

★ **Top Tips**

◦ Queues can be huge and get longer throughout the day, especially during the summer months – arrive as early as possible.

◦ Pick up an audio-guide (€5, including treasury admission) from Notre Dame's information desk, just inside the entrance.

◦ Free 45-minute English-language tours take place at 2pm Wednesday to Friday, and at 2.30pm Monday, Tuesday and Saturday.

✕ **Take a Break**

Pop across to adjacent Île St-Louis for a drink, snack or meal at Café Saint Régis (p146).

Buy a creatively stuffed baguette and a cake from Huré (p146) and picnic on a tree-shaded bench with flying-buttress views in square Jean XXIII.

10am-5.30pm Oct-Mar), the cathedral's bell towers. Climb the 400-odd spiralling steps to the top of the western façade of the North Tower, where gargoyles grimace and grin on the rooftop **Galerie des Chimères** (Gargoyles Gallery). These grotesque statues divert rainwater from the roof to prevent masonry damage, with the water exiting through the elongated, open mouth; they also, purportedly, ward off evil spirits. Although they appear medieval, they were installed by Eugène Viollet-le-Duc in the 19th century. From the rooftop there's a spectacular view over Paris.

In the South Tower hangs Emmanuel, the cathedral's original 13-tonne bourdon bell (all of the cathedral's bells are named). During the night of 24 August 1944,

when the Île de la Cité was retaken by French, Allied and Resistance troops, the tolling of the Emmanuel announced Paris' approaching liberation. Emmanuel's peal purity comes from the precious gems and jewels Parisian women threw into the pot when it was recast from copper and bronze in 1631.

As part of 2013's celebrations for Notre Dame's 850th anniversary since construction began, nine new bells were installed, replicating the original medieval chimes.

Treasury

Pay a small fee to enter the **trésor** (treasury; €5/3; ⏰ 9.45am-5.30pm), dazzling treasure chest of sacred jewels and gems squirrelled away in the cathedral's southeastern transept. The **Ste-Couronne** (Holy

Trésor exhibit

PHOTOGOLFER/SHUTTERSTOCK ©

Notre Dame Timeline

1160 The Bishop of Paris, Maurice de Sully, orders the demolition of the original cathedral, the 4th-century Saint Étienne (St Stephen's).

1163 Notre Dame's cornerstone is laid and construction begins on the new cathedral.

1182 The apse and choir are completed.

Early 1200s Work commences on the western façade.

1225 The western façade is completed.

1250 Work is finished on the western towers and north rose window.

Mid-1200s To 'modernise' the cathedral, the transepts are remodelled in the Rayonnant style.

1345 The cathedral reaches completion.

1548 Huguenots storm and damage the cathedral following the Council of Trent.

1793 Damage during the most radical phase of the French Revolution sees many of Notre Dame's treasures plundered or destroyed.

1845–64 Following petitions to save the by-then-derelict cathedral from demolition, architect Eugène Viollet-le-Duc carries out extensive repairs and architectural additions.

1991 A lengthy maintenance and restoration program is initiated.

2013 Notre Dame celebrates 850 years since construction began.

Crown), purportedly the wreath of thorns placed on Jesus' head before he was crucified, is only exhibited between 3pm and 4pm on the first Friday of each month, 3pm to 4pm every Friday during Lent, and 10am to 5pm on Good Friday.

Easier to visit is the treasury's wonderful collection, **Les Camées des Papes** (Papal cameos). Sculpted with incredible finesse in shell and framed in silver, the 268-piece collection depicts every pope in miniature from St Pierre to the present day, ending with Pope Benoit XVI. Note the different posture, hand gestures and clothes of each pope.

The Mays

Walk past the **choir**, with its carved wooden stalls and statues representing the Passion of the Christ, to admire the cathedral's wonderful collection of paintings in its nave side chapels. From 1449 onwards, city goldsmiths offered to the cathedral each year on 1 May a tree strung with

Cathédrale Notre Dame De Paris

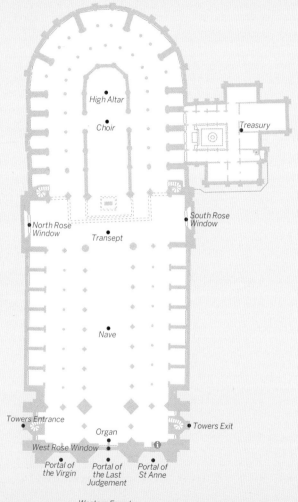

High Altar

Choir

Treasury

North Rose Window

South Rose Window

Transept

Nave

Towers Entrance

Organ

Towers Exit

West Rose Window

Portal of the Virgin

Portal of the Last Judgement

Portal of St Anne

Western Facade

devotional ribbons and banners to honour the Virgin Mary – to whom Notre Dame (Our Lady) is dedicated. Fifty years later the goldsmiths' annual gift, known as a May, had become a tabernacle decorated with scenes from the Old Testament, and, from 1630, a large canvas – 3m tall – commemorating one of the Acts of the Apostles, accompanied by a poem or literary explanation. By the early 18th century, when the brotherhood of goldsmiths was dissolved, the cathedral had received 76 such monumental paintings – just 13 can be viewed today.

Music at Notre Dame

Music has been a sacred part of Notre Dame's soul since birth. The best day to appreciate its musical heritage is on Sunday at a Gregorian or polyphonic Mass (10am and 6.30pm respectively) or a free organ recital (4.30pm).

October to June the cathedral stages evening concerts (tickets €15 and €25); find the program online at www.musique-sacree-notredamedeparis.fr.

If you can't make it in person, tune into Sunday's 6.30pm Mass on Radio Notre Dame 1 (100.7 FM), or streamed on the cathedral's website.

Landmark Occasions

Historic events that have taken place at Notre Dame include Henry VI of England's 1431 coronation as King of France; the 1558 marriage of Mary, Queen of Scots, to the Dauphin Francis (later Francis II of France); the 1804 coronation of Napoléon I by Pope Pius VII; and the 1909 beatification and 1920 canonisation of Joan of Arc.

The Heart of Paris

Notre Dame is very much the heart of Paris – so much so that distances from Paris to every part of metropolitan France are measured from Parvis Notre Dame – place Jean-Paul II, the vast square in front of the Cathedral of Our Lady of Paris, where crowds gather in the afternoon sun to admire the cathedral's façade. A bronze star across the street from the cathedral's main entrance marks the exact location of **Point Zéro des Routes de France**.

Crypt

Beneath the square in front of Notre Dame is the **Archaeological Crypt** (Archaeological Crypt; ☎01 55 42 50 10; www.crypte.paris.fr; 7 Parvis Notre Dame – place Jean-Paul II, 4e; adult/child €8/free; ☉10am-6pm Tue-Sun; MCité). The 117m-long and 28m-wide area displays the remains of structures built on this site during the Gallo-Roman period, a 4th-century enclosure wall, the foundations of the medieval foundlings hospice and a few of the original sewers sunk by Haussman. A highly worthwhile 30-minute audioguide costs €5.

Notre Dame & the Islands

A Q du Louvre
B
C R de Rivoli
D

R Bertin Poirée
R Jean Lantier
R St-Denis

Bd de Sébastopol

1
Seine
Q de la Megisserie
Théâtre
Musical
de Paris

Pont
Neuf
Châtelet Ⓜ
Pl du
Châtelet

Av Victoria

Théâtre
de la Ville

Square du
Vert-Galant
Pl du
Pont
Neuf
4

Q de l'Hortoge

Pont au
Change

Pont
Notre
Dame

Pont
Neuf
Q de Conti
2
✕ 13
✕ 9
R Henri
Robert
3
11 ✕
🍴 ✕
15
Pl
Dauphine

1ER

Q des Orfèvres

Conciergerie;
Palais de
Justice

2
Conciergerie

Tribunal de
Commerce

Cité Ⓜ
18

Hôpital
Hôtel
Dieu

Q des Grands Augustins
R Dauphine
R des Grands Augustins
R Séguier
Gt-le-Cœur

3
Sainte-
Chapelle
1
Bd du Palais
Pl Louis
Lépin

Île de la
Cité

R de Lutèce
R de la Cité

Pont
St-Michel
Préfecture de
Police

Q du Marché Neuf

St-Michel–
Notre Dame

St-Michel–
Notre Dame
Pl St-
Michel
R St-André des Arts
St-Michel Ⓜ
Pl St-André
des Arts

Q St-Michel

St-Michel Ⓜ

Parvis NotreDame–
Pl Jean-Paul II
Petit
Pont

Pont du
Double

4
6E
R Danton
R de la Harpe
Bd St-Michel
Église
St-Séverin
R St-Jacques
R Galande
R Dante
R Lagrange

Sq R
Viviani

Pl H
Mondor
Bd St- Germain
R de l'École de Médecine

5
Cluny–La
Sorbonne Ⓜ
5E

Maubert –
Mutualité
R du Sommerard
R des Carmes

Sq et
Place Paul
Painlevé
Pl
Maubert

Sorbonne
(Universités
Paris III & IV)
R des Écoles

For reviews see	
◉ Top Sights	p136
◉ Sights	p144
✕ Eating	p145
🍴 Drinking	p148
🔒 Shopping	p150

6

E

R de la Verrerie

R du Renard

F

R du Temple

G

N 0 ——————— 200 m
0 ——————— 0.1 miles

1

R Ste-Croix de la
Bretonnerie

R des Archives

R de la Verrerie

R Vieille du Temple

Bazar de
l'Hôtel de
Ville (BHV)

R de la
Coutellerie

Ⓜ Hôtel de
Ville

Ⓜ

Ⓜ
Châtelet

Pl de
l'Hôtel
de Ville

R de Rivoli

Ⓜ Hôtel de
Ville

Pl du
Bourg
Tibourg

R du Roi de Sicile

R des Écouffes

2

Q des Gesvres

Hôtel de
Ville

R de l'Obau

Pl Baudoyer

R du Pont Louis-Philippe

R François Miron

Q de la Corse

Pont
d'Arcole

Pl St-
Gervais

Église
St-Gervais -
St-Protais

4E

R de Jouy

3

Ⓧ
10

Q de l'Hôtel de Ville

R de l'Hôtel de Ville

R Geoffroy l'Asnier

Sq
A Schweitzer

R des Nonnains d'Hyères

Q d'Arcole

R Chanoinesse

Seine

Pont
Louis-Philippe

Pl du Bataillon
Français de
l'ONU en Corée

Ⓜ
Pont
Marie

4

R aux Fleurs

4E

R du Cloître Notre Dame

Pont
Marie

Ⓞ
Notre Dame

R Jean
du Bellay

Ⓧ8
Ⓐ22

Q de Bourbon

R des Deux Ponts

Pont
Marie

Q d'Anjou

Ⓧ
16

Île
St-Louis

12 Ⓧ

R le Regrattier

Sq
Jean
XXIII

Sq
de l'Île
de France

Ⓐ
20

R Boutarel

Ⓐ
21

14

R Budé

Ⓐ

17

19 Ⓐ

R St-Louis en l'Île

R le Poulletier

5

Q de
Montebello

Ⓢ
Pont de
l'Archevêché

5 Ⓞ
Mémorial des
Martyrs de la
Déportation

Q d'Orléans

7 Ⓧ

6 Ⓞ

Église St-Louis
en l'Île

Q de Béthune

R de Bièvre

R des Bernardins

Q de la Tournelle

Pont de la
Tournelle

Seine

R Monge

Bd St-Germain

R de Poissy

R du Cardinal
Lemoine

Musée de
la Sculpture
en Plein Air

Pont
de Sully

6

E

F

G

H

Notre Dame & the Islands

Sights

Sainte-Chapelle CHAPEL

1 MAP P142, C3

Try to save Sainte-Chapelle for a sunny day, when Paris' oldest, finest stained glass is at its dazzling best. Enshrined within the Palais de Justice (Law Courts), this gemlike Holy Chapel is Paris' most exquisite Gothic monument. It was completed in 1248, just six years after the first stone was laid, and was conceived by Louis IX to house his personal collection of holy relics, including the famous Holy Crown (now in Notre Dame). (☎01 53 40 60 80, concerts 01 42 77 65 65; www.sainte-chapelle.fr; 8 bd du Palais, 1er; adult/child €10/free, joint ticket with Conciergerie €15; ⊙9am-7pm Apr-Sep, to 5pm Oct-Mar; Ⓜ Cité)

Conciergerie MONUMENT

2 MAP P142, C2

A royal palace in the 14th century, the Conciergerie later became a prison. During the Reign of Terror (1793–94) alleged enemies of the Revolution were incarcerated here before being brought before the Revolutionary Tribunal next door in the **Palais de Justice**. Top-billing exhibitions take place in the beautiful, Rayonnant Gothic **Salle des Gens d'Armes**, Europe's largest surviving medieval hall. (☎01 53 40 60 80; www.paris-conciergerie.fr; 2 bd du Palais, 1er; adult/child €9/free, joint ticket with Sainte-Chapelle €15; ⊙9.30am-6pm; Ⓜ Cité)

Pont Neuf BRIDGE

3 ⊙ MAP P142, A2

Paris' oldest bridge, misguidingly named 'New Bridge', has linked the western end of Île de la Cité with both riverbanks since 1607, when king Henri IV inaugurated it by crossing it on a white stallion. View the bridge's arches (seven on the northern stretch and five on the southern span), decorated with 381 *mascarons* (grotesque figures) depicting barbers, dentists, pickpockets, loiterers etc, from a spot along the river or afloat. (Ⓜ Pont Neuf)

Square du Vert-Galant PARK

4 ⊙ MAP P142, A2

Chestnut, yew, black walnut and weeping willow trees grace this picturesque park at the westernmost tip of the Île de la Cité, along with migratory birds including mute swans, pochard and tufted ducks, black-headed gulls and wagtails. Sitting at the islands' original level, 7m below their current height, the waterside park is reached by stairs leading down from the Pont Neuf. It's romantic at any time of day, but especially so in the evening as the sun sets over the river. (place du Pont Neuf, 1er; ⊙24hr; Ⓜ Pont Neuf)

Mémorial des Martyrs de la Déportation MONUMENT

5 ⊙ MAP P142, F5

The Memorial to the Victims of the Deportation, erected in 1962, remembers the 200,000 French residents (including 76,000 Jews, of whom 11,000 were children) who were deported to and murdered in Nazi concentration camps during WWII. A single barred 'window' separates the bleak, rough-concrete courtyard from the waters of the Seine. Inside lies the **Tomb of the Unknown Deportee**. (☏01 46 33 87 56; square de l'Île de France, 1er; admission free; ⏰10am-7pm Apr-Sep, to 5pm Tue-Sun Oct-Mar; Ⓜ︎Cité, ☒RER St-Michel–Notre Dame)

Église St-Louis en l'Île   CHURCH

6 ◉ MAP P142, H5

French baroque Église St-Louis en l'Île was built between 1664 and 1726. It hosts classical music and organ concerts some Sundays; check the agenda online. (☏01 46 24 11 69; www.saintlouisenlile.

catholique.fr; 19 rue St-Louis en l'Île, 4e; ⏰9.30am-1pm & 2-7.30pm Mon-Sat, 9am-1pm & 2-7pm Sun; Ⓜ︎Pont Marie)

Eating

Berthillon   ICE CREAM €

7 🍴 MAP P142, H5

Founded here in 1954, this esteemed *glacier* (ice-cream maker) is still run by the same family. Its 70-plus all-natural flavours include fruit sorbets (pink grapefruit, raspberry and rose) and richer ice creams made from fresh milk and eggs (salted caramel, candied Ardèche chestnuts, Armagnac and prunes). Watch for tempting new seasonal flavours. (www.berthillon.fr; 29-31 rue St-Louis en l'Île, 4e; 1/2/3/4 scoops take away

Conciergerie

The Hunchback of Notre Dame

The damage inflicted on Notre Dame during the French Revolution saw it fall into ruin, and it was destined for demolition. Salvation came with the widespread popularity of Victor Hugo's 1831 novel *The Hunchback of Notre Dame*, which sparked a petition to save it.

The novel opens in 1482 on the Epiphany (6 January), the day of the 'Feast of Fools', with the eponymous hunchback, Quasimodo, the deafened bell-ringer at Notre Dame, crowned the King of Fools. Much of the ensuing action (such as the scene where the dancer Esmeralda is being led to the gallows and Quasimodo swings down by a bell rope to rescue her) takes place in and around the cathedral, which effectively becomes another 'character' in the novel. Subsequently, in 1845, architect Eugène Emmanuel Viollet-le-Duc began the cathedral's grand-scale renovations.

€3/4.50/6/7.50; ⏱10am-8pm Wed-Sun, closed mid-Feb–early Mar & Aug; MPont Marie)

Café Saint Régis

CAFE €

 MAP P142, F4

Waiters in long white aprons, a ceramic-tiled interior and retro vintage decor make hip Le Saint Régis a deliciously Parisian hang-out any time of day – for eating or drinking. From breakfast pastries, organic eggs and bowls of fruit-peppered granola to mid-morning pancakes or waffles, lunchtime salads, burgers, dusk-time oysters and late-night cocktails, it is the hobnobbing hot spot on the islands. (☏01 43 54 59 41; www.cafesaintregisparis.com; 6 rue Jean du Bellay, 4e; breakfast & snacks €3.50-15.50, mains €18-32; ⏱6.30am-2am, kitchen 8am-midnight; 🛜; MPont Marie)

Sequana

MODERN FRENCH €€€

9 🍴 MAP P142, A2

At home in a chic steel-grey dining room with 1950s-style banquet-seating on Île de la Cité's south-western tip, sleek Sequana evokes the Gallo-Roman goddess of the River Seine. In the kitchen are well-travelled Philippe and Eugénie, whose childhood in Senegal finds its way into colourful combos such as wild turbot with spinach, mallard and butternut pumpkin, parsnip and China black tea. (☏01 43 29 78 81; http://sequana.paris; 72 quai des Orfèvres, 1er; 2-/3-/4-course lunch menu €24/32/50, 4-/6-course dinner menu €50/70; ⏱noon-2.30pm & 7.30-11pm Tue-Fri, 7.30-11pm Sat; MPont Neuf)

Huré

BAKERY €

10 🍴 MAP P142, E3

'Createur de plaisir' (creator of pleasure) is the titillating strapline

of this contemporary, street-smart *boulangerie* (bakery) where glass cabinets burst with feisty savoury tarts and quiches, jumbo salads, giant cookies and a rainbow of cakes. For a light, alfresco lunch to eat in a park, you'll be hard-pushed to find a better-value spot near Notre Dame. (www.facebook.com/HureCreateurDe Plaisir/; 1 rue d'Arcole, 4e; sandwiches €4.40; ☺6.30am-8pm Mon-Sat; MSt-Michel Notre Dame, Châtelet)

Le Caveau du Palais

MODERN FRENCH €€

 11 🗙 MAP P142, B2

Even when the western Île de la Cité shows few other signs of life, the Caveau's half-timbered dining areas and (weather permitting) alfresco terrace are packed with diners tucking into bountiful fresh fare: pan-seared scallops with artichokes, grilled codfish with smoked haddock cream and coriander-spiced cauliflower, or vegetable risotto. (📞01 43 26 04 28; www.caveaudupalais.fr; 19 place Dauphine, 1er; mains €20-27; ☺noon-2.30pm & 7-10pm; MPont Neuf)

Les Fous de l'Île

FRENCH €€

12 🗙 MAP P142, H4

Families flock to this island brasserie with a rustic cockerel theme celebrating the French national symbol and female chef Anaïs Dutilleul in the kitchen. Comforting French fare includes *parmentier de boeuf confit* (French 'shepherd's pie'), smoked haddock with creamy leeks, and fried snails with

Café Saint Régis

goat's cheese foam and blinis. Vegetarians are catered for with a daily *belle assiette vegetarienne du moment* (seasonal veggie dish). (📞01 43 25 76 67; www.lesfousde lile.com; 33 rue des Deux Ponts, 4e; 2-/3-course menus lunch €21/26, dinner €27/33, mains €17-20; ⏰noon-11pm; 🛜; Ⓜ Pont Marie)

Ma Salle à Manger   BISTRO €€

13 MAP P142, B2

Framed by a pretty blue-and-white striped awning and colourful pavement tables, bistro-wine bar 'My Dining Room' chalks its daily menu on the blackboard. No-fuss dishes include French onion soup, wine-baked Camembert, duck confit with baked apple, crayfish risotto and a feather-light crème brûlée. Its terrace overlooking enchanting place Dauphine, with purple-and-cream rugs to cuddle up in on friskier days, is idyllic in summer. (📞01 43 29 52 34; 26 place Dauphine, 1er; mains €20; ⏰9am-10.30pm; 🚼; Ⓜ Pont Neuf)

L'Îlot Vache   FRENCH €€

14 MAP P142, G5

Named for one of the Île St-Louis' previous two islands and decorated with cow statuettes, this former butcher shop flickers with candles that give its exposed stone walls and dark wood beams a romantic glow. Traditional French classics range from Burgundy snails in parsley butter to bœuf bourguignon grandma-style, duck breast with raspberry *jus,* and

roast seasonal fruits with blackcurrant sorbet. (📞01 46 33 55 16; www.lilotvache.fr; 35 rue St-Louis en l'Île, 4e; menu €39, mains €24.50-35; ⏰7-11pm; 🛜; Ⓜ Pont Marie)

Drinking

Le Bar du Caveau   WINE BAR

15 MAP P142, B2

The wine bar of neighbouring restaurant Le Caveau du Palais (p147) is not only a good spot for a glass of wine from France's flagship regions, but also small, inexpensive dishes such as salads, *tartines* (open-faced sandwiches), and croques madame and monsieur (toasted ham and cheese sandwiches, the former with a fried egg on top). (www.barducaveau.fr; 17 place Dauphine, 1er; ⏰bar 8am-6.30pm Mon-Fri, kitchen noon-4pm Mon-Fri; Ⓜ Pont Neuf)

Le Flore en l'Île   CAFE

16 MAP P142, F4

A tourist crowd piles into this green-and-gold awning-shaded, old-world people-watching spot with prime views of the buskers on Pont St-Louis. There's an extensive menu of brasserie-style fare ranging from salads to steaks; if you're looking to linger over a Berthillon ice cream, note it's pricier here than other spots around the island, including Berthillon's own nearby premises (p145). (📞01 43 29 88 27; www.lefloreenlile.fr; 42 quai d'Orléans, 4e; ⏰8am-2am; Ⓜ Pont Marie)

Understanding the French Revolution

Beginnings

By the late 1780s, the extravagance of Louis XVI and his queen, Marie Antoinette, had alienated virtually every segment of society and the king grew increasingly isolated as unrest and dissatisfaction reached boiling point. When he tried to neutralise the power of the more reformminded delegates at a meeting of the États-Généraux (States-General), the masses took to the streets. On 14 July 1789, a mob raided the Hôtel des Invalides for rifles, seizing 32,000 muskets, and then stormed the prison at Bastille. The French Revolution had begun.

Girondins vs Jacobins

At first the Revolution was in the hands of moderate republicans called the Girondins. France was declared a constitutional monarchy and reforms were introduced, including the adoption of the Déclaration des Droits de l'Homme et du Citoyen (Declaration of the Rights of Man and of the Citizen). But as the masses armed themselves against the external threat to the new government by Austria, Prussia and the exiled French nobles, patriotism and nationalism combined with extreme fervour to both popularise and radicalise the Revolution. It was not long before the Girondins lost out to the extremist Jacobins, who abolished the monarchy and declared the First Republic in 1792. The Assemblée Nationale (National Assembly) was replaced by an elected Revolutionary Convention.

End of the Monarchy

Louis XVI, who had unsuccessfully tried to flee the country, was convicted of 'conspiring against the liberty of the nation' and guillotined at today's place de la Concorde in January 1793. Marie Antoinette was later executed in October 1793.

The Jacobins set up the notorious Committee of Public Safety to deal with national defence and to apprehend and try 'traitors'. This body had dictatorial control over the city and the country during the Reign of Terror (from September 1793 to July 1794), which saw thousands beheaded, most religious freedoms revoked and churches closed to worship and desecrated.

After the Reign of Terror faded, moderate republicans set themselves up to rule the republic. A group of royalists bent on overthrowing them were led by Napoléon, whose victories would soon turn him into an independent political force.

Shopping

38 Saint Louis

FOOD & DRINKS

17 🔒 MAP P142, H5

Not only does this contemporary, creamy white-fronted *fromagerie* (cheese shop) have an absolutely superb selection of first-class French cheese, it also offers Saturday wine tastings, artisan fruit juices and prepared dishes to go such as sheep's-cheese salad with truffle oil, and wooden boxes filled with vacuum-packed cheese to take home. (38 rue St-Louis en l'Île, 4e; ⏰8.30am-10pm Tue-Sat, 9.30am-4pm Sun; Ⓜ Pont Marie)

Île St-Louis: Two Islands in One

Today's Île St-Louis was actually two uninhabited islets called Île Notre Dame (Our Lady Isle) and Île aux Vaches (Cows Island) in the early 17th century. That was until building contractor Christophe Marie and two financiers worked out a deal with Louis XIII to create one island and build two stone bridges to the mainland. In exchange they could subdivide and sell the newly created real estate, and by 1664 the entire island was covered with fine houses facing the quays and the river, which remain today.

Marché aux Fleurs Reine Elizabeth II

MARKET

18 🔒 MAP P142, D3

Blooms have been sold at this flower market since 1808, making it the oldest market of any kind in Paris. On Sunday (from 8am to 7pm) it transforms into a cacophonous bird market, the **Marché aux Oiseaux**. (place Louis Lépin, 4e; ⏰8am-7.30pm Mon-Sat; Ⓜ Cité)

Librairie Ulysse

BOOKS

19 🔒 MAP P142, H5

Stuffed to the rafters with anti-quarian and new travel guides, *National Geographic* back editions and maps, this bijou boutique was the world's first travel bookshop when it was opened in 1971 by the intrepid Catherine Domaine. Hours vary, but ring the bell and Catherine will open up if she's around. (📞01 43 25 17 35; www.ulysse.fr; 26 rue St-Louis en l'Île, 4e; ⏰2-8pm Tue-Fri, mornings & Sat by appointment; Ⓜ Pont Marie)

L'Îles aux Images

ART

20 🔒 MAP P142, G5

Original and rare vintage posters, photographs and lithographs dating from 1850 onwards from artists including Man Ray, Salvador Dalí, Paul Gauguin and Picasso are stocked at this gallery-boutique. Many depict Parisian scenes and make evocative home decorations. Framing can be arranged. (📞01 56 24 15

Marché aux Fleurs Reine Elizabeth II

22; www.vintage-photos-lithos-paris. com; 51 rue Saint-Louis en l'Île, 4e; ⊙2-7pm Mon-Sat & by appointment; Ⓜ Pont Marie)

Clair de Rêve   TOYS

21 🅐 MAP P142, G5

Stringed marionettes made of papier mâché, leather and porcelain bob from the ceiling of this endearing little shop. It also sells wind-up toys and music boxes. (📞01 43 29 81 06; www.clairdereve.com; 35 rue St-Louis en l'Île, 4e; ⊙11am-1pm & 1.30-7.15pm Mon-Sat; Ⓜ Pont Marie)

Il Campiello   ARTS & CRAFTS

22 🅐 MAP P142, G4

Venetian carnival masks – intricately crafted from papier mâché, ceramics and leather – are the speciality of this exquisite shop, which also sells jewellery made from Murano glass beads. It was established by a native of Venice, to which the Île St-Louis bears more than a passing resemblance. (📞01 44 27 00 22; www.ilcampiello. com; 88 rue St-Louis en l'Île, 4e; ⊙noon-7pm; Ⓜ Pont Marie)

Explore ◈
The Latin Quarter

*So named because international students commu-
nicated in Latin here until the French Revolution, the
Latin Quarter remains the hub of academic life in Paris.
Centred on the Sorbonne's main university campus,
graced by fountains and lime trees, this lively area is
also home to lovely museums and churches, along with
Paris' beautiful art deco mosque and botanic gardens.*

*The Batobus stops at Paris' botanic gardens, the
Jardin des Plantes (p159), so consider cruising here
first and exploring its natural history museums (p160)
and small zoo. Then make your way to the Mosquée de
Paris (p158) and enjoy sweet mint tea in its courtyard.
Check out amazing Arab art and ingenious architecture at the Institut du Monde Arabe (p158) and
pay your respects to some of France's most illustrious thinkers and innovators at the Panthéon (p158)
mausoleum. Browse late-night bookshops such as
charming Shakespeare & Company (p169), then catch
jazz at the Caveau de la Huchette (p169).*

Getting There & Around

Ⓜ St-Michel (line 4) and the connected St-Michel–Notre
Dame (RER B and C) is the neighbourhood's gateway.

Ⓜ Cluny–La Sorbonne (line 10) and Place Monge (line 7)
are also handy metro stations.

🚢 The hop-on, hop-off Batobus stops in the Latin Quarter
opposite Notre Dame and near the Jardin des Plantes.

Neighbourhood Map on p156

Jardin des Plantes (p159) PETER FORSBERG/ALAMY ©

Walking Tour 🥾

A Stroll along Rue Mouffetard

Originally a Roman road, rue Mouffetard acquired its name in the 18th century, when the now underground River Bievre became the communal waste disposal for local tanners and wood-pulpers. The odours gave rise to the name Mouffettes ('skunks'), which evolved into Mouffetard. Today the aromas on 'La Mouffe', as it's nicknamed, are infinitely more enticing, particularly at its market.

Walk Facts

Start Marché Mouffetard;
Ⓜ Censier Daubenton

Finish Chez Nicos;
Ⓜ Place Monge

Length 500m, 30 minutes

❶ Market Shopping

Grocers, butchers, fishmongers and other food purveyors set their goods out on stall stalls along this sloping, cobbled street during the **Marché Mouffetard** (rue Mouffetard, 5e; ⊘8am-7.30pm Tue-Sat, to noon Sun; Ⓜ Censier Daubenton).

❷ Fine Cheeses

You won't even have to worry about aromas if you're taking home something scrumptious from the *fromagerie* (cheese shop) **Androuet** (☑01 45 87 85 05; www.androuet.com; 134 rue Mouffetard, 5e; ⊘9.30am-1pm & 4-7.30pm Tue-Thu, 9.30am-7.30pm Fri & Sat, 9.30am-1.30pm Sun; Ⓜ Censier Daubenton); all of its cheeses can be vacuum-packed for free. (Be sure to look up to see the beautiful murals on the building's façade!)

❸ Delicious Deli

Stuffed olives and capsicums, and marinated eggplant are among the picnic goodies at gourmet Italian deli **Delizius** (☑01 42 17 00 23; 134 rue Mouffetard, 5e; ⊘9.30am-8pm Tue-Sat, 9am-2pm Sun; Ⓜ Censier Daubenton), which also sells hot meals, and fresh and dried pasta.

❹ Movie Time

Even locals find it easy to miss the small doorway leading to cinema **L'Epée de Bois** (☑08 92 68 75 35; www.cine-epeedebois.fr; 100 rue Mouffetard, 5e; adult/child €7.90/5; Ⓜ Censier Daubenton), which screens both art-house flicks and big-budget blockbusters.

❺ Sweet Treats

Light, luscious macarons in flavours such as jasmine, raspberry and blackcurrant, plus a tempting range of chocolates, are laid out like jewels at **Mococha** (☑01 47 07 13 66; www.chocolatsmococha.com; 89 rue Mouffetard, 5e; ⊘11am-8pm Tue-Sun; Ⓜ Censier Daubenton). They are the creations of three *maîtres chocolatiers* (master chocolate-makers) – Fabrice Gillotte, Jacques Bellanger and Patrice Chapoare.

❻ Caffeine Hit

Dip into Paris' blossoming craft-coffee scene with a serious espresso at **Dose** (www.dosedealer-decafe.fr; 73 rue Mouffetard, 5e; ⊘8am-6pm Mon-Fri, 9am-7pm Sat & Sun; 🛜; Ⓜ Place Monge), a new-generation coffee shop and organic juice bar. Beans are supplied by Breton roastery Caffè Cataldi. Lounge on lovely cushioned benches in a heated alley outside or with a line-up of digital creatives plugged into various devices in the book-lined galley space.

❼ Crêpes at Chez Nicos

The signboard outside crêpe artist Nicos' unassuming little shop, **Chez Nicos** (☑01 45 87 28 13; www.facebook.com/ChezNicos; 44 rue Mouffetard, 5e; crêpes €1.50-5.50; ⊘10am-2am; 👶; Ⓜ Place Monge), lists dozens of fillings. Ask for his masterpiece 'La Crêpe du Chef', stuffed with eggplant, feta, mozzarella, lettuce, tomatoes and onions. There's a handful of tables; otherwise, head to a nearby park.

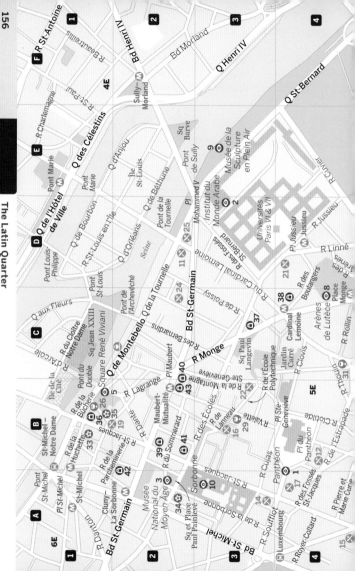

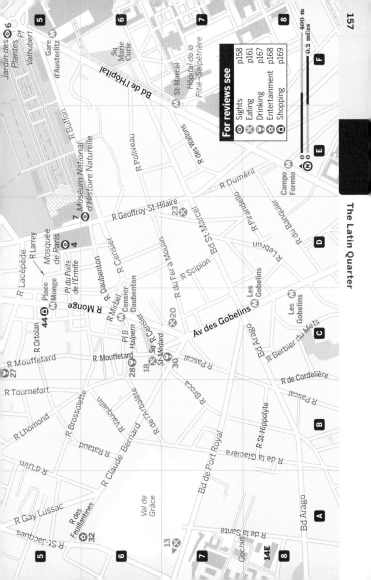

The Latin Quarter

For reviews see

◉ Sights		p158
⊗ Eating		p161
◑ Drinking		p167
◉ Entertainment		p168
⊕ Shopping		p169

400 m
0.2 miles

Jardin des 6 ◉
Plantes
Valhubert Pl
Gare
d'Austerlitz

Sq
Marie
Curie

Bd de l'Hôpital

Hôpital de la
Pitié-Salpêtrière

Ⓜ St-Marcel

Campo
Formio Ⓜ

R des Wallons

R Poliveau

R Duméril

R Pirandello

R du Banquier

R Lebrun

Muséum National
d'Histoire Naturelle 7 ◉

R Geoffroy-St-Hilaire 23 ⊗

Bd St-Marcel

R du Fer à Moulin

R Scipion

Les Ⓜ
Gobelins
Les Ⓜ
Gobelins

R Censier

R Daubenton

Mosquée
de Paris 4 ◉

R Larrey

R Lacépède

Place Ⓜ
Monge

Pl du Puits
de l'Ermite

R Monge

R Mirbel

Ⓜ Censier
Daubenton

R Daubenton

Av des Gobelins

Bd Arago

R Berbier du Mets

R de Cordelière

R Pascal

R Ortolan

44 ◉

R Mouffetard
27 ◉

Pl B
Halpern

Sq R-Cassin

18 ⊗
St-Médard
30 ⊗

28 ◉
R Mouffetard

R Pascal

R Broca

R de l'Arbalète

R Vauquelin

R St-Hippolyte

Bd de Port Royal

Bd de la Glacière

R Tournefort

R Lhomond

R Brossolette

R Rataud

R Claude-Bernard

R d'Ulm

R Gay Lussac

R des
Feuillantines 32 ◉

Val de
Grâce

13 ⊗

Bd de Port Royal

R de la Santé

Cochin

14E ⊗

Bd Arago

R St-Jacques

Sights

Panthéon
MAUSOLEUM

1 MAP P156, A4

The Panthéon's stately neoclassical dome is an icon of the Parisian skyline. Its vast interior is an architectural masterpiece: originally an abbey church dedicated to Ste Geneviève and now a mausoleum, it has served since 1791 as the resting place of some of France's greatest thinkers, including Voltaire, Rousseau, Braille and Hugo. A copy of Foucault's pendulum, first hung from the dome in 1851 to demonstrate the rotation of the earth, takes pride of place. (01 44 32 18 00; www.paris-pantheon.fr; place du Panthéon, 5e; adult/child €9/ free; 10am-6.30pm Apr-Sep, to 6pm Oct-Mar; Maubert-Mutualité or RER Luxembourg)

Institut du Monde Arabe
MUSEUM

2 MAP P156, D3

The Arab World Institute was jointly founded by France and 18 Middle Eastern and North African nations in 1980, with the aim of promoting cross-cultural dialogue. It hosts temporary exhibitions and a fascinating museum of Arabic culture and history (4th to 7th floors). The stunning building, designed by French architect Jean Nouvel, was inspired by latticed-wood windows (*mashrabiya*) traditional to Arabic architecture: thousands of modern-day photo-

electrically sensitive apertures cover its sparkling glass facade. (Arab World Institute; 01 40 51 38 38; www.imarabe.org; 1 place Mohammed V, 5e; adult/child €8/4; 10am-6pm Tue-Fri, to 7pm Sat & Sun; Jussieu)

Musée National du Moyen Âge
MUSEUM

3 MAP P156, A2

Undergoing renovation until late 2020, the National Museum of the Middle Ages is considered one of Paris' top small museums. It showcases a series of sublime treasures, from medieval statuary, stained glass and objets d'art to its celebrated series of tapestries, *The Lady with the Unicorn* (1500). Other highlights include ornate 15th-century mansion Hôtel de Cluny and the *frigidarium* (cold room) of an enormous Roman-era bathhouse. (01 53 73 78 16; www.musee-moyenage.fr; 6 place Paul Painlevé, 5e; adult/child €8/ free; 9.15am-5.45pm Wed-Mon; Cluny–La Sorbonne)

Mosquée de Paris
MOSQUE

4 MAP P156, D5

Paris' central mosque, with a striking 26m-high minaret, was completed in 1926 in an ornate art deco Moorish style. You can visit the interior to admire the intricate tile work and calligraphy. A separate entrance leads to the wonderful North African–style **hammam** (01 43 31 14 32; admission €18, spa package from €43; ⊙10am-9pm Wed-Mon), **restaurant** (📞01 43 31 14 32; www.restaurant auxportesdelorient.com; mains €10-28; ⊙kitchen noon-midnight) and **tearoom** (📞01 43 31 38 20; www.restaurantauxportesdelorient. com; ⊙noon-midnight), and a small *souk* (actually more of a gift shop). Visitors must be modestly dressed. (📞01 45 35 97 33; www. mosqueedeparis.net; 2bis place du Puits de l'Ermite, 5e; adult/child €3/2; ⊙9am-noon & 2-7pm Sat-Thu Apr-Sep, 9am-noon & 2-6pm Sat-Thu Oct-Mar; Ⓜ Place Monge)

Square René Viviani   PARK

5 ◉ MAP P156, B1

Opened in 1928 on the site of the former graveyard of adjoining

church Église St-Julien le Pauvre (p169), this picturesque little park is home to the oldest tree in Paris. The black locust (*Robinia pseudo-acacia*) was planted here in 1602 by royal gardener, Jean Robin, and is now supported by concrete pillars disguised as branches and trunks. A fountain installed by Georges Jeanclos in 1995 depicts the legend of St Julien. Roses bloom here during spring and summer. (quai de Montebello, 5e; ⊙24hr; Ⓜ St-Michel)

Jardin des Plantes   PARK

6 ◉ MAP P156, F5

Founded in 1626 as a medicinal herb garden for Louis XIII, Paris' 24-hectare botanic gardens – visually defined by the double

Foucault's pendulum, the Panthéon

A Pivotal Year: 1968

The year 1968 was a watershed. In March a large demonstration in Paris against the Vietnam War gave impetus to protests by students of the University of Paris. In May police broke up yet another demonstration, prompting angry students to occupy the Sorbonne and erect barricades in the Latin Quarter. Workers quickly joined in, with six million people across France participating in a general strike that virtually paralysed the country.

But while workers wanted to reap greater benefits from the consumer market, the students supposedly wanted to destroy it. De Gaulle took advantage of this division and appealed to people's fear of anarchy. A 100,000-strong crowd of Gaullists marched in support for the government, quashing any idea of revolution.

Once stability was restored the re-elected government immediately decentralised the higher education system, and implemented a series of reforms (including lowering the voting age to 18 and enacting an abortion law) throughout the 1970s to create the modern society France is today.

alley of plane trees that run the length of the park – are an idyllic spot to stroll around, break for a picnic (watch out for the automatic sprinklers!) and escape the city concrete for a spell. Three museums from the Muséum National d'Histoire Naturelle and a small zoo, **La Ménagerie** (Le Zoo du Jardin des Plantes; www.zoodujardindesplantes.fr; 57 rue Cuvier, 5e; adult/child €13/10; ⏰9am-6pm Mon-Sat, to 6.30pm Sun Mar-Oct, to 5pm or 5.30pm Nov-Feb), add to the appeal of the Jardin de Plantes. (www.jardindesplantes.net; place Valhubert & 36 rue Geoffroy-St-Hilaire, 5e; ⏰7.30am-8pm early Apr–mid-Sep, shorter hours rest of year; Ⓜ️Gare d'Austerlitz, Censier Daubenton, Jussieu)

Muséum National d'Histoire Naturelle   MUSEUM

7 ◉ MAP P156, D6

Despite the name, the National Museum of Natural History is not a single building, but a collection of sites throughout France. Its historic home is in the Jardin des Plantes, and it's here that you'll find the greatest number of branches: the excellent **Grande Galerie de l'Évolution** (☎01 40 79 54 79; www.grandegaleriedelevolution.fr; adult/child €9/free, with Galeries des Enfants €11/9; ⏰10am-6pm Wed-Mon) for taxidermied animals; the **Galeries d'Anatomie Comparée et de Paléontologie** (☎01 40 79 56 01; adult/child €7/free; ⏰10am-6pm Wed-Mon Apr-Sep, to 5pm Wed-

Mon Oct-Mar) for fossils and dinosaur skeletons; and the **Galerie de Minéralogie et de Géologie** (☎01 40 79 56 01; www.galeriedeminer alogieetgeologie.fr; adult/child €7/5; ⏱10am-6pm Wed-Mon Apr-Sep, to 5pm Wed-Mon Oct-Mar) for meteorites and crystals. (www.mnhn.fr; place Valhubert & 36 rue Geoffroy-St-Hilaire, 5e; Ⓜ Gare d'Austerlitz, Censier Daubenton, Jussieu)

Arènes de Lutèce RUINS

8 ◉ MAP P156, C4

The 2nd-century Roman amphitheatre Lutetia Arena once seated 10,000 people for gladiatorial combats and other events. Found by accident in 1869 when rue Monge was under construction, it's now used by locals playing football and, especially, boules (similar to lawn bowls). Hours can vary. (49 rue Monge, 5e; admission free; ⏱8am-9.30pm May-Aug, to 8.30pm Apr & Sep, shorter hours rest year; Ⓜ Place Monge)

Musée de la Sculpture en Plein Air MUSEUM

9 ◉ MAP P156, E3

Along quai St-Bernard, this open-air sculpture museum (also known as the Jardin Tino Rossi) has more than 50 late-20th-century unfenced sculptures, and makes a great picnic spot. A salad beneath a César or a baguette beside a Brancusi is a pretty classy way to see the Seine up close. (quai St-Bernard, 5e; admission free; Ⓜ Gare d'Austerlitz)

Sorbonne UNIVERSITY

10 ◉ MAP P156, A3

The crème de la crème of academia flock to this distinguished university, one of the world's most famous. Today 'La Sorbonne' embraces most of the 13 autonomous universities – some 45,215 students in all – created when the University of Paris was reorganised after the student protests of 1968. Visitors are not permitted to enter. (www.sorbonne.fr; 12 rue de la Sorbonne, 5e; Ⓜ Cluny–La Sorbonne or RER Luxembourg)

Eating

Restaurant AT GASTRONOMY €€€

11 ✕ MAP P156, D2

Trained by some of the biggest names in gastronomy (Pierre Gagnaire included), chef Atsushi Tanaka showcases abstract artlike masterpieces incorporating rare ingredients (charred bamboo, kohlrabi turnip cabbage, juniper berry powder, wild purple fennel, Nepalese Timut pepper) in a blank-canvas-style dining space on stunning outsized plates. Ingeniously, dinner menus can be paired with wine (€70) or juice (€45). Reservations essential. (☎01 56 81 94 08; www.atsushitan aka.com; 4 rue du Cardinal Lemoine, 5e; 6-course lunch menu €55, 12-course dinner tasting menu €105; ⏱12.15-2pm & 8-9.30pm Mon-Sat; Ⓜ Cardinal Lemoine)

Café de la Nouvelle Mairie

CAFE €

12  MAP P156, B4

Shhhh...just around the corner from the Panthéon (p158) but hidden away on a small, fountained square, this hybrid cafe-restaurant and wine bar is a tip-top neighbourhood secret, serving natural wines by the glass and delicious seasonal bistro fare from oysters and ribs (à la française) to grilled lamb sausage over lentils. It takes reservations for dinner but not lunch – arrive early. (📞 01 44 07 04 41; 19 rue des Fossés St-Jacques, 5e; mains €10-20; ⏰ 8am-midnight Mon-Fri, kitchen noon-2.30pm & 8-10.30pm Mon-Thu, 8-10pm Fri; Ⓜ Cardinal Lemoine)

La Bête Noire

MEDITERRANEAN €

13 MAP P156, A7

Funky music and a small, fashionably minimalist interior with open kitchen ensure bags of soul at this off-the-radar 'cantine gastronomique', a showcase for the sensational home cooking of passionate chef-owner Maria. Inspired by her Russian-Maltese heritage, she cooks just one meat and one vegetarian dish daily using seasonal products sourced from local farmers and small producers, washed down with Italian wine. (📞 06 15 22 73 61; www.facebook.com/labetenoire-paris; 58 rue Henri Barbusse, 5e; mains lunch €12-15, dinner €20, brunch €25; ⏰ 8am-5pm Tue, 8am-11pm Wed-Fri, 9.30am-5.30pm Sat & Sun; 🛜 📶; Ⓜ RER Port Royal)

Restauant on rue Mouffetard (p154)

Croq' Fac

SANDWICHES €

14 🍴 MAP P156, A3

Latin Quarter students pack out this *sandwicherie* (sandwich bar) at lunchtime and for good reason. Delicious, made-to-measure sandwiches embrace dozens of bread types (wraps, ciabatta, panini, bagels, *pan bagnat* etc) and fillings (the world's your oyster). Arrive before noon to ensure a table – inside or on the people-watching pavement terrace – or takeaway. (160 rue St-Jacques, 5e; sandwich menu €5.50; ⏰8am-7pm Mon-Sat; Ⓜ Cardinal Lemoine)

Les Papilles

BISTRO €€

15 🍴 MAP P156, A4

This hybrid bistro, wine cellar and *épicerie* (specialist grocer) with a sunflower-yellow façade is one of those fabulous Parisian dining experiences. Meals are served at simply dressed tables wedged beneath bottle-lined walls, and fare is market driven: each weekday cooks up a different *marmite du marché* (market casserole). But what really sets it apart is its exceptional wine list. (☎01 43 25 20 79; www.lespapillesparis.fr; 30 rue Gay Lussac, 5e; 2-/4-course menus €28/35; ⏰noon-2pm & 7-10.30pm Tue-Sat; Ⓜ Raspail or RER Luxembourg)

Le Coupe-Chou

FRENCH €€

16 🍴 MAP P156, B3

This maze of candlelit rooms inside a vine-clad 17th-century townhouse is overwhelmingly romantic. Ceilings are beamed, furnishings are antique, open fireplaces crackle and background classical music mingles with the intimate chatter of diners. As in the days when Marlene Dietrich dined here, reservations are essential. Timeless French dishes on offer include Burgundy snails, steak tartare and bœuf bourguignon. (☎01 46 33 68 69; www.lecoupechou.com; 9 & 11 rue de Lanneau, 5e; menu lunch €15, 2-/3-course dinner €27/33, mains €17.50-29.50; ⏰noon-1.30pm & 7-10.30pm Mon-Sat, 7-10.30pm Sun Sep-Jun, 7-10.30pm Jul & Aug; Ⓜ Maubert-Mutualité)

Le Comptoir du Panthéon

CAFE €

17 🍴 MAP P156, A4

Enormous, creative, meal-size salads are the reasons to choose this cafe as a dining spot. Magnificently placed across from the domed Panthéon (p158) and on the shady side of the street, the pavement terrace of Le Comptoir du Panthéon is big, busy and quintessentially Parisian – turn your head away from Voltaire's burial place and the Eiffel Tower pops into view. The bar stays open to 1.45am daily. (☎01 43 54 75 36; 5 rue Soufflot, 5e; salads €12.10-13.90, mains €15-18; ⏰kitchen 7am-11pm Mon-Sat, 8am-11pm Sun; 📶; Ⓜ Cardinal Lemoine or RER Luxembourg)

La Salle à Manger   FRENCH €

18 ⊗ MAP P156, C6

With a sunny pavement terrace beneath trees enviably placed at the foot of foodie street rue Mouffetard, the 'Dining Room' is prime real estate. Its 360-degree outlook – market stalls, fountain, church and garden with a play-ground for tots – couldn't be pret-tier, and its salads, *tartines* (open sandwiches), tarts and pastries ensure packed tables at breakfast, lunch and weekend brunch. (📋01 55 43 91 99; 138 rue Mouffetard, 5e; mains €10-18, weekend brunch €18-34; 🕐9am-5pm Wed-Sun; 🛜; Ⓜ Censier Daubenton)

Odette   PATISSERIE €

19 ⊗ MAP P156, B1

Odette's ground-floor space sells *choux* (pastry puffs) with seasonal flavoured cream fillings (nine on offer at any one time), such as coffee, lemon, green tea, salted caramel, pistachio and forest ber-ries. Upstairs, its art deco tearoom plays 1920s music and serves *choux* along with tea, coffee and Champagne. The black-painted timber façade, fronted by tables, and a geranium-filled 1st-floor window box are charming. (📋01 43 26 13 06; www.odette-paris.com; 77 rue Galande, 5e; 1/6/12 pastry puffs €1.90/10.90/19.80; 🕐noon-8pm Mon-Fri, 10am-8pm Sat & Sun; Ⓜ St-Michel)

Dans Les Landes   BASQUE, TAPAS €€

20 ⊗ MAP P156, C7

Treat yourself to a trip to the Basque Country: Gascogne chef Julien Duboué presents his artful, tapas-size take on southwestern cuisine, with whimsical shared plates that range from duck hearts with parsley and chilli-smothered *xistoria* (Basque sau-sages) to fried camembert with green apple, duck-neck confit and jars of foie gras. It's one of the best places in Paris for Basque wines. (📋01 45 87 06 00; http://dansleslandes.fr; 119bis rue Monge, 5e; tapas €9-17; 🕐noon-2.30pm & 7-11pm Mon-Fri, noon-11pm Sat & Sun; Ⓜ Censier Daubenton)

Le Buisson Ardent   MODERN FRENCH €€

21 ⊗ MAP P156, D4

Housed in a former coach house, this time-worn bistro (front-room murals date to the 1920s) serves classy, exciting French fare. The menu changes every week and includes varied dishes such as grilled tuna with capers and black olives, veal cutlets with candied ginger sauce and beef in porto. End on a sweet high with home-made vanilla, pistachio and choco-late profiteroles. (📋01 43 54 93 02; www.lebuissonardent.fr; 25 rue Jussieu, 5e; 2-/3-course lunch menus €19/24, mains €22-38; 🕐noon-2.30pm & 7.30-10.30pm; Ⓜ Jussieu)

Living in Paris

Within the Walls

Paris is defined by its walls (that is, the Périphérique or ring road). *Intramuros* (Latin for 'within the walls'), the 105-sq-km interior has a population of just under 2.2 million, while the greater metropolitan area (the Île de France région, encircled by rivers) has some 12 million inhabitants, about 19% of France's total population. This makes Paris – the capital of both the région and the highly centralised nation – in effect an 'island within an island' (or, as residents elsewhere might say, a bubble).

Communal Living

Paris isn't merely a commuter destination, however – its dense inner-city population defines city life. Paris' shops, street markets, parks and other facets of day-to-day living evoke a village atmosphere, and its almost total absence of high-rises gives it a human scale. Single-occupant dwellings make up around half of central Paris' households. And space shortages mean residential apartments are often minuscule. As a result, communal areas are the living and dining rooms and backyards of many Parisians, while neighbourhood shops are cornerstones of community life. This high concentration of city dwellers is why there are few late-night bars and cafes or inner-city nightclubs, due to noise restrictions. It's also why so many pet dogs live in Paris. Hefty fines for owners who don't clean up after them have meant the pavements are the cleanest they've ever been.

Beyond the Walls

The Grand Paris (Greater Paris) redevelopment project connects the outer suburbs with the city proper. This is a significant break in the physical and conceptual barrier that the Périphérique has imposed. Its crux is a massive decentralised metro expansion, with four new metro lines, the extension of several existing lines, and a total of 68 new stations, with a target completion date of 2030. The principal goal is to connect the suburbs with one another, instead of relying on a central inner-city hub from which all lines radiate outwards (the current model). Ultimately, the surrounding suburbs – Vincennes, Neuilly, Issy, St-Denis etc – will lose their autonomy and become part of a much larger Grand Paris governed by the Hôtel de Ville.

Les Pipos

FRENCH €€

22 ⓧ MAP P156, B3

Natural wines are the speciality of this *bar à vins,* which it keeps in its vaulted stone cellar. First-rate food – served all day – includes a fish of the day and oysters from Brittany, along with standards such as confit of duck and a mouthwatering cheese board, which includes all the French classics (Comté, Bleu d'Auvergne, Brie de Meaux, Rocamadour and St-Marcellin). (☎01 43 54 11 40; www.facebook.com/lespiposbara-vins; 2 rue de l'École Polytechnique, 5e; 2-course weekday menu €14.50, mains €11.90-19.90; ⊘9am-midnight Mon-Sat, kitchen 11.30am-11pm; ⓜMaubert-Mutualité)

L'Agrume

BISTRO €€

23 ⓧ MAP P156, D7

Reserve a table in advance (online or by telephone) at this chic bistro where you can watch chefs work with seasonal products in the open kitchen while you dine at a table or the *comptoir* (counter). Lunch is magnificent value and a real gourmet experience. Evening dining is an exquisite, no-choice *dégustation* (tasting) medley of five courses that changes daily. (☎01 43 31 86 48; http://restaurant-lagrume.fr; 15 rue des Fossés St-Marcel, 5e; 2-/3-course lunch menu €23/26, dinner menu €48; ⊘12.15-2.30pm & 7.30-10.30pm Tue-Sat; ⓜCensier Daubenton)

Le Petit Pontoise

BISTRO €€

24 ⓧ MAP P156, C2

Entering this tiny bistro with tra-ditional lace curtains and simple wooden tables is like stepping into old-world Paris. And the kitchen lives up to expectation with fantas-tic old-fashioned classics including calf kidneys, veal liver cooked in raspberry vinegar, roast quail, *cassoulette d'escargots* (snail stew) and honey- and almond-baked camembert (out of this world). Everything is deliciously *fait maison* (homemade). (☎01 43 29 25 20; www.lepetitpontoise. fr; 9 rue de Pontoise, 5e; 2-/3-course weekday lunch menu €23/29, 3-course weekend lunch menu €34, mains €21-30; ⊘noon-2.30pm & 6.30-10.30pm; ⓜMaubert-Mutualité)

La Tour d'Argent

GASTRONOMY €€€

25 ⓧ MAP P156, D2

The venerable Michelin-starred 'Silver Tower' is famous for its *caneton* (duckling), rooftop garden with glimmering Notre Dame views and fabulous history harking back to 1582 – from Henry III's inau-guration of the first fork in France to inspiration for the winsome animated film *Ratatouille*. Its wine cellar is one of Paris' best; dining is dressy and exceedingly fine. (☎01 43 54 23 31; www.latourdargent.com; 15 quai de la Tournelle, 5e; lunch menu €105, dinner menus €280-350, mains €78-146; ⊘12.30-2pm & 7-10pm Tue-Sat, closed Aug; ⓜCardinal Lemoine)

Drinking

Shakespeare & Company Café

CAFE

26 MAP P156, B1

Instant history was made when this literary-inspired cafe opened in 2015 adjacent to magical bookshop Shakespeare & Company (p169). It was designed from long-lost sketches to fulfil a dream of late bookshop founder George Whitman from the 1960s. Organic chai tea, turbo-power juices and specialist coffee by Parisian roaster Café Lomi are served alongside soups, salads, bagels and pastries by Bob's Bake Shop. (01 43 25 95 95; www.shakespeareandcompany.com; 2 rue St-Julien le Pauvre, 5e; 9.30am-7pm Mon-Fri, to 8pm Sat & Sun; ; M St-Michel)

Little Bastards

COCKTAIL BAR

27 MAP P156, C5

Only house-creation cocktails (€12) are listed on the menu at uberhip Little Bastards – among them Balance Ton Cochon (bacon-infused rum, egg white, lime juice, oak wood–smoked syrup and bitters) and Deep Throat (Absolut vodka, watermelon syrup and Pernod). The barmen will mix up classics too if you ask. (01 43 54 28 33; www.facebook.com/lilbastards; 5 rue Blainville, 5e; 6pm-2am Mon-Thu, 6pm-4am Fri & Sat; M Place Monge)

Shakespeare & Company Café

PETER FORSBERG/PEOPLE/ALAMY ©

Le Verre à Pied
CAFE

28 🚇 MAP P156, C6

This *café-tabac* (cafe plus a tobac-conist) is a pearl of a place where little has changed since 1870. Its nicotine-hued mirrored wall, moulded cornices and original bar make it part of a dying breed, but it epitomises the charm, glamour and romance of an old Paris every-one loves, including stallholders from the rue Mouffetard market who yo-yo in and out. (📞01 43 31 15 72; 118bis rue Mouffetard, 5e; ⏰9am-9pm Tue-Sat, 9.30am-4pm Sun; 🚇Censier Daubenton)

Pub St-Hilaire
PUB

29 🚇 MAP P156, B3

'Buzzing' fails to do justice to the pulsating vibe inside this student-loved pub. Generous happy hours last from 5pm to 9pm and the place is kept packed with a trio of pool tables, board games, music on two floors, hearty bar food and various gimmicks to rev up the party crowd (a metre of cocktails, 'be your own barman' etc). (📞01 46 33 52 42; www.facebook.com/pub-sthilaire; 2 rue Valette, 5e; ⏰4pm-2am Mon-Thu, to 5am Fri & Sat; 🚇Maubert-Mutualité)

Cave La Bourgogne
BAR

30 🚇 MAP P156, C7

A prime spot for soaking up rue Mouffetard's contagious 'saunter-all-day' spirit, this neighbourhood hangout sits on square St-Médard, one of the Latin Quarter's loveliest,

with flower-bedecked fountain, centuries-old church and market stalls spilling across one side. Inside, locals and their pet dogs meet for coffee around dark wood tables alongside a local wine-sipping set. In summer everything spills outside. (📞01 47 07 82 80; 144 rue Mouffetard, 5e; ⏰7am-2am Mon-Sat, to 11pm Sun; 🚇Censier Daubenton)

Café Delmas
CAFE

31 🚇 MAP P156, C4

Enviably situated on tree-studded place de la Contrescarpe, Delmas is perfect for *un café,* all-day breakfast or St-Germain Spritz (St-Germain liqueur, Prosecco and peach coulis) at sunset. Get cosy beneath overhead heaters outside and soak up the street atmosphere or snuggle between books in the library-style interior – awash with students from the nearby universi-ties. (📞01 43 26 51 26; www.cafe delmas.com; 2 place de la Contrescarpe, 5e; ⏰7.30am-2am Sun-Thu, to 4am Fri & Sat; 🛜; 🚇Place Monge)

Entertainment

Café Universel
JAZZ, BLUES

32 ⭐ MAP P156, A6

Café Universel hosts a brilliant ar-ray of live concerts with everything from bebop and Latin sounds to vocal jazz sessions. Plenty of freedom is given to young produc-ers and artists, and its convivial relaxed atmosphere attracts a mix of students and jazz lovers. Concerts are free, but you should tip the artists when they pass the hat around. (☏01 43 25 74 20; www.facebook.com/cafeuniverseljazzbar; 267 rue St-Jacques, 5e; ⊙8.30pm-1.30am Tue-Sat; 🛜; Ⓜ Censier Daubenton or RER Port Royal)

Caveau de la Huchette
JAZZ, BLUES

33 ⭐ MAP P156, B1

Housed in a medieval *caveau* (cellar) used as a courtroom and torture chamber during the Revolution, this club is where virtually all the jazz greats (Georges Brassens, Thibault...) have played since the end of WWII. It attracts its fair share of tourists, but the atmosphere can be more electric than at the more serious jazz clubs. Sessions start at 10pm. (☏01 43 26 65 05; www.caveaudelahuchette.fr; 5 rue de la Huchette, 5e; admission €13-15; ⊙9pm-2.30am Sun-Thu, to 4am Fri & Sat; Ⓜ St-Michel)

Le Champo
CINEMA

34 ⭐ MAP P156, A2

This is one of the most popular of the many Latin Quarter cinemas, featuring classics and retrospectives looking at the films of such actors and directors as Alfred Hitchcock, Jacques Tati, Alain Resnais, Frank Capra, Tim Burton and Woody Allen. One of the two *salles* (cinemas) has wheelchair access. (www.cinema-lechampo.com; 51 rue des Écoles, 5e; tickets adult/child €9/4; Ⓜ Cluny–La Sorbonne)

Église St-Julien le Pauvre
CLASSICAL MUSIC

35 ⭐ MAP P156, B1

Piano recitals (Chopin, Liszt) are staged at least two evenings a week in one of the oldest churches in Paris. Higher-priced tickets directly face the stage. Payment is by cash only at the door. (☏01 42 26 00 00; www.concertinparis.com; 1 rue St-Julien le Pauvre, 5e; hours vary; Ⓜ St-Michel)

Shopping

Shakespeare & Company
BOOKS

36 🔒 MAP P156, B1

Enchanting nooks and crannies overflow with new and second-hand English-language books. The original shop (12 rue l'Odéon, 6e; closed by the Nazis in 1941) was run by Sylvia Beach and became the meeting point for Hemingway's 'Lost Generation'. Readings by emerging and illustrious authors take place at 7pm most Mondays and there's a wonderful cafe (p167) next door. (☏01 43 25 40 93; www.shakespeareandcompany.com; 37 rue de la Bûcherie, 5e; ⊙10am-10pm; Ⓜ St-Michel)

Le Bonbon au Palais
FOOD

37 🔒 MAP P156, C3

Kids and kids-at-heart will adore this sugar-fuelled *tour de France*. The school-geography-themed boutique stocks rainbows of artisan sweets from around the country. Old-fashioned glass jars brim with treats such as *calissons* (diamond-shaped, icing-sugar-topped ground fruit and almonds from Aix-en-Provence), *rigolettes* (fruit-filled pillows from Nantes), *berlingots* (striped, triangular boiled sweets from Carpentras and elsewhere) and *papalines* (herbal liqueur-filled pink-chocolate balls from Avignon). (📞01 78 56 15 72; www.bonbonsau palais.fr; 19 rue Monge, 5e; ⏱10.30am-7.30pm Tue-Sat; Ⓜ Cardinal Lemoine)

Bières Cultes Jussieu   DRINKS

38 📍 MAP P156, C4

At any one time this beer-lovers' fantasyland stocks around 500 different craft and/or international brews, along with two on tap to taste on the spot. Just some of its wares when you visit might include US-brewed Alaskan Smoked Porter, German smoked Aecht Schlenkerla Rauchbier from Bamberg and New Zealand Monteith's. Check its website and Facebook page for events and seasonal releases. (📞09 51 27 04 84; http://bierescultes.fr; 44 rue des Boulangers, 5e; ⏱noon-2pm & 3-9pm Tue, Wed & Fri, to 11pm Thu & Fri; Ⓜ Cardinal Lemoine)

Album   COMICS

39 📍 MAP P156, B2

Album specialises in *bandes dessinées* (comics and graphic novels), which have an enormous following in France, with everything from Tintin and Babar to erotic comics and the latest Japanese manga.

Latin Quarter jazz club

JOHN NORMAN/ALAMY ©

Serious comic collectors – and anyone excited by Harry Potter wands, *Star Wars, Superman* and other superhero figurines and T-shirts (you know who you are!) – shouldn't miss it. (📞01 53 10 00 60; www.albumcomics.com; 67 bd St-Germain, 5e; ⏰10am-6pm Mon-Sat, noon-7pm Sun; Ⓜ Cluny–La Sorbonne)

Fromagerie Laurent Dubois
CHEESE

40 🔒 MAP P156, C2

One of the best *fromageries* (cheese shops) in Paris, this cheese-lover's nirvana is filled with to-die-for delicacies, such as St-Félicien with Périgord truffles. Rare, limited-production cheeses include blue Termignon and Tarentaise goat's cheese. All are appropriately cellared in warm, humid or cold environments. (📞01 43 54 50 93; www.fromageslaurentdubois. fr; 47ter bd St-Germain, 5e; ⏰8.30am-7.30pm Tue-Sat, 8.30am-1pm Sun; Ⓜ Maubert-Mutualité)

Au Vieux Campeur
SPORTS & OUTDOORS

41 🔒 MAP P156, B2

This outdoor store has colonised the Latin Quarter, with 30-odd different boutiques scattered around its original shop that opened on rue St-Jacques in 1941 (actually a few doors down at No 38). Each space is devoted to a different sport: climbing, skiing, diving, camping, biking, water sports and so on. (📞01 53 10 48 48; www. auvieuxcampeur.fr; 48 rue des Écoles, 5e; ⏰11am-7.30pm Mon-Wed & Fri, 11am-9pm Thu, 10am-7.30pm Sat; Ⓜ Maubert-Mutualité)

Abbey Bookshop
BOOKS

42 🔒 MAP P156, A2

Inside 18th-century Hôtel Dubuisson, this chaotic but welcoming Canadian-run bookshop serves free coffee (sweetened with maple syrup) to sip while you browse thousands upon thousands of new and used books. Watch for occasional literary events. (📞01 46 33 16 24; https://abbeybookshop.word press.com; 29 rue de la Parcheminerie, 5e; ⏰10am-7pm Mon-Sat; Ⓜ Cluny– La Sorbonne)

Marché Maubert
MARKET

43 🔒 MAP P156, B2

Shop for fruit and veg (some organic), cheese, bread and so on at this welcoming, village-like food market that spills across place Maubert thrice weekly. (place Maubert, 5e; ⏰7am-2.30pm Tue & Thu, 7am-3pm Sat; Ⓜ Maubert-Mutualité)

Marché Monge
MARKET

44 🔒 MAP P156, C5

Open-air Marché Monge is laden with wonderful cheeses, baked goods and a host of other temptations. (place Monge, 5e; ⏰7am-2pm Wed, Fri & Sun; Ⓜ Place Monge)

Walking Tour 🥾

Southeastern Discovery

Spanning both banks of the Seine, Paris' south-east is an eclectic mix of quartiers (quarters) that makes for a fascinating stroll if you've stood in one tourist queue too many. But while it's an authentic slice of local life, there are plenty of big-hitting attractions here too, including France's national cinema institute and national library.

Getting There

Southeastern Paris is about 3km southeast of Notre Dame.

Ⓜ Metro Gare de Lyon (lines 1 and 14) and Place d'Italie (lines 5, 6 and 7) are convenient start/end points.

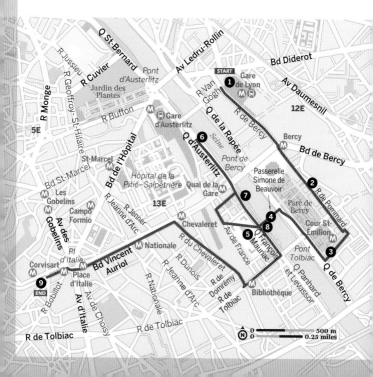

❶ Railway Splendour

Start your journey in style with a drink or classical fare at belle époque showpiece **Le Train Bleu** (☎ 01 43 43 09 06; www.le-train-bleu. com; 1st fl, Gare de Lyon, 26 place Louis Armand, 12e; 2-/3-/6-course menus €49/65/110, mains €29-48; ⏱ restaurant 11.30am-2.45pm & 7-10.45pm, bar 7.30am-10.30pm Mon-Sat, 9am-10pm Sun; 🛜 👪; Ⓜ Gare de Lyon).

❷ Cinematic History

Cinephiles shouldn't miss **Cinémathèque Française** (☎ 01 71 19 33 33; www.cinematheque.fr; 51 rue de Bercy, 12e; adult/child €5/2.50, with film €8; ⏱ noon-7pm Wed-Mon; Ⓜ Bercy), which showcases the history of French cinema and screens classic and edgy new films.

❸ Village Spirit

There are more cinemas at **Bercy Village** (www.bercyvillage.com; Cour St-Émilion, 12e; ⏱ shops 11am-9pm, restaurants & bars to 2am; Ⓜ Cour St-Émilion), but its main draw is its strip of former wine warehouses, now home to shops, eateries and bars.

❹ Crossing the Bridge

Opened in 2006 the oak-and-steel foot and cycle bridge, **Passerelle Simone de Beauvoir**, links the Right and Left Banks.

❺ Hitting the Books

Topped by four sunlit glass towers shaped like open books, the **Bibliothèque Nationale de France** (☎ 01 53 79 59 59; www.bnf.fr; 11 quai François Mauriac, 13e; €3-9; ⏱ 10am-7pm Tue-Sat, 1-7pm Sun, closed two weeks in Sep; Ⓜ Bibliothèque) mounts exhibitions revolving around 'the word'.

❻ Dockside Fashion

Transformed warehouse **Les Docks** (Cité de la Mode et du Design; ☎ 01 76 77 25 30; www.citemode design.fr; 34 quai d'Austerlitz, 13e; ⏱ 10am-midnight; Ⓜ Gare d'Austerlitz) is the French fashion institute's HQ, with exhibitions and events.

❼ Swimming on the Seine

Splash at floating pool **Piscine Joséphine Baker** (☎ 01 56 61 96 50; www.piscine-baker.fr; quai François Mauriac, 13e; adult/child €6.20/3.10; ⏱ 7-9am & 10am-11pm Mon-Fri, 10am-8pm Sat & Sun Jun-Sep, shorter hours rest of year; Ⓜ Quai de la Gare).

❽ Floating Nightlife

Board floating bar-restaurant-clubs like the red tugboat **Le Batofar** (☎ 01 53 60 37 85; www.batofar.fr; opposite 11 quai François Mauriac, 13e; ⏱ 6pm-7am Wed-Sat, to midnight Sun-Tue; Ⓜ Quai de la Gare, Bibliothèque).

❾ Heading to the 'Hood

The pavement terrace of **La Butte aux Piafs** (☎ 09 70 38 55 11; www. labutteauxpiafs-paris.fr; 31 bd Auge Blanqui, 13e; mains €14.10-16.90; ⏱ noon-midnight Mon-Fri, noon-3.30pm & 6pm-midnight Sat; Ⓜ Place d'Italie) is the best spot to lap up the quietly fashionable vibe of La Butte aux Cailles.

Explore

Musée d'Orsay & St-Germain des Prés

Literary buffs, antique collectors and fashionistas flock to this fabled part of Paris. Artists and writers such as Hemingway and Fitzgerald hung out here and further south in Montparnasse, where you'll find surviving brasseries alongside redevelopments underway on its train station and landmark skyscraper.

Pay homage to writers Sartre and de Beauvoir and singer Serge Gainsbourg in the Cimetière du Montparnasse (p186) and get a contemporary-art fix at the Fondation Cartier pour l'Art Contemporain (p186). Stroll through the beautiful Jardin du Luxembourg (p178) en route to viewing Delacroix' works in the Église St-Sulpice (p184) and Musée National Eugène Delacroix (p184). Stop by the Église St-Germain des Prés (p184) and famous literary cafes such as Les Deux Magots (p192). Entry to the Musée d'Orsay (p176) is cheaper in the late afternoon, so it's an ideal time to check out its breathtaking collections.

Getting There & Around

Ⓜ St-Germain des Prés (line 4), Mabillon (line 10) and Odéon (lines 4 and 10) are in the heart of the action.

Ⓜ Montparnasse Bienvenüe (lines 4, 6, 12 and 13) is Montparnasse's hub.

The hop-on, hop-off Batobus stops outside the Musée d'Orsay and at quai Malaquais in St-Germain des Prés.

Neighbourhood Map on p182

Top Sight 📷

Musée d'Orsay

The home of France's national collection from the impressionist, postimpressionist and art nouveau movements spanning from 1848 to 1914 is the glorious former Gare d'Orsay railway station – itself an art nouveau showpiece – where a roll-call of masters and their world-famous works are on display.

◉ MAP P182, C1

www.musee-orsay.fr

1 rue de la Légion d'Honneur, 7e

adult/child €12/free

🕐 9.30am-6pm Tue, Wed & Fri-Sun, to 9.45pm Thu

Ⓜ Assemblée Nationale, RER Musée d'Orsay

The Building

The Gare d'Orsay's platforms were built for the 1900 Exposition Universelle – by 1939 they were too short for trains, and in a few years all rail services ceased. In 1962 Orson Welles filmed Kafka's *The Trial* in the then-abandoned building before the government set about transforming it into the country's premier showcase for art created between 1848 and 1914. Don't miss the panorama through the station's giant glass clockface and from the adjacent terrace.

Painting Collections

Masterpieces include Manet's *On the Beach*; Monet's gardens at Giverny and *Rue Montorgueil, Paris, Festival of June 30, 1878*; Cézanne's card players, *Green Apples* and *Blue Vase*; Renoir's *Ball at the Moulin de la Galette* and *Girls at the Piano*; Degas' ballerinas; Toulouse-Lautrec's cabaret dancers; Pissarro's *The Harvest*; Sisley's *View of the Canal St-Martin*; and Van Gogh's *Starry Night*.

Decorative Arts Collections

Household items from 1848 to 1914, such as hat stands, desks, chairs, bookcases, vases, water pitchers, decorated plates, goblets, bowls – and even kettles and cutlery – are true works of art and incorporate exquisite design elements.

Sculptures

Sculptures by Degas, Gauguin, Camille Claudel, Renoir and Rodin are magnificently displayed in the soaring building.

Graphic Arts Collections

Drawings and sketches from major artists are another of the Musée d'Orsay's highlights. Look for Georges Seurat's crayon on paper work *The Black Bow* (c 1882) and Paul Gauguin's poignant self-portrait (c 1902–03).

★ Top Tips

○ Musée d'Orsay admission drops to €9 after 4.30pm (after 6pm on Thursday).

○ Combined tickets with the Musée de l'Orangerie (p78) cost €16, while combined tickets with the Musée Rodin (p40) are €18; both combination tickets are valid for a single visit to the museums within three months.

✕ Take a Break

The ground-floor **Café de l'Ours** (⊙9.30am-4.45pm Tue, Wed & Fri-Sun, to 8pm Thu) overlooks Francois Pompon's sculpted *Polar Bear* (1923–33).

Alternatively, try the museum's orange-and-turquoise **Café Campana** (dishes €9-19; ⊙10.30am-5pm Tue, Wed & Fri-Sun, 11am-9pm Thu) or dine at the Gare Orsay's original **Le Restaurant** (☑ 01 45 49 47 03; 2-/3-course lunch menu €22.50, mains €18-27; ⊙11.45am-5.30pm Tue, Wed & Fri-Sun, 11.45am-2.45pm & 7-9.30pm Thu; ♿).

Top Sight 📷
Jardin du Luxembourg

This inner-city oasis of formal terraces, chestnut groves and lush lawns has a special place in Parisians' hearts. Napoléon dedicated the 23 gracefully laid-out hectares of the Luxembourg Gardens to the children of Paris, and many residents spent their childhood prodding little wooden sailboats with long sticks on the octagonal pond, watching puppet shows and riding the carousel or ponies.

⊙ MAP P182, E5

www.senat.fr/visite/jardin

🕑 hours vary

Ⓜ Mabillon, St-Sulpice, Rennes, Notre Dame des Champs, RER Luxembourg

Grand Bassin

All ages love the octagonal Grand Bassin, a serene ornamental pond where adults can lounge and kids can play with 1920s **toy sailboats** (sailboat rental per 30min €4; ⊙11am-6pm Apr-Oct). Nearby, littlies can take **pony rides** (☎06 07 32 53 95; www.animaponey.com; 600m/900m pony ride €6/8.50; ⊙3-6pm Wed, Sat, Sun & school holidays) or romp around the **playgrounds** (adult/child €1.50/2.50; ⊙hours vary) – the green half is for kids aged seven to 12 years, the blue half for under-sevens.

Puppet Shows

You don't have to be a kid or be able to speak French to be delighted by marionette shows, which have entertained audiences in France since the Middle Ages. The lively puppets perform in the Jardin du Luxembourg's little **Théâtre du Luxembourg** (☎01 43 29 50 97; www.marionnettesduluxembourg.fr; tickets €6.40; ⊙Wed, Sat & Sun, daily during school holidays). Show times can vary; check the program online and arrive half an hour ahead.

Musée du Luxembourg

Prestigious temporary art exhibitions take place in the **Musée du Luxembourg** (☎01 40 13 62 00; http://museeduluxembourg.fr; 19 rue de Vaugirard, 6e; most exhibitions €13; ⊙10.30am-7pm Sat-Thu, to 10pm Fri; Ⓜ St-Sulpice, RER Luxembourg).

Around the back of the museum, lemon and orange trees, palms, grenadiers and oleanders shelter from the cold in the palace's **orangery**.

Palais du Luxembourg

The **Palais du Luxembourg** (www.senat.fr; rue de Vaugirard, 6e; Ⓜ Mabillon, RER Luxembourg), pictured left, was built in the 1620s and has been home to the Sénat (French Senate) since 1958. It's occasionally visitable by guided tour.

★ **Top Tips**

● Kiosks and cafes are dotted throughout the park.

● The elegantly manicured lawns are off-limits apart from a small wedge on the southern boundary. Do as Parisians do, and corral one of the iconic 1923-designed green metal chairs and find your own favourite part of the park.

✕ **Take a Break**

Polidor (☎01 43 26 95 34; www.polidor. com; 41 rue Monsieur le Prince, 6e; menus €22 & €35, mains €13-20; ⊙noon-2.30pm & 7pm-12.30am Mon-Sat, to 11pm Sun; Ⓜ Odéon) and its decor date from 1845 and it still serves family-style French cuisine.

Tearoom **Angelina** (www.angelina-paris. fr; 19 rue de Vaugirard, 6e; ⊙10am-7.30pm Sun-Thu, to 11.30pm Fri & Sat; Ⓜ St-Sulpice) adjoins the Musée du Luxembourg.

Walking Tour 🥾

Left Bank Literary Loop

It wasn't only Paris' reputation for liberal thought and relaxed morals that lured writers in the early 20th century – Left Bank Paris was cheap and, unlike Prohibition-era America, you could drink to your heart's content. This walk through the area's long-gentrified streets takes in pivotal places from the era.

Walk Facts

Start Rue du Cardinal Lemoine; mCardinal Lemoine

Finish Rue Notre Dame des Champs; mVavin

Length 6.5km; three hours

❶ Rue du Cardinal Lemoine

Walk southwest along rue du Cardinal Lemoine, peering down the passageway at No 71, where James Joyce finished *Ulysses* in apartment E. From 1922 to 1923, Ernest Hemingway lived at No 74.

❷ Paul Verlaine's Garret

Hemingway wrote in the top-floor garret of a hotel at 39 rue Descartes – the same hotel where the poet Paul Verlaine died. Ignore the incorrect plaque.

❸ George Orwell's Boarding House

In 1928 George Orwell stayed in a **boarding house** (6 rue du Pot de Fer, 5e; M Place Monge), which he called 'rue du Coq d'Or' in *Down and Out in Paris & London* (1933).

❹ Jack Kerouac's Hotel

The **Relais Hôtel du Vieux Paris** at 9 rue Gît le Coeur was a favourite of poet Allen Ginsberg and Beat writer Jack Kerouac in the 1950s.

❺ Shakespeare & Company

The original Shakespeare & Company bookshop (p169) stood at 12 rue de l'Odéon, where owner Sylvia Beach lent books to Hemingway and published *Ulysses* for Joyce in 1922. It was closed during WWII's Nazi occupation.

❻ Henry Miller's Room

Henry Miller stayed on the 5th floor of 36 rue Bonaparte in 1930; he wrote about the experience in *Letters to Emil* (1989).

❼ Oscar Wilde's Hotel

The former Hôtel d'Alsace, now **L'Hôtel** (www.l-hotel.com; 13 rue des Beaux Arts, 6e; M St-Germain des Prés), is where Oscar Wilde died in 1900.

❽ Hemingway's First Night in Paris

Hemingway spent his first night in the city at the **Hôtel d'Angleterre** (www.hotel-dangleterre.com; 44 rue Jacob, 6e; M St-Germain des Prés).

❾ Gertrude Stein's Home

Ezra Pound and Hemingway were among those entertained at 27 rue de Fleurus, where Gertrude Stein lived with Alice B Toklas.

❿ Rue Notre Dame des Champs

Pound lived at 70bis rue Notre Dame des Champs, while Hemingway's first apartment in this area was above a sawmill at No 113.

Musée d'Orsay & St-Germain des Prés Left Bank Literary Loop

Musée d'Orsay & St-Germain des Prés

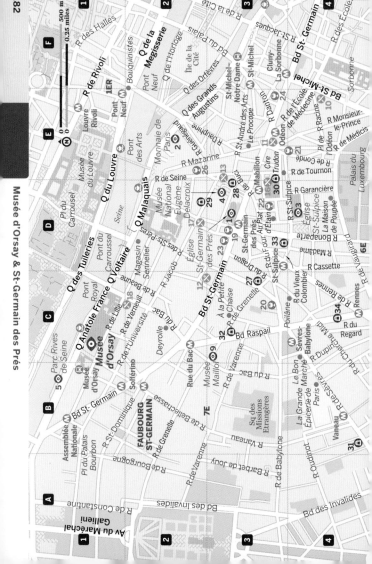

500 m
0.25 miles

1ER

6E

7E

**FAUBOURG
ST-GERMAIN**

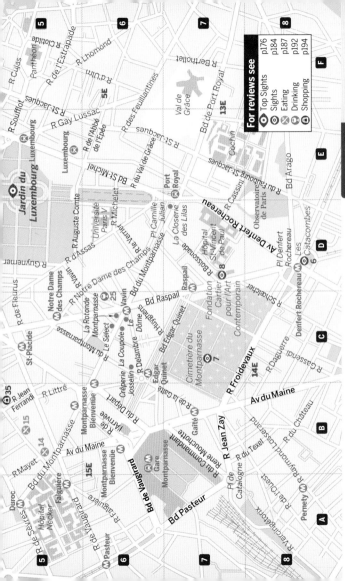

Musée d'Orsay & St-Germain des Prés

For reviews see

◉	Top Sights	p176
⊙	Sights	p184
✕	Eating	p187
✕	Drinking	p192
⛉	Shopping	p194

R Cujas
Panthéon
R Clotilde
R de l'Estrapade
R L'homond
R d'Ulm
R Berthollet
R Soufflot
R St-Jacques
5E
Luxembourg
R Gay Lussac
R de l'Abbé de l'Epée
R des Feuillantines
Val de Grâce
13E
Bd de Port Royal
Jardin du Luxembourg
Luxembourg
R du Val de Grâce
R St-Jacques
Cochin
R Guynemer
R Auguste Comte
Université Paris V
R Michelet
Bd St-Michel
Port Royal
Port Royal
Cassini
Observatoire de Paris
Bd Arago
R du Faubourg St-Jacques
E
Notre Dame des Champs
St-Placide
R de Fleurus
R d'Assas
R de Vaugirard
R Notre Dame des Champs
Pl Camille Julian
La Closerie des Lilas
Hôpital St-Vincent de Paul
Raspail
R Cassini
R Cassin
Observatoire de Paris
Les Catacombes
Pl Denfert Rochereau
Denfert Rochereau
Av Denfert Rochereau
D
R Gassendi
R Daguerre
C
25
La Rotonde
Le Select
Vavin
Montparnasse
Bd du Montparnasse
Le Dôme
La Coupole
R Delambre
R Huyghens
Bd Raspail
Fondation Cartier pour l'Art Contemporain
R Schœlcher
35
R Jean Ferrandi
R Littré
Montparnasse Bienvenüe
Crêperie Josselin
Edgar Quinet
Bd Edgar Quinet
Cimetière du Montparnasse
14E
R Froidevaux
Av du Maine
B
R Mayet
15
14
R de Sèvres
Duroc
Hôpital Necker
Falguière
R Falguière
Av du Maine
R du Départ
Montparnasse Bienvenüe
15E
Montparnasse Bienvenüe
Gare Montparnasse
R du Commandant René Mouchotte
R Jean Zay
Gaîté
R de la Gaîté
Pasteur
Bd Pasteur
Pl de Catalogne
R du Château
R du Texel
R Raymond Losserand
Pernety
R de l'Ouest
A
R Vercingétorix

Sights

Église St-Germain des Prés

CHURCH

1 ⊙ MAP P182, D3

Paris' oldest standing church, the Romanesque St Germanus of the Fields, was built in the 11th century on the site of a 6th-century abbey and was the main place of worship in Paris until the arrival of Notre Dame. It's since been altered many times. The oldest part, **Chapelle de St-Symphorien** is to the right as you enter; St Germanus (496–576), the first bishop of Paris, is believed to be buried there. (☎01 55 42 81 18; www.eglise-saintgermaindespres.fr; 3 place St-Germain des Prés, 6e; ⊙9am-7.45pm; Ⓜ St-Germain des Prés)

Monnaie de Paris

MUSEUM

2 ⊙ MAP P182, E2

The 18th-century royal mint, Monnaie de Paris, houses the **Musée du 11 Conti**, an interactive museum exploring the history of French coinage from antiquity onwards, plus edgy contemporary-art exhibitions. The impeccably restored, neoclassical building, with one of the longest façades on the Seine stretching 116m long, squirrels away five sumptuous courtyards, the Hôtel de Conti designed by Jules Hardouin Mansart in 1690, engraving workshops, the original foundry (now the museum boutique), Guy Savoy's flagship restaurant (p187) and the fashionable cafe **Frappé by Bloom** (http://

frappe.bloom-restaurant.fr). (☎01 40 46 56 66; www.monnaiedeparis.fr; 11 quai de Conti, 6e; adult/child €10/free; ⊙11am-7pm Tue & Thu-Sun, to 9pm Wed; Ⓜ Pont Neuf)

Église St-Sulpice

CHURCH

3 ⊙ MAP P182, D4

In 1646 work started on the twin-towered Church of St Sulpicius, lined inside with 21 side chapels, and it took six architects 150 years to finish. It's famed for its striking Italianate façade with two rows of superimposed columns, its Counter-Reformation-influenced neoclassical decor and its frescoes by Eugène Delacroix – and its setting for a murderous scene in Dan Brown's The Da Vinci Code. You can hear the monumental, 1781-built organ during 10.30am Mass on Sunday or the occasional Sunday-afternoon concert. (☎01 42 34 59 98; www.pss75.fr/saint-sulpice-paris; place St-Sulpice, 6e; admission free; ⊙7.30am-7.30pm; Ⓜ St-Sulpice)

Musée National Eugène Delacroix

MUSEUM

4 ⊙ MAP P182, D3

In a courtyard off a pretty tree-shaded square, this museum is housed in the romantic artist's home and studio at the time of his death in 1863. It contains a collection of his oil paintings, watercolours, pastels and drawings, including many of his more intimate works, such as An Unmade Bed (1828) and his paintings of Morocco. A ticket from the Musée du Louvre (p68) allows same-day entry here (you can also buy tickets here and skip the Louvre's ticket queues). (📞01 44 41 86 50; www.musee-delacroix.fr; 6 rue de Furstenberg, 6e; adult/child €7/free; 🕙9.30am-5pm Wed-Mon, to 9pm 1st Thu of month; Ⓜ Mabillon)

Parc Rives de Seine

PARK

5 ◎ MAP P182, B1

A breath of fresh air, this 2.3km-long expressway-turned-riverside prom-enade on the Left Bank is a favour-ite spot in which to run, cycle, skate, play board games or take part in a packed program of events. Equally it's a great place to hang out – in a Zzz shipping-container hut (reserve at the information point just west of the Musée d'Orsay), on the archipelago of floating gardens, or

at the burgeoning restaurants and bars (some floating aboard boats and barges). (btwn Musée d'Orsay & Pont de l'Alma, 7e; 🕙information point noon-7pm Tue-Sun May-Sep, shorter hours Oct-Apr; Ⓜ Solférino, Assemblée Nationale, Invalides)

Les Catacombes

CEMETERY

6 ◎ MAP P182, D8

Paris' most macabre sight is its un-derground tunnels lined with skulls and bones. In 1785 it was decided to rectify the hygiene problems of Paris' overflowing cemeteries by exhuming the bones and storing them in disused quarry tunnels and the Catacombes were created in 1810. After descending 20m (via 130 narrow, dizzying spiral steps), follow dark, subterranean passages to the ossuary (1.5km in all). Exit

Les Catacombes

Station F Start-ups

Some 3000 resident entrepreneurs beaver away on ground-breaking ideas at the world's largest start-up campus, **Station F** (https://stationf.co/fr/campus/; 55 bd Vincent Auriol, 13e; admission free; ⏰tours noon Mon, Wed & Fri; Ⓜ Chevaleret, Bibliothèque). **Guided tours** (English available; book well in advance) take visitors on a 45-minute waltz through the gargantuan steel, glass and concrete hangar – a railway depot constructed in 1927–29 to house new trains servicing nearby Gare de Austerlitz.

In its Chill Zone, gigantic restaurant **La Felicità** has five different kitchens, a vast pavement terrace, bar, and dining in two train carriages.

via a minimalist all-white 'transition space' with gift shop onto 21bis av René Coty, 14e. Buy tickets in advance online to avoid queueing. (📞01 43 22 47 63; www.catacombes.paris.fr; 1 av Colonel Henri Roi-Tanguy, 14e; adult/child €13/free, online booking incl audioguide €29/5; ⏰10am-8.30pm Tue-Sun; Ⓜ Denfert Rochereau)

Cimetière du Montparnasse CEMETERY

7 MAP P182, C7

This 19-hectare cemetery opened in 1824 and is Paris' second largest after Père Lachaise (p132).

Famous residents include writer Guy de Maupassant, playwright Samuel Beckett, sculptor Constantin Brancusi, photographer Man Ray, industrialist André Citroën, Captain Alfred Dreyfus of the infamous Dreyfus Affair, legendary singer Serge Gainsbourg and philosopher-writers Jean-Paul Sartre and Simone de Beauvoir. (www.paris.fr; 3 bd Edgar Quinet, 14e; admission free; ⏰8am-6pm Mon-Fri, 8.30am-6pm Sat, 9am-6pm Sun; Ⓜ Edgar Quinet)

Fondation Cartier pour l'Art Contemporain GALLERY

8 MAP P182, D7

Designed by Jean Nouvel, this stunning glass-and-steel building is a work of art in itself. It hosts temporary exhibits on contemporary art (from the 1980s to today) in a diverse variety of media – from painting and photography to video and fashion, as well as performance art. Artist Lothar Baumgarten created the wonderfully rambling garden. (📞01 42 18 56 50; http://fondation.cartier.com; 261 bd Raspail, 14e; adult/child €12/8.50; ⏰11am-10pm Tue, to 8pm Wed-Sun; Ⓜ Raspail)

Musée Maillol MUSEUM

9 MAP P182, C3

Located in the stunning 18th-century Hôtel Bouchardon, this splendid little museum focuses on the work of sculptor Aristide Maillol (1861–1944), whose creations primarily occupy several rooms on the 2nd floor, and also includes works by Matisse, Gauguin, Kandinsky, Cézanne and Picasso. All are from the private collection of Odessa-born Dina Vierny (1919–2009), Maillol's principal model for 10 years from the age of 15. Major temporary exhibitions (included in the admission price) regularly take place here. (Fondation Dina Vierny; www.museemaillol.com; 61 rue de Grenelle, 7e; adult/child €13/11; ⊙10.30am-6.30pm Sat-Thu, to 9.30pm Fri; Ⓜ Rue du Bac)

and ceramic tiling, was built in 1906 to feed market workers. Despite the magnificent interior, the food – inspired by age-old recipes – is no afterthought but superbly executed (stuffed, spit-roasted suckling pig, pork shank in Rodenbach red beer, scallops and shrimps with lobster coulis). (🖉 01 44 32 15 60; www.bouillonracine.com; 3 rue Racine, 6e; 2-course weekday lunch menu €16.90, 3-course menu €35, mains €16-27.50; ⊙noon-11pm; 👫; Ⓜ Cluny-La Sorbonne)

Eating

Bouillon Racine   BRASSERIE €€

10 ❌ MAP P182, E4

Inconspicuously situated in a quiet street, this heritage-listed art nouveau 'soup kitchen', with mirrored walls, floral motifs

Restaurant Guy Savoy   GASTRONOMY €€€

If you're considering visiting a three-Michelin-star temple to gastronomy, this should certainly be on your list (see 2 ◎ Map p182, E2). The world-famous chef needs no introduction (he trained Gordon

---

Paris' Oldest Restaurant & Cafe

St-Germain claims the city's oldest restaurant and its oldest cafe:

À la Petite Chaise (Map p182, C3; 🖉 01 42 22 13 35; www.alapetitechaise. fr; 36 rue de Grenelle, 6e; 2-/3-course lunch menu €25/33, 3-course dinner menu €26, mains €21; ⊙noon-2pm & 7-11pm; Ⓜ Sèvres-Babylone) Hides behind an iron gate that's been here since it opened in 1680, when pioneering wine merchant Georges Rameau served food to accompany his wares. Classical decor and cuisine (onion soup, venison terrine with hazelnuts) make it worth a visit above and beyond its history.

Le Procope (Map p182, E3; 🖉 01 40 46 79 00; www.procope.com; 13 rue de l'Ancienne Comédie, 6e; 2-/3-course menu €21.90/28.90; ⊙11.30am-midnight Sun-Wed, to 1am Thu-Sat; Ⓜ Odéon) Welcoming its first patrons in 1686, it was frequented by Voltaire, Molière and Balzac. House specialities include coq au vin, calf kidneys with violet mustard, and homemade ice cream.

Rue Daguerre

Paris' traditional village atmosphere thrives along rue Daguerre, 14e. Tucked just southwest of the Denfert-Rochereau metro and RER stations, this narrow street – pedestrianised between av du Général-Leclerc and rue Boulard – is lined with florists, *fromageries* (cheese shops), *boulangeries* (bakeries), patisseries, greengrocers, delis (including Greek, Asian and Italian) and classic cafes where you can watch the local goings on.

Shops set up market stalls on the pavement; Sunday mornings are especially lively. It's a great option for lunch before or after visiting Les Catacombes, or packing a picnic to take to one of the area's parks or squares.

Ramsay, among others) but his flagship, entered via a red-carpeted staircase, is ensconced in the gorgeously refurbished neoclassical Monnaie de Paris (p184). Monumental cuisine to match includes Savoy icons such as artichoke and black-truffle soup with layered brioche. (📞01 43 80 40 61; www.guysavoy.com; 11 quai de Conti, 6e, Monnaie de Paris; lunch menu via online booking €130, tasting menu €415; ⊙noon-2pm & 7-10.30pm Tue-Fri, 7-10.30pm Sat; M Pont Neuf)

L'Avant Comptoir de la Mer
SEAFOOD €

11 MAP P182, E3

This is just one of Yves Camdeborde's stunning line-up of St-Germain hors d'oeuvre bars. It serves succulent Cap Ferret oysters (straight, Bloody Mary–style or with chipolata sausages), herring tartine, cauliflower and trout roe, blood-orange razor clams, roasted scallops and salmon croquettes, complemented by fantastic artisan bread, hand-churned flavoured butters, sea salt and Kalamata olives. (📞01 42 38 47 55; www.hotel-paris-relais-saint-germain.com; 3 Carrefour de l'Odéon, 6e; tapas €5-25, oysters per six €17; ⊙noon-11pm; M Odéon)

Clover
BISTRO €€

12 MAP P182, C2

Dining at hot-shot chef Jean-François Piège's casual bistro is like attending a private party: the galley-style open kitchen adjoining the 20 seats (online reservations open just 15 days in advance) is part of the dining-room decor, putting customers at the front and centre of the culinary action. Light, luscious dishes range from tomato gazpacho with pea sorbet to cabbage leaves with smoked herring *crème* and chestnuts. (📞01 75 50 00 05; www.clover-paris.com; 5 rue Perronet, 7e; 2-/3-course lunch menu €37/47, 3-/5-course dinner menu €60/73; ⊙12.30-2pm & 7-10pm

Tue-Fri, 12.30-2.30pm & 7-10pm Sat;
M St-Germain des Prés)

Semilla

NEOBISTRO €€

13 MAP P182, E3

Stark concrete floor, beams and an open kitchen (in front of which you can book front-row 'chef seats') set the factory-style scene for edgy, modern, daily changing dishes such as scallops cooked in Vin Jaune wine with crunchy endives or trout with passionfruit and ginger. Desserts are equally creative and irresistible. Be sure to book. (01 43 54 34 50; www.semillaparis. com; 54 rue de Seine, 6e; 2-/3-course weekday lunch menu €34/40, mains €24-40; 12.30-2.30pm & 7-11pm Mon-Sat, to 10pm Sun, closed early–mid-Aug; M Mabillon)

Chez Dumonet

BISTRO €€

14 MAP P182, B5

Fondly known by its former name, Joséphine, this lace-curtained, mosaic-tiled place with white-cloth covered tables inside and out is the classic Parisian bistro of many people's dreams. Chez Dumonet serves timeless standards such as confit of duck and grilled châteaubriand steak with Béarnaise sauce. Order its enormous signature Grand Marnier soufflé at the start of your meal. Mains, unusually, are available in full or half-portion size. (Joséphine; 01 45 48 52 40; 117 rue du Cherche Midi, 6e; mains €24-40; noon-2.30pm & 7.30-9.30pm Mon-Fri; M Duroc)

Le Procope (p187)

PETR KOVALENKOV/ALAMY ©

'Little Brittany'

Gare Montparnasse links Paris with Brittany, and the station's surrounding streets, especially rue du Montparnasse and rue d'Odessa, 14e, are lined with dozens of authentic crêperies.

Breton savoury buckwheat-flour galettes and sweet crêpes, with traditional toppings such as *caramel au beurre salé* (salty caramel), are served on a plate and eaten using cutlery.

Try lace-curtain-screened **Crêperie Josselin** (Map p182, C6; ☑ 01 43 20 93 50; 67 rue du Montparnasse, 14e; crêpes €5-10.50; ☺ 11am-11.30pm Wed-Sun; ⊛; Ⓜ Edgar Quinet).

Anicia FRENCH €€

 15 ⊗ MAP P182, B5

An advance online booking is essential at this glorious 'bistro nature', showcase for the earthy but refined cuisine of chef François Gagnaire who ran a Michelin-starred restaurant in the foodie town of Puy-en-Velay in the Auvergne before uprooting to the French capital. He still sources dozens of regional products – Puy lentils, Velay snails, St-Nectaire cheese – from small-time producers in central France, to stunning effect. (☑ 01 43 35 41 50; http://anicia-bistrot.com; 97 rue du Cherche Midi, 6e; 2-/3-course weekday lunch

menu €24/29, 3-/5-course dinner menu €49/58, mains €27-34; ☺ noon-10.30pm Tue-Sat; Ⓜ Duroc, Vaneau)

L'Étable Hugo Desnoyer FRENCH €€

 16 ⊗ MAP P182, D3

Duck beneath the elegant stone arches of Marché St-Germain to uncover the stylish steakhouse of Paris' superstar butcher Hugo Desnoyer. Vegetarians be warned, there are some delicious veggie dishes too, but some of the walls in the sharp design interior are clad in ginger-and-cream cow-hide and the menu is essentially for meat lovers. (☑ 01 42 39 89 27; www.hugodesnoyer.com; 15 rue Clément, 6e; lunch menu €24.50, mains €30-40; ☺ noon-2.30pm & 7.30-10.30pm Tue-Sat; Ⓜ Mabillon)

Au Pied de Fouet BISTRO €

17 ⊗ MAP P182, D2

At this tiny, lively, cherry-red bistro, wholly classic dishes such as *entrecôte* (steak), *confit de canard* (duck cooked slowly in its own fat) with creamy potatoes and *foie de volailles sauté* (pan-fried chicken livers) are astonishingly good value. Round off your meal with a tarte Tatin (upside-down apple tart), wine-soaked prunes, or deliciously rich *fondant au chocolat*. (☑ 01 42 96 59 10; 3 rue St-Benoît, 6e; mains €9-12.50; ☺ noon-2.30pm & 7-11pm Mon-Sat; Ⓜ St-Germain des Prés)

Les Climats

FRENCH €€€

18 MAP P182, C2

Like the neighbouring Musée d'Orsay, this is a magnificent art-nouveau treasure. Once a 1905-built former home for female telephone, telegram and postal workers, it features soaring vaulted ceilings and original stained glass, along with a lunchtime summer garden and glassed-in winter garden. Exquisite Michelin-starred dishes complement its 150-page list of wines, sparkling wines and whiskies purely from the Burgundy region. (☑ 01 58 62 10 08; http://lesclimats.fr; 41 rue de Lille, 7e; lunch/dinner menu €45/130, mains €52-72; ☺ 12.15-2.30pm & 7-10pm Tue-Sat; M Solférino)

Montparnasse Brasseries

🍴

After WWI, avant-garde writers, poets and artists shifted from Montmartre to the area around bd du Montparnasse.

Artists Chagall, Modigliani, Léger, Soutine, Miró, Matisse, Kandinsky and Picasso, composer Stravinsky, and writers Hemingway, Ezra Pound and Cocteau were among those who hung out here. It remained a creative hub until the mid-1930s. Historic brasseries that recall their legacy include the following:

La Rotonde Montparnasse (Map p182, C6; ☑ 01 43 26 48 26; 105 bd du Montparnasse, 6e; 3-course menu €46, mains €16-48, seafood platters €29.50-118.50; ☺ 6am-2am, kitchen noon-3pm & 7-11pm; M Vavin), opened in 1911.

Le Select (Map p182, C6; www.leselectmontparnasse.fr; 99 bd du Montparnasse, 6e; ☺ 7am-2am Sun-Thu, to 3am Fri & Sat; 🛜; M Vavin) The first of the area's grand cafes to stay open late into the night; founded 1923.

La Coupole (Map p182, C6; ☑ 01 43 20 14 20; www.lacoupole-paris.com; 102 bd du Montparnasse, 14e; 2-/3-course lunch menu €31/39, mains €18-42; ☺ 8am-11pm Mon, 8am-midnight Tue-Fri, 8.30am-midnight Sat, 8.30am-11pm Sun; 🛜; M Vavin) This 450-seat, 1927-opened brasserie has muralled columns painted by artists including Chagall.

La Closerie des Lilas (Map p182, D7; ☑ 01 40 51 34 50; www.closeriedeslilas.fr; 171 bd du Montparnasse, 6e; 3-course lunch menu €52, mains restaurant €28-52, brasserie €17-27; ☺ restaurant noon-2.30pm & 7-11.30pm, brasserie noon-12.30am, piano bar 11am-1.30am; M Vavin or RER Port Royal) Hemingway's favourite (established 1847).

Le Dôme (Map p182, C6; ☑ 01 43 35 25 81; www.restaurant-ledome.com; 108 bd du Montparnasse, 14e; mains €42-67, seafood platters €85-148; ☺ noon-3pm & 7-11pm; M Vavin) Shellfish specialist and art deco extravaganza.

Drinking

Les Deux Magots
CAFE

19 MAP P182, D3

If ever there was a cafe that summed up St-Germain des Prés' early-20th-century literary scene, it's this former hang-out of anyone who was anyone. You'll spend substantially more here than elsewhere to sip *un café* (€4.70) in a wicker-woven bistro chair on the pavement terrace shaded by dark-green awnings and geraniums spilling from window boxes, but it's an undeniable piece of Parisian history. (☏ 01 45 48 55 25; www.lesdeuxmagots.fr; 170 bd St-Germain, 6e; 🕑 7.30am-1am; M St-Germain des Prés)

Au Sauvignon
WINE BAR

20 MAP P182, C3

Grab a table in the evening light at this wonderfully authentic wine bar or head to the quintessential bistro interior, with original zinc bar, tightly packed tables and hand-painted ceiling celebrating French viticultural tradition. A plate of *casse-croûtes au pain Poilâne* (toast with ham, pâté, terrine, smoked salmon and foie gras) is the perfect accompaniment. (☏ 01 45 48 49 02; http://ausauvignon.com; 80 rue des Sts-Pères, 7e; 🕑 8am-11pm Mon-Sat, 9am-10pm Sun; M Sèvres-Babylone)

Cod House
COCKTAIL BAR

21 MAP P182, E4

'Oh my cod!' screams the turquoise-neon 'tag' on the wall, and indeed, this achingly cool cocktail bar with a gold-and-blue, Scandinavian-style interior does excite. Sake-based cocktails play around with matcha-infused cachaça, cinnamon-infused pisco, homemade lemongrass syrup and fresh yuzu. Creative small plates (€5 to €16) titillate tastebuds with shrimp tempura, yellow-tail carpaccio with fresh chilli and a yuzu sauce, and deep-fried chicken ravioli. (☏ 01 42 49 35 59; www.thecodhouse.fr; 1 rue de Condé, 6e; 🕑 noon-3pm & 7.30-2am Mon-Sat; M Odéon)

Tiger
COCKTAIL BAR

22 MAP P182, D3

Suspended bare-bulb lights and fretted timber make this split-level space a stylish spot for specialist gins (130 varieties). Signature cocktails include a Breakfast Martini (gin, triple sec, orange marmalade and lemon juice) and Oh My Dog (white-pepper-infused gin, lime juice, raspberry and rose cordial and ginger ale). Dedicated G&T aficionados can work their way through a staggering 1040 combinations. (www.tiger-paris.com; 13 rue Princesse, 6e; 🕑 6.30pm-2am Mon-Sat; M Mabillon)

Café de Flore CAFE

23 MAP P182, D3

The red upholstered benches, mirrors and marble walls at this art deco landmark haven't changed much since the days when Jean-Paul Sartre and Simone de Beauvoir essentially set up office here, writing in its warmth during the Nazi occupation. Watch for monthly English-language *philocafé* (philosophy discussion) sessions. (☏ 01 45 48 55 26; http://cafedeflore.fr; 172 bd St-Germain, 6e; ⊕ 7.30am-1.30am; Ⓜ St-Germain des Prés)

Castor Club COCKTAIL BAR

24 MAP P182, E3

Discreetly signed, this superb underground cocktail bar has

an intimate English gentleman's club–style upstairs bar with vintage wall lamps and slinky, red velour stools. But it's downstairs, in the 18th-century stone cellar with hole-in-the-wall booths, that the real cocktail-sipping action happens. Smooth '50s, '60s and '70s tracks only add to the already cool vibe. (☏ 09 50 64 99 38; 14 rue Hautefeuille, 6e; ⊕ 7pm-2am Tue & Wed, 7pm-4am Thu-Sat; Ⓜ Odéon)

La Quincave WINE BAR

25 MAP P182, C6

Bar stools at this lively wine bar and shop are fashioned from wine barrels, but on summer evenings most of the action spills onto the tiny street out front. Over 200 varieties of natural wines are

Café de Flore

available by the bottle, along with tasty charcuterie and cheese platters to soak them up. (09 67 02 80 14; www.facebook.com/quincave; 17 rue Bréa, 6e; 11am-1pm & 5-11.30pm Tue-Thu, 11am-11.30pm Fri & Sat; M Vavin)

La Palette CAFE

26 MAP P182, E2

In the heart of gallery land, this timeless *fin de siècle* cafe and erstwhile stomping ground of Paul Cézanne and Georges Braque attracts a grown-up set of fashion-industry professionals and local art dealers. Its summer terrace is beautiful. (www.cafelapaletteparis.com; 43 rue de Seine, 6e; 8am-2am; ; M Mabillon)

Shopping

Sabbia Rosa FASHION & ACCESSORIES

27 MAP P182, C3

Only French-sourced fabrics (silk from Lyon, lace from Calais) are used by lingerie designer Sabbia Rosa for her ultra-luxe range at this upmarket boutique, open since 1976. Every piece is unique; items can be custom-made in 48 hours. The list of celebrity clients reads like a who's who: Serge Gainsbourg, Madonna, Naomi Campbell, Claudia Schiffer and George Clooney have all shopped here. (01 45 48 88 37; 73 rue des Sts-Pères, 6e; 10am-7pm Mon-Sat; M St-Germain des Prés)

Wine shop, St-Germain des Prés

La Dernière Goutte   WINE

28 🔒 MAP P182, D3

'The Last Drop' is the brainchild of Cuban-American sommelier Juan Sánchez, whose tiny wine shop is packed with exciting, mostly organic French *vins de proprié-taires* (estate-bottled wines) made by small independent producers. Wine classes lasting two hours (two white tastings, five red) regularly take place in English (per person €55); phone for schedules and reservations. Free tastings with winemakers take place most Saturdays. (📞01 43 29 11 62; www. ladernieregoutte.net; 6 rue du Bourbon le Château, 6e; ⏱3.30-8pm Mon, 10.30am-1.30pm & 3-8pm Tue-Fri, 10.30am-8pm Sat, 11am-7pm Sun; Ⓜ Mabillon)

Gab & Jo   FASHION & ACCESSORIES

29 🔒 MAP P182, D2

For quality local gifts, browse the shelves of this tiny concept store stocking only made-in-France items. Designers include La Note Parisienne (scented candles for each Parisian *arrondissement,* such as the 6e, with notes of lipstick, cognac, orange blossom, tuberose, jasmine, rose and fig), Marius Fabre (Marseille soaps), Germaine-des-Prés (lingerie), MILF (sunglasses) and Monsieur Marcel (T-shirts). (www.gabjo.fr; 28 rue Jacob, 6e; ⏱11am-7pm Mon-Sat; Ⓜ St-Germain des Prés)

Book Stalls

With some 3km of forest-green boxes lining the Seine – containing over 300,000 secondhand (and often out-of-print) books, rare magazines, postcards and old advertising posters – Paris' **bouquinistes** (Map p182, F2; quai Voltaire, 7e, to quai de la Tournelle, 5e, & Pont Marie, 4e, to quai du Louvre, 1er; ⏱11.30am-dusk) are as integral to the cityscape as Notre Dame. Many open only from spring to autumn (and many shut in August), but year-round you'll still find some to browse.

Gérard Mulot   FOOD

30 🔒 MAP P182, E3

Fruit tarts (peach, lemon, apple), *tarte normande* (apple cake) and *clafoutis* (cherry flan) are among this celebrated pastry chef's specialities sold at his delightfully quaint patisserie with candyfloss pink-and-white striped canopy. Head to his tearoom, **L'Amaryllis de Gérard Mulot** (📞01 43 26 91 03; 12 rue des Quartre Vents, 6e; lunch menu €25, afternoon tea €15; ⏱11am-6.30pm Tue-Sat; Ⓜ Odéon) to sit down and indulge. (📞01 43 26 85 77; www.gerard-mulot.com; 76 rue de Seine, 6e; ⏱7am-8pm; Ⓜ Mabillon)

St-Germain des Prés' Historic Shops

St-Germain des Prés is filled with antique and vintage dealers and a trove of historic small shops.

Cire Trudon (Map p182, E3; ☎ 01 43 26 46 50; https://trudon.com; 78 rue de Seine, 6e; ☺11am-7pm Mon, 10am-7pm Tue-Sat; Ⓜ Odéon) Claude Trudon began selling candles here in 1643, and officially supplied Versailles and Napoléon with light. It is now the world's oldest candlemaker (look for the plaque to the left of the awning).

Au Plat d'Étain (Map p182, D3; ☎ 01 43 54 32 06; www.soldats-plomb-au-plat-etain.fr; 16 rue Guisarde, 6e; ☺10.30am-6.30pm Tue-Sat; Ⓜ Mabillon, St-Sulpice) Miniature tin and lead soldiers have been sold at this tiny shop since 1775.

La Maison de Poupée (Map p182, D4; ☎ 06 09 65 58 68; 40 rue de Vaugirard, 6e; ☺2.30-7pm Mon-Sat, by appointment Sun; Ⓜ St-Sulpice or RER Luxembourg) The teensy shop sells its namesake doll's houses as well as *poupées anciennes* (antique dolls).

Le Bon Marché (Map p182, C4; ☎ 01 44 39 80 00; http://lebonmarche. com; 24 rue de Sèvres, 7e; ☺10am-8pm Mon-Wed, Fri & Sat, 10am-8.45pm Thu, 11am-8pm Sun; Ⓜ Sèvres-Babylone) Designed by Gustave Eiffel, this 1852-opened department store houses fashion, homewares and food hall **La Grande Épicerie de Paris** (Map p182, B4; www.lagrandeepicerie. com; 36 rue de Sèvres, 7e; ☺8.30am-9pm Mon-Sat, 10am-8pm Sun), with fantastical displays of chocolates, biscuits, cheeses and more.

Poilâne (Map p182, C4; ☎ 01 45 48 42 59; www.poilane.com; 8 rue du Cherche Midi, 6e; ☺7am-8.30pm Mon-Sat; Ⓜ Sèvres-Babylone) Pierre Poilâne opened his *boulangerie* (bakery) in 1932. Today his granddaughter runs the company, which still turns out wood-fired, rounded sourdough loaves made with stonemilled flour and Guérande sea salt.

Deyrolle (Map p182, C2; ☎ 01 42 22 30 07; www.deyrolle.com; 46 rue du Bac, 7e; ☺10am-1pm & 2-7pm Mon, 10am-7pm Tue-Sat; Ⓜ Rue du Bac) Overrun with creatures such as lions, tigers, zebras and storks, this taxidermist opened in 1831.

Magasin Sennelier (Map p182, D2; ☎ 01 42 60 72 15; www.magasinsennelier.com; 3 quai Voltaire, 7e; ☺2-6.30pm Mon, 10am-12.45pm & 2-6.30pm Tue-Sat; Ⓜ St-Germain des Prés) Cézanne and Picasso were among the artists who helped develop products for this 1887-founded art supplier, which retains exquisite timber cabinetry and glass display cases.

Fromagerie Quatrehomme
CHEESE

31 🔒 MAP P182, B4

Buy the best of French cheeses, many with an original take (eg Epoisses boxed in chestnut leaves, Mont d'Or flavoured with black truffles, spiced honey and Roquefort bread), at this king of *fromageries* (cheese shops), at home in the 'hood since 1953. (☏ 01 47 34 33 45; www.quatrehomme. fr; 62 rue de Sèvres, 7e; ⏰ 9am-7.45pm Tue-Sat; Ⓜ Vaneau)

Fermob
HOMEWARES

32 🔒 MAP P182, C3

Fermob is famed for manufacturing iconic French garden furniture, including the Jardin du Luxembourg's signature sage-green chairs, actually available in a spectacular rainbow of colours for your own garden or terrace. Fermob has another **branch** (81-83 av Ledru-Rollin, 12e; ⏰ 10am-7pm Mon-Sat; Ⓜ Ledru-Rollin) across the river near Bastille. (☏ 01 45 44 10 28; www.paris.fermob.com; 17 bd Raspail, 7e; ⏰ 10am-7pm Tue-Sat; Ⓜ Rue du Bac)

Pierre Hermé
FOOD

33 🔒 MAP P182, D3

Leading *pâtissier* and chocolatier Pierre Hermé has several boutiques in Paris including this one in the heart of St-Germain. The size of a chocolate box, it's a veritable feast of perfectly presented petits fours, cakes, chocolates, nougats, jams and dazzling macarons. (www. pierreherme.com; 72 rue Bonaparte, 6e; ⏰ 10am-7pm Sun-Fri, to 8pm Sat; Ⓜ Odéon)

Marché Raspail
MARKET

34 🔒 MAP P182, C4

A traditional open-air market on Tuesday and Friday, Marché Raspail is especially popular on Sunday, when it's filled with *biologique* (organic) produce. (bd Raspail, btwn rue de Rennes & rue du Cherche Midi, 6e; ⏰ 7am-2.30pm Tue & Fri, organic market 9am-1.30pm Sun; Ⓜ Rennes)

Smallable Concept Store
CHILDREN'S CLOTHING

35 🔒 MAP P182, B5

'Dream big' is the inviting strapline of this Parisian-chic space, a one-stop shop for accessories, fashion and homewares for babies, children and teens. Premium brands include Little Eleven Paris, Chloé Kids, Petit Bateau, Pom d'Api and Zadig & Voltaire. It is also one of the few places in Paris to buy exquisite, French-made Maison de Vacances cushions and linens. (☏ 01 40 46 01 15; www.smallable. com; 81 rue du Cherche Midi, 6e; ⏰ 2-7.30pm Mon, 10.30am-7.30pm Tue-Sat; Ⓜ Vaneau)

Worth a Trip 🔭
Versailles

The opulent-and-then-some Château de Versailles sits amid 900 hectares of gardens, parks and woods. Louis XIV transformed his father's hunting lodge into the colossal Château de Versailles in the mid-17th century and the baroque palace was the kingdom's political capital from 1682 until 1789, when revolutionaries massacred the palace guard. Louis XVI and Marie Antoinette were ultimately dragged back to Paris and ingloriously guillotined.

www.chateauversailles.fr

place d'Armes, Versailles

adult/child passport ticket incl estate-wide access €20/ free, with musical events €27/ free, palace €18/free except during musical events

🕙 9am-6.30pm Tue-Sun Apr-Oct, to 5.30pm Tue-Sun Nov-Mar

Château de Versailles in Numbers

Louis XIV ordered 700 rooms, 2153 windows, 352 chimneys and 11 hectares of roof for the 580m-long main palace. It housed the entire court of 6000 (plus 5000 servants). The finest talent of the day installed some 6300 paintings, 2000 sculptures and statues, 15,000 engravings and 5000 furnishings and objets d'art.

Hall of Mirrors

The palace's opulence peaks in its shimmering, sparkling Galerie des Glaces (Hall of Mirrors). This 75m-long ballroom has 17 giant mirrors on one side and an equal number of windows on the other.

King's & Queen's State Apartments

Luxurious, ostentatious appointments – frescoes, marble, gilt and woodcarvings, with themes and symbols drawn from Greek and Roman mythology – emanate from every last moulding, cornice, ceiling and door in the palace's Grands Appartements du Roi et de la Reine.

Guided Tours

To access areas that are otherwise off-limits and learn more about Versailles' history, take a 90-minute **guided tour** (☎01 30 83 77 88; €10, plus palace entry; ✆English-language tours 9.30am Tue-Sun) of the Private Apartments of Louis XV and Louis XVI and the Opera House or Royal Chapel. Tours include access to the most famous parts of the palace; book online.

The Gardens

Celebrated landscape artist André Le Nôtre was commissioned by Louis XIV to design the château's magnificent **gardens** (free except during musical events; ✆8am-8.30pm Apr-Oct, to 6pm Nov-Mar, park 7am-8.30pm Apr-Oct, 8am-6pm Nov-Mar).

★ Top Tips

o Versailles has several train stations; the most convenient way to reach the château is to take RER C5 (return €7.10, 40 minutes, frequent) from Paris' Left Bank RER stations to Versailles-Château–Rive Gauche station.

o Tuesday, Saturday and Sunday are the palace's busiest days.

o Versailles is free on the first Sunday of every month from November to March.

✗ Take a Break

Restaurants within the estate include Alain Ducasse's **Ore** (☎01 30 84 12 96; www.ducasse-chateau versailles.com; 1st floor, Pavillon Dufour; breakfast menus €12-20, mains €20-36, afternoon-tea platters €35; ✆9am-6.30pm Tue-Sun Apr-Oct, to 5.30pm Nov-Mar; 🛜👶).

In the town of Versailles, rue de Satory is lined with restaurants and cafes. More local options can be found on and around rue de la Paroisse.

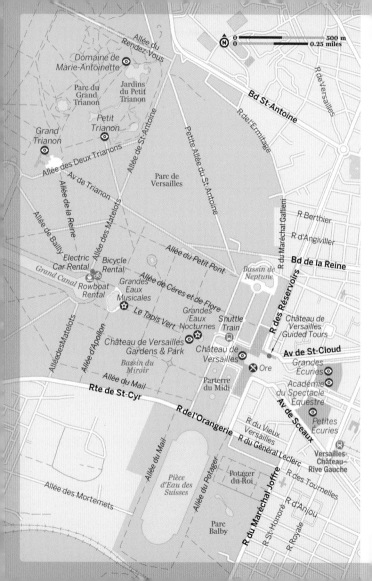

N 0 500 m
0 0.25 miles

Allée du Rendez-Vous

Domaine de Marie-Antoinette

Parc du Grand Trianon

Jardins du Petit Trianon

Bd St-Antoine

R de Versailles

R de l'Ermitage

Petit Trianon

Grand Trianon

Allée des Deux Trianons

Av de Trianon

Allée de St-Antoine

Petite Allée du St-Antoine

Parc de Versailles

Allée de la Reine

Allée de Bailly

Allée des Matelots

R Berthier

R d'Angiviller

R du Maréchal Gallieni

Allée du Petit Pont

Bd de la Reine

Electric Car Rental

Bicycle Rental

Grand Canal

Rowboat Rental

Grandes Eaux Musicales

Allée de Cérès et de Flore

Bassin de Neptune

Château de Versailles Guided Tours

R des Réservoirs

Le Tapis Vert

Grandes Eaux Nocturnes

Shuttle Train

Av de St-Cloud

Allées des Matelots

Allée d'Apollon

Château de Versailles Gardens & Park

Bassin du Miroir

Château de Versailles

✕ Ore

Grandes Écuries

Académie du Spectacle Équestre

Av de Sceaux

Allée du Mail

Rte de St-Cyr

Parterre du Midi

Petites Écuries

R de l'Orangerie

R du Vieux Versailles

R du Général Leclerc

Versailles-Château–Rive Gauche

Allée du Mail

Pièce d'Eau des Suisses

Allée du Potager

Potager du Roi

R des Tournelles

R du Maréchal Joffre

R d'Anjou

Allée des Mortemets

Parc Balby

R St-Honoré

R Royale

The best view over the rectangular pools is from the Hall of Mirrors. Pathways include the Royal Walk's verdant 'green carpet', with smaller paths leading to leafy groves.

The Canals

Oriented to reflect the sunset, the **Grand Canal**, 1.6km long and 62m wide, is traversed by the 1km-long **Petit Canal**, creating a cross-shaped body of water with a perimeter of more than 5.5km.

Marie Antoinette's Estate

Northwest of the main palace is the **Domaine de Marie-Antoinette** (Marie Antoinette's Estate; adult/child €12/free, free with passport ticket; ⏰noon-6.30pm Tue-Sun Apr-Oct, to 5.30pm Tue-Sat Nov-Mar). Tickets include the Grand and Petit Trianon palaces, and the **Hameau de la Reine** (Queen's Hamlet), a mock village of thatched cottages where Marie Antoinette played milkmaid.

Trianon Palaces

The pink-colonnaded **Grand Trianon** was built in 1687 for Louis XIV and his family as a place of escape from the rigid etiquette of the court, and renovated under Napoléon I in the Empire style. The ochre-coloured 1760s **Petit Trianon** was redecorated in 1867 by the consort of Napoléon III, Empress Eugénie, who added Louis XVI-style furnishings.

Musical Fountain Shows

Try to time your visit for the magical **Grandes Eaux Musicales** (www.chateauversailles-spectacles.fr; adult/child €9.50/8; ⏰9am-7pm Tue, Sat & Sun mid-May–late Jun, 9am-7pm Sat & Sun Apr–mid-May & late Jun-Oct) or the after-dark **Grandes Eaux Nocturnes** (www.chateauversailles-spectacles.fr; adult/child €24/20; ⏰8.30-11.30pm Sat mid-Jun–mid-Sep), 'dancing water' displays set to baroque- and classical-era music.

Getting Around

The estate is so vast that the only way to see it all is to hire a four-person **electric car** (📞01 39 66 97 66; www.versailles-tourisme.com; car hire per hr €34; ⏰10am-6.45pm Apr-Oct, to 5.30pm Feb & Mar, to 5pm Nov & Dec) or hop aboard the **shuttle train** (www.train-versailles.com; adult/child €8/6.10, audioguide €4; ⏰every 20min 11.10am-6.50pm Apr-Oct, to 5.10pm Nov-Mar); you can also rent a **bike** (📞01 39 66 97 66; bike hire per hr/day €8.50/20; ⏰10am-6.45pm Apr-Oct, to 5.30pm mid-Feb–Mar, to 5pm early–mid-Nov) or a **rowboat** (📞01 39 66 97 66; www.versailles-tourisme.com; boat hire per 30 min/hr €13/17; ⏰10am-6.45pm Jul & Aug, shorter hrs Mar-Jun & Sep–mid-Nov).

Survival Guide

Before You Go   204
Book Your Stay 204
When to Go 204

Arriving in Paris   205

Getting Around   208
Metro & RER 208
Bus 208
Bicycle 208
Boat 210
Taxi 210

Essential Information   210
Accessible Travel 210
Business Hours 211
Discount Cards 211
Electricity 212
Emergency 212
Internet Access 212
Money 213
Public Holidays 213
Safe Travel 213
Telephone 213
Toilets 214
Tourist Information 214
Visas 214

Language   215

Arc de Triomphe (p54) STOCKBRUNET/SHUTTERSTOCK ©

Before You Go

Book Your Stay

o Paris has a wealth of accommodation for all budgets, but it's often full well in advance. Reservations are recommended year-round and essential April to October and public and school holidays.

o Although marginally cheaper, accommodation outside central Paris is invariably a false economy given travel time and costs. Choose somewhere within Paris' 20 *arrondissements* (city districts) to experience Parisian life the moment you step out the door.

o The city levies a *taxe de séjour* (tourist tax) per person per night on all accommodation, from €0.88 to €4.40 per person per night (normally added to your bill).

o Breakfast is rarely included; cafes often offer better value.

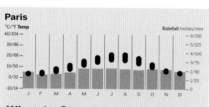

When to Go

Winter (Nov–Feb)
Cold and dark, occasional snow. Museums are quieter and accommodation prices are lower.

Spring (Mar–May)
Mild, sometimes wet. Major sights start getting busier; parks and gardens begin to come into their own.

Summer (Jun–Aug)
Warm to hot, generally sunny. Main tourist season. Some businesses close for August.

Autumn (Sep–Nov)
Mild, generally sunny. Cultural life moving into top gear after the summer lull.

Useful Websites

Lonely Planet (www.lonelyplanet.com/france/paris/hotels) Reviews of Lonely Planet's top choices.

Paris Attitude (www.parisattitude.com) Thousands of apartment rentals, professional service, reasonable fees.

Haven In (https://havenin.com) Charming Parisian apartments.

Best Budget

Hôtel du Dragon (www.hoteldudragon.com) Home-made jam is on the breakfast menu at this heart-warming spot.

Hôtel Diana (http://hotel-diana-paris.com) Contemporary meets retro in the Latin Quarter.

Cosmos Hôtel (www.cosmos-hotel-paris.com) Brilliant value and footsteps from the nightlife of the 11e.

Hôtel du Nord – Le Pari Vélo (www.hoteldunord-leparivelo.com) Bric-a-brac charm and bikes for loan.

Mama Shelter (www.mamashelter.com)

Philippe Starck–designed property with a cool in-house pizzeria.

Hôtel Port Royal (www.port-royal-hotel.fr) Spotless vintage-furnished hotel with a peaceful courtyard garden.

Best Midrange

Hôtel Paris Bastille Boutet (www.sofitel.com) One-time chocolate factory with beautiful art deco tiling and a basement pool.

Hoxton (www.thehoxton.com) Paris' outpost of the hot-shot design group occupies an 18th-century residence in the hip Sentier neighbourhood.

Hôtel Providence (www.hotelprovidenceparis.com) Rooms at this luxurious property come with bespoke cocktail bars.

Familia Hôtel (www.familiahotel.com) Sepia murals and flower-bedecked balconies in the Latin Quarter.

Edgar (www.edgarparis.com) A former convent now contains 13 rooms by different artists and designers.

Best Top End

Les Bains (www.lesbains-paris.com) Nineteenth-century thermal baths turned nightclub turned rockstar-hot hotel.

Hôtel Crayon (www.hotelcrayon.com) Line drawings, retro furnishings and coloured-glass shower doors.

Hôtel du Jeu de Paume (http://jeudepaumehotel.com) Romantic haven on the serene Île St-Louis.

Hôtel Molitor (www.mltr.fr) Stunningly restored art deco swimming pool with gallery-style poolside rooms.

Arriving in Paris

Charles de Gaulle Airport

Most international airlines fly to **Aéroport de Charles de Gaulle** (CDG; ☎ 01 70 36 39 50; www.parisaeroport.fr), 28km northeast of central Paris. In French the airport is commonly called 'Roissy' after the suburb in which it is located. A high-speed train link between Charles de Gaulle and Gare de l'Est in central Paris is planned, but no track will be laid until 2019. When complete in 2024, the CDG Express will cut the current 50-minute journey to 20 minutes. Inter-terminal shuttle services are free. A fourth terminal is due to open by 2025.

Train

CDG is served by the RER B line (€11.40, child four to nine €7.90, approximately 50 minutes, every 10 to 20 minutes), which connects with central Paris stations including Gare du Nord, Châtelet–Les Halles and St-Michel–Notre Dame. Trains run from 4.50am to 11.50pm (from Gare du Nord 4.53am to 12.15am) every six to 15 minutes.

Bus

There are six main bus lines.

Le Bus Direct line 2 (www.lebusdirect.com; €17, one hour, every 30 minutes from 5.45am to

11pm) Links the airport with the Arc de Triomphe via an **Eiffel Tower stop** (16-20 av de Suffren, 15e) and Trocadéro.

Le Bus Direct line 4 (€17, 50 to 80 minutes, every 30 minutes from 6am to 10.30pm from the airport, 5.30am to 10.30pm from Montparnasse) Links the airport with **Gare Montparnasse** (rue du Commandant René Mouchotte, 14e; 80 minutes) in southern Paris via **Gare de Lyon** (20bis bd Diderot, 12e; 50 minutes) in eastern Paris.

Noctilien buses 140 and 143 (€8 or four metro tickets) Part of the RATP night service, Noctilien has two buses that link CDG with **Gare de l'Est** (rue du 8 Mai 1945, 10e) in northern Paris via nearby Gare du Nord: bus 140 (1am to 4am; from Gare de l'Est 1am to 3.40am) takes 80 minutes, and bus 143 (12.32am to 4.32am; from Gare de l'Est 12.55am to 5.08am) takes 55 minutes.

RATP bus 350 (www.ratp.fr; €6 or three metro tickets, 70 minutes, every 30 minutes from 5.30am to 11pm) Links

the airport with **Gare de l'Est** (bd de Strasbourg, 10e, Gare de l'Est).

RATP bus 351 (€6 or three metro tickets, 70 minutes, every 30 minutes from 5.30am to 11pm) Links the airport with **place de la Nation** (2 av du Trône, 12e; Ⓜ Nation) in eastern Paris.

Roissybus (€12.50, one hour, from CDG every 15 to 20 minutes from 6am to 12.30am; from Paris every 15 minutes from 5.15am to 12.30am) Links the airport with **Opéra** (11 rue Scribe, 9e).

Taxi

○ A taxi to the city centre takes 40 minutes. Fares are a flat rate: €50 to the Right Bank and €55 to the Left Bank. The fare increases by 15% between 7pm and 7am and on Sundays.

○ Only take taxis at a clearly marked rank. Never follow anyone who approaches you at the airport and claims to be a driver.

Orly Airport

Aéroport d'Orly (ORY; ☏ 01 70 36 39 50; www.parisaeroport.fr) is

19km south of central Paris but, despite being closer than CDG, it is not as frequently used by international airlines, and public-transport options aren't quite as straightforward. That will change by 2024, when metro line 14 will be extended to the airport. A TGV station is due to arrive here in 2025.

Orly's south and west terminals are currently being unified into one large terminal suitable for bigger planes such as A380s; completion is due in 2019.

Train

There is currently no direct train to/from Orly; you'll need to change halfway. Note that while it is possible to take a shuttle to the RER C line, this service is quite long and not recommended.

RER B (€13.25, children four to nine €6.60, 35 minutes, every four to 12 minutes) This line connects Orly with the St-Michel–Notre Dame, Châtelet–Les Halles and Gare du Nord stations in the city centre. In order to get from

Orly to the RER station (Antony), you must first take the Orlyval automatic train. The service runs from 6am to 11.35pm. You only need one ticket to take the two trains.

Tram

Tramway T7 (€1.90, 40 minutes, every six minutes from 5.30am to 12.30am) This tramway links Orly with Villejuif–Louis Aragon metro station in southern Paris; buy tickets from the machine at the tram stop as no tickets are sold on board.

Bus

Two bus lines serve Orly:

Le Bus Direct line 1 (www.lebusdirect.com; €12, one hour, every 20 minutes from 5.50am to 11.30pm from Orly, 4.50am to 10.30pm from the Arc de Triomphe) Runs to/from the Arc de Triomphe (one hour) via **Gare Montparnasse** (40 minutes), **La Motte-Picquet** (88 av de Suffren, 15e) and Trocadéro.

Orlybus (€8.70, 30 minutes, every 15 to 20 minutes from 6am

to 12.30am from Orly, 5.35am to midnight from Paris) Runs to/from **place Denfert-Rochereau** (3 place Denfert-Rochereau, 14e) in southern Paris.

Taxi

A taxi to the city centre takes roughly 30 minutes. Standardised flat-rate fares since 2016 mean a taxi costs €30 to the Left Bank and €35 to the Right Bank. The fare increases by 15% between 7pm and 7am and on Sunday.

Beauvais Airport

Aéroport de Beauvais (BVA; ☎ 08 92 68 20 66; www.aeroportbeauvais.com) is 75km north of Paris and is served by a few low-cost flights. Before you snap up that bargain, though, consider whether the post-arrival journey is worth it.

The Beauvais *navette* (shuttle bus; €17, 1¼ hours) links the airport with **Parking Pershing** (16-24 bd Pershing, 17e; **M** Porte Maillot) on central Paris' western edge; services are coordinated with flight

times. See the airport website for details and tickets.

A taxi to central Paris during the day/night costs around €170/210 (probably more than the cost of your flight!).

Gare du Nord

Gare du Nord (www.gares-sncf.com; rue de Dunkerque, 10e) is the terminus for northbound domestic trains as well as several international services. Located in northern Paris.

Eurostar (www.eurostar.com) The London–Paris line runs from St Pancras International to Gare du Nord. Voyages take 2¼ hours.

Thalys (www.thalys.com) Trains pull into Paris' Gare du Nord from Brussels, Amsterdam and Cologne.

Other Mainline Train Stations

○ Paris has five other stations for long-distance trains, each with its own metro station: Gare d'Austerlitz, Gare de l'Est, Gare de Lyon, Gare Montparnasse and Gare St-Lazare. The station used depends on the direction from Paris.

○ Contact Voyages SNCF (www.voyages-sncf.com) for connections throughout France and continental Europe.

Getting Around

Metro & RER

Paris' underground network is run by RATP (www.ratp.fr). It consists of two separate but linked systems: the metro and the Réseau Express Régional (RER) suburban train line. The metro has 14 numbered lines; the RER has five main lines (but you'll probably only need to use A, B and C). When buying tickets consider how many zones your journey will cover; there are five concentric transport zones rippling out from Paris (zone 5 being the furthest); if you travel from Charles de Gaulle airport to Paris, for instance, you will have to buy a ticket for zones 1 to 5.

○ Metro lines are identified by both their number (eg *ligne* 1 – line 1) and their colour, listed on official metro signs and maps.

○ Signs in metro and RER stations indicate the way to the correct platform for your line. The *direction* signs on each platform indicate the terminus. On lines that split into several branches (such as lines 7 and 13), the terminus of each train is indicated on the cars and on signs on each platform giving the number of minutes until the next and subsequent train.

○ Signs marked *correspondance* (transfer) show how to reach connecting trains. At stations with many intersecting lines, like Châtelet and Montparnasse Bienvenüe, walking from one platform to the next can take a very long time.

○ Different station exits are indicated by white-on-blue *sortie* (exit) signs. You can get your bearings by checking the *plan du quartier* (neighbourhood maps) posted at exits.

○ Each line has its own

schedule, but trains usually start at around 5.30am, with the last train beginning its run between 12.35am and 1.15am (2.15am on Friday and Saturday).

Bus

○ Paris' bus system, operated by the RATP, runs from approximately 5am to 1am Monday to Saturday; services are drastically reduced on Sunday and public holidays. Hours vary substantially depending on the line.

○ The RATP runs night-bus lines known as Noctilien (www.vianavigo.com), which depart hourly from 11.45pm to 6am. The services pass through the main train stations and cross the major axes of the city before leading out to the suburbs. Look for navy-blue N or Noctilien signs at bus stops.

Bicycle

○ The **Vélib'** (☎01 76 49 12 34; www.velib-metropole.fr; day/week subscription for up to 5 people €5/15, standard bike hire up to 30/60min free/€1, electric bike €1/2) bike-share scheme changed operators in

Tickets & Passes

o The same RATP tickets are valid on the metro, the RER (for travel within the city limits), buses, trams and the Montmartre funicular.

o A ticket – white in colour and called *Le Ticket t+* – costs €1.90 (half price for children aged four to nine years) if bought individually; a *carnet* (book) of 10 costs €14.90 for adults.

o Tickets are sold at all metro stations. Some automated machines take notes and coins, though not all. Ticket windows accept most credit cards; however, machines do not accept credit cards without embedded chips (and even then, not all foreign chip-embedded cards are accepted).

o One ticket lets you travel between any two metro stations (no return journeys) for a period of 1½ hours, no matter how many transfers are required. You can also use it on the RER for travel within zone 1, which encompasses all of central Paris.

o Transfers from the metro to buses or vice versa are not possible.

o Always keep your ticket until you exit from your station; if you are stopped by a ticket inspector, you will have to pay a fine if you don't have a valid ticket.

o If you're staying in Paris for a week or more, ask at metro station offices about rechargeable Navigo (www.navigo.fr) passes.

o Mobilis and Paris Visite passes cover transport.

2018; check the website for the latest information. When the handover is complete, it will put tens of thousands of bikes (30% of which will be electric) at the disposal of Parisians and visitors at some 1400 stations throughout Paris, accessible around the clock.

o For longer rentals, places generally require a deposit (usually €150 for a standard bike, €300 for electric bikes).

Take ID and your bank or credit card.

Freescoot (☎ 01 44 07 06 72; www.freescoot.com; 63 quai de la Tournelle, 5e; 50/125cc scooters per 24hr from €65/75, bicycle/ tandem/electric-bike rental per 24hr from €25/40/50; ⊙ 9am-1pm & 2-7pm mid-Apr–mid-Sep, closed Sun & Wed mid-Sep–mid-Apr; Ⓜ Maubert-Mutualité)

Gepetto et Vélos (☎ 01 43 54 19 95; www. gepetto-velos.com; 28 rue des Fossées St-Bernard,

5e; bike rental per hour/ day/weekend €4/16/20, tandem €8/30/45; ⊙ 9am-7pm Tue-Sat; Ⓜ Cardinal Lemoine)

Paris à Vélo, C'est Sympa (☎ 01 48 87 60 01; www.parisvelosympa. fr; 22 rue Alphonse Baudin, 11e; half-day/full day/24hr bike from €12/15/20, electric bike €20/30/40; ⊙ 9.30am-1pm & 2-6pm Mon-Fri, 9am-7pm Sat & Sun Apr-Oct, shorter hours Nov-Mar; Ⓜ Richard Lenoir)

Boat

Batobus (www.batobus. com; adult/child 1-day pass €17/8, 2-day pass €19/10; ⊙10am-9.30pm late Apr-Aug, shorter hours Sep-late Apr) runs glassed-in trimarans that dock every 20 to 25 minutes at nine small piers along the Seine: Beaugrenel-le, Eiffel Tower, Musée d'Orsay, St-Germain des Prés, Notre Dame, Jardin des Plantes/ Cité de la Mode et du Design, Hôtel de Ville, Musée du Louvre and Champs-Élysées.

Buy tickets online, at ferry stops or at tourist offices. Two-day passes must be used on consecutive days. You can also buy a Pass+ that includes **L'Open Tour buses** (☏01 42 66 56 56; www. paris.opentour.com; 1-day pass adult/child €33/17, night tour €27/17), to be used on consecutive days. A two-day pass per adult/child costs €46/21; a three day-pass is €50/21.

Taxi

o The *prise en charge* (flagfall) is €4. Within the city limits, it costs €1.07 per kilometre for travel between 10am and 5pm Monday to Saturday (*Tarif A;* white light on taxi roof and meter).

o At night (5pm to 10am), on Sunday from 7am to midnight, and in the inner suburbs the rate is €1.29 per kilometre (*Tarif B;* orange light).

o Travel in the city limits and inner suburbs on Sunday night (midnight to 7am Monday) and in the outer suburbs is at *Tarif C,* €1.56 per kilometre (blue light).

o The minimum taxi fare for a short trip is €7.10.

o There are flat-fee fares to/from the major airports (Charles de Gualle from €50, Orly from €30).

o A fifth passenger incurs a €4 surcharge.

o There's no additional charge for luggage.

o Flagging down a taxi in Paris can be difficult; it's best to find an official taxi stand.

o To order a taxi, call or reserve online with **Taxis G7** (☏3607, 01 41 27 66 99; www.g7.fr) or **Alpha Taxis** (☏01 45 85 85 85; www. alpha-taxis-paris.fr).

Essential Information

Accessible Travel

o Visit www.parisinfo. com/accessibility for a wealth of useful info.

o For information about which cultural venues in Paris are accessible to people with disabilities, visit Accès Culture (http://accesculture.org).

o **Mobile en Ville** (☏09 52 29 60 51; www.mobileen ville.org; 8 rue des Mariniers, 14e) works hard to make independent travel within the city easier for people in wheelchairs. Among other things it organises wheelchair *randonnées* (walks) in and around Paris; those in wheelchairs are pushed by 'walkers' on roller skates; contact the association well ahead of your visit to take part.

o Download Lonely Planet's free *Accessible Travel Online Resources* from http://lptravel. to/AccessibleTravel for heaps more useful websites, including travel agents and tour operators.

Transport

o Info Mobi (📞 09 70 81 93 95; www.vianavigo.com/accessibilite) has detailed information about public transport in the Île-de-France region surrounding Paris, filterable by disability type.

o Taxis G7 (📞 3607, 01 41 27 66 99; www.g7.fr) has hundreds of low-base cars, 120 cars equipped with ramps, and drivers trained in helping passengers with disabilities. Guide dogs are accepted in its entire fleet.

Business Hours

The following list covers *approximate* standard opening hours. Many places close in August for summer holidays.

Banks 9am to 1pm and 2 to 5pm Monday to Friday; some open on Saturday morning

Bars & Cafes 7am to 2am

Museums 10am to 6pm; closed Monday or Tuesday

Post Offices 8am to 7pm Monday to Friday, and until noon Saturday

Restaurants noon to 2pm and 7.30 to 10.30pm

Shops 10am to 7pm Monday to Saturday; they occasionally close in the early afternoon for lunch and sometimes all day Monday. Hours are longer for shops in defined ZTIs (international tourist zones).

Discount Cards

Paris Museum Pass (http://en.parismuseumpass.com; two/four/six days €48/62/74) Gets you into 50-plus venues in and around Paris; a huge advantage is that pass holders usually enter larger sights at a different entrance, meaning you bypass (or substantially reduce) ridiculously long ticket queues.

Paris Passlib' (www.parisinfo.com; two/three/five days €109/129/155) Sold at the Paris Convention & Visitors Bureau (p214) and on its website, this handy city pass covers unlimited public transport in zones 1 to 3, admission to some 50 museums in the Paris region (aka a Paris Museum Pass), temporary exhibitions at most municipal museums, a one-hour **Bateaux**

Parisiens (📞 08 25 01 01 01; www.bateauxparisiens.com; Port de la Bourdonnais, 7e; adult/child €15/7; Ⓜ Bir Hakeim or RER Pont de l'Alma) boat cruise along the Seine, and a one-day hop-on, hop-off open-top bus sightseeing service around central Paris' key sights with L'Open Tour (p24). There's an optional €20 supplement for a skip-the-line ticket to levels one and two of the Eiffel Tower.

Mobilis and **Paris Visite** passes are valid on the metro, the RER, SNCF's suburban lines, buses, night buses, trams and the Montmartre funicular railway. No photo is needed, but write your full name and date of use on the ticket. Passes are sold at larger metro and RER stations, SNCF offices in Paris, and the airports. Passes operate by date (rather than 24-hour periods), so activate early in the day for the best value.

Mobilis Allows unlimited travel for one day and costs €7.50 (for two zones) to €17.80 (five zones). Buy it at any metro, RER or SNCF station in the Paris region. Depending on how many times you plan to hop on/off the metro in a day, a *carnet* (book of 10 tickets) might work out cheaper.

Paris Visite Allows unlimited travel as well as discounted entry to certain museums and other bonuses. The 'Paris+ Suburbs+ Airports' pass includes transport to/from the airports and costs €25.25/38.35/53.75/65.80 for one/two/ three/five days. The cheaper 'Paris Centre' pass, valid for zones 1 to 3, costs €12/19.50/26.65/38.35 for one/two/ three/five days. Children aged four to 11 years pay half price.

Electricity

Type E
230V/50Hz

Dos & Don'ts

Overall, communication tends to be formal and reserved, but this shouldn't be mistaken for unfriendliness.

Greetings Always greet/farewell anyone you interact with, such as shopkeepers, with *'Bonjour (bonsoir* at night)/Au revoir'*.

Shops Particularly in smaller upmarket boutiques, staff may not appreciate your touching the merchandise until you have been invited to do so, nor taking photographs.

Speech Parisians don't speak loudly – modulate your voice to a similarly low pitch.

Terms of address *Tu* and *vous* both mean 'you', but *tu* is only used with people you know very well, children or animals. Use *vous* until you're invited to use *tu*.

Conversation topics Discussing financial affairs (eg salaries or spending outlays) is generally taboo in public.

Waitstaff Never use 'garçon' (literally 'boy') to summon a waiter, rather 'Monsieur' or 'Madame'.

Emergency

Ambulance (SAMU)
☏15

Fire ☏18

Police ☏17

EU-wide emergency
☏112

Internet Access

o Wi-fi (pronounced *'wee-fee'* in France) is available in most Paris hotels, usually at no

extra cost, and in some museums.

o Many cafes and bars have free wi-fi for customers; you may need to ask for the code.

o Free wi-fi is available in hundreds of public places, including parks, libraries and municipal buildings; look for a purple 'Zone Wi-fi' sign. To connect, select the 'PARIS_WI-FI_' network. Sessions are limited to two hours (renewable). For complete details and a map of hot spots, see www.paris.fr/wifi.

○ Co-working cafes have sprung up across Paris; you typically pay for a set amount of time, with wi-fi, drinks and snacks included.

Money

○ France uses the euro (€). For updated exchange rates, check www.xe.com.

○ Visa is the most widely accepted credit card, followed by MasterCard. American Express and Diners Club cards are accepted only at more exclusive establishments. Some restaurants don't accept credit cards.

○ Many automated services, such as ticket machines, require a chip-and-PIN credit card (even some foreign chip-enabled cards won't work). Ask your bank for advice before you leave.

Public Holidays

A *jour férié* (public holiday) is celebrated strictly on the day on which it falls. If it falls on a Saturday or Sunday,

no provision is made for an extra day off.

New Year's Day (Jour de l'An) 1 January

Easter Sunday & Monday (Pâques & Lundi de Pâques) Late March/April

May Day (Fête du Travail) 1 May

Victory in Europe Day (Victoire 1945) 8 May

Ascension Thursday (L'Ascension) May, celebrated on the 40th day after Easter

Whit Monday (Lundi de Pentecôte) Mid-May to mid-June on the seventh Monday after Easter

Bastille Day/National Day (Fête Nationale) 14 July

Assumption Day (L'Assomption) 15 August

All Saints' Day (La Toussaint) 1 November

Armistice Day/ Remembrance Day (Le Onze Novembre) 11 November

Christmas (Noël) 25 December

Safe Travel

Overall, Paris is well lit and safe, and random street assaults are rare.

○ Stay alert for pickpock-

ets and take precautions: don't carry more cash than you need, and keep cards and passports in a concealed pouch.

○ Common 'distraction' scams include would-be pickpockets pretending to 'find' a gold ring, brandishing fake petitions, dropping items, and tying 'friendship bracelets' to your wrist.

○ Metro stations best avoided late at night include Châtelet–Les Halles, Château Rouge, Gare du Nord, Strasbourg St-Denis, Réaumur Sébastopol, Stalingrad and Montparnasse Bienvenüe. Marx Dormoy, Porte de la Chapelle and Marcadet–Poissonniers can be sketchy day and night.

○ *Bornes d'alarme* (alarm boxes) are located in the centre of metro/RER platforms and some station corridors.

Telephone

○ Check with your provider about roaming costs before you leave home, or ensure your phone's unlocked to use a French SIM card (available cheaply in Paris).

○ There are no area codes in France – you

always dial the 10-digit number.

○ France's country code is 33.

○ To call abroad from Paris, dial France's international access code (00), the country code, the area code (drop the initial '0', if there is one) and the local number.

Toilets

○ Public toilets in Paris are signposted *toilettes* or *WC*. On main roads, *sanisettes* (self-cleaning cylindrical toilets) are open 24 hours and are free of charge. Look for the words *libre* ('available'; green-coloured) or *occupé* ('occupied'; red-coloured).

○ Cafe owners do not appreciate your using their facilities if you are not a paying customer (a coffee can be a good investment); however, if you have young children they may make an exception (ask first!). Other good bets are big hotels and major department stores (the latter may incur a charge).

○ There are free public toilets in front of Notre Dame cathedral, near the Arc de Triomphe, down the steps at Sacré-Cœur (to the east and west) and at the northwestern entrance to the Jardins des Tuileries.

Tourist Information

Information desks are located at Charles de Gaulle and Orly airports.

Paris Convention & Visitors Bureau (Paris Office de Tourisme; ☑ 01 49 52 42 63; www.parisinfo. com; 29 rue de Rivoli, 4e; ⏰ 9am-7pm; ☎; Ⓜ Hôtel de Ville) Paris' main tourist office is at the Hôtel de Ville. It sells tickets for tours and several attractions, plus museum and transport passes.

Gare du Nord Welcome Desk (www. parisinfo.com; 18 rue de Dunkerque, 10e; ⏰ 8.30am-6.30pm) Inside Gare du Nord station, under the glass roof of the Île-de-France departure and arrival area (eastern end of station).

Syndicate d'Initiative de Montmartre (☑ 01 42 62 21 21; www. montmartre-guide.com; 21 place du Tertre, 18e; ⏰ 10am-5pm Mon-Fri, 10am-1pm & 2-5pm Sat & Sun; Ⓜ Abbesses) Locally run tourist office and shop on Montmartre's most picturesque square. It sells maps of Montmartre and organises guided tours.

Visas

○ There are no entry requirements for nationals of EU countries and a handful of other European countries (including Switzerland). Citizens of Australia, the USA, Canada and New Zealand do not need visas to visit France for up to 90 days.

○ Everyone else needs a Schengen Visa, named after the Schengen Agreement that has abolished passport controls among 26 EU countries and that has also been ratified by the non-EU governments of Iceland, Norway and Switzerland. A visa for any of these countries should be valid throughout the Schengen area, but it pays to doublecheck with the embassy or consulate of each country you plan to visit.

○ Check www.diplomatie. gouv.fr for the latest visa regulations and the closest French embassy to your current residence.

Language

The sounds used in spoken French can almost all be found in English. There are a couple of exceptions: nasal vowels (represented in our pronunciation guides by 'o' or 'u' followed by an almost inaudible nasal consonant sound 'm', 'n' or 'ng'), the 'funny' u sound ('ew' in our guides) and the deep-in-the-throat r. Bearing these few points in mind and reading our pronunciation guides below as if they were English, you'll be understood just fine. The markers (m) and (f) indicate the forms for male and female speakers.

To enhance your trip with a phrasebook, visit **lonelyplanet.com**. Lonely Planet iPhone phrasebooks are available in the Apple App store.

Basics

Hello.
Bonjour.   bon·zhoor

Goodbye.
Au revoir.   o·rer·vwa

How are you?
Comment   ko·mon
allez-vous?   ta·lay·voo

I'm fine, thanks.
Bien, merci.   byun mair·see

Please.
S'il vous plaît.   seel voo play

Thank you.
Merci.   mair·see

Excuse me.
Excusez-moi.   ek·skew·zay·mwa

Sorry.
Pardon.   par·don

Yes./No.
Oui./Non.   wee/non

I don't understand.
Je ne comprends   zher ner kom·pron
pas.   pa

Do you speak English?
Parlez-vous   par·lay·voo
anglais?   ong·glay

Eating & Drinking

..., please.
..., s'il vous plaît.   ... seel voo play

A coffee	*un café*	un ka·fay
A table for two	*une table pour deux*	ewn ta·bler poor der
Two beers	*deux bières*	der bee·yair

I'm a vegetarian.
Je suis   zher swee
végétarien/   vay·zhay·ta·ryun/
végétarienne. (m/f) vay·zhay·ta·ryen

That was delicious!
C'était délicieux!   say·tay day·lee·syer

The bill, please.
L'addition,   la·dee·syon
s'il vous plaît.   seel voo play

Shopping

I'd like to buy ...
Je voudrais   zher voo·dray
acheter ...   ash·tay ...

I'm just looking.
Je regarde.   zher rer·gard

How much is it?
C'est combien?   say kom·byun

It's too expensive.
C'est trop cher.   say tro shair

Can you lower the price?
Vous pouvez   voo poo·vay
bay·say
baisser le prix?   ler pree

Emergencies

Help!
Au secours!   o skoor

Call the police!
Appelez la police!   a·play la po·lees

Call a doctor!
Appelez un   a·play un
médecin!   mayd·sun

I'm sick.
Je suis malade.   zher swee ma·lad

I'm lost.
Je suis perdu/   zhe swee pair·dew
perdue. (m/f)

Where are the toilets?
Où sont les   oo son lay
toilettes?   twa·let

Time & Numbers

What time is it?
Quelle heure   kel er
est-il?   ay til

It's (eight) o'clock.
Il est (huit)   il ay (weet)
heures.   er

It's half past (10).
Il est (dix) heures   il ay (deez) er
et demie.   ay day·mee

morning	matin	ma·tun
afternoon	après-midi	a·pray·mee·dee
evening	soir	swar
yesterday	hier	yair
today	aujourd'hui	o·zhoor·dwee
tomorrow	demain	der·mun

Monday	lundi	lun·dee
Tuesday	mardi	mar·dee
Wednesday	mercredi	mair·krer·dee
Thursday	jeudi	zher·dee
Friday	vendredi	von·drer·dee
Saturday	samedi	sam·dee
Sunday	dimanche	dee·monsh

1	un	un
2	deux	der
3	trois	trwa
4	quatre	ka·trer
5	cinq	sungk
6	six	sees
7	sept	set
8	huit	weet
9	neuf	nerf
10	dix	dees
100	cent	son
1000	mille	meel

Transport & Directions

Where's ...?
Où est ...?   oo ay ...

What's the address?
Quelle est l'adresse?   kel ay la·dres

Can you show me (on the map)?
Pouvez-vous   poo·vay·voo
m'indiquer   mun·dee·kay
(sur la carte)?   (sewr la kart)

I want to go to ...
Je voudrais   zher voo·dray
aller à ...   a·lay a ...

Does it stop at (Amboise)?
Est-ce qu'il   es·kil
s'arrête à   sa·ret a
(Amboise)?   (om·bwaz)

I want to get off here.
Je veux   zher ver
descendre ici.   day·son·drer ee·see

Behind the Scenes

Send Us Your Feedback

We love to hear from travellers – your comments help make our books better. We read every word, and we guarantee that your feedback goes straight to the authors. Visit **lonelyplanet.com/contact** to submit your updates and suggestions.

Note: We may edit, reproduce and incorporate your comments in Lonely Planet products such as guidebooks, websites and digital products, so let us know if you don't want your comments reproduced or your name acknowledged. For a copy of our privacy policy visit lonelyplanet.com/privacy.

Acknowledgements

Cover photograph: Eiffel Tower, Alessandro Saffo/4Corners ©

Catherine's Thanks

Merci mille fois first and foremost to Julian and to the innumerable Parisians who provided insights, inspiration and great times. Huge thanks too to my Paris co-writers Chris and Nicola, Destination Editor Daniel Fahey and everyone at Lonely Planet. As ever, a heartfelt *merci encore* to my parents, brother, *belle-soeur, neveu* and *nièce* for sustaining my lifelong love of Paris and France.

Christopher's Thanks

Special thanks to my two great co-writers for their advice and input and to all the crew at Lonely Planet who have put so much hard work into making this book what it is. Also thanks to Neil Fazakerley for providing company and conversation for a day. *Bises* as always to the Pavillard clan, and my dearest partners in crime: Perrine, Elliot and Céleste.

Nicola's Thanks

Heartfelt *bisous* to the many friends and professionals who aided and abetted me in tracking down the best of Paris, including the more-Parisian-than-Parisian and hugely knowledgeable Elodie Berta; savvy local in the 13e, Mary Winston-Nicklin; New Yorker in Le Marais, Kasia Dietz; Rachel Vanier at Station F; Chinatown queen, Stéphanie Ruch; and Maria and Bartolomeo at La Bête Noire. Love and thanks too to my formidable, trilingual *'Paris en famille'* research team, Matthias, Niko, Mischa and Kaya Luefkens.

This Book

This 6th edition of Lonely Planet's *Pocket Paris* guidebook was researched and written by Catherine Le Nevez, Christopher Pitts and Nicola Williams. They also researched and wrote the previous two editions. This guidebook was produced by the following:

Destination Editor
Daniel Fahey

Senior Product Editor
Genna Patterson

Product Editor
Kate Mathews

Senior Cartographer
Mark Griffiths

Book Designers Clara Monitto, Michael Weldon

Assisting Editors Sarah Bailey, Judith Bamber, Lucy Cowie, Melanie Dankel, Andrea Dobbin, Kristin Odijk, Fionnuala Twomey

Cover Researcher
Naomi Parker

Thanks to Loubna El Amine, Jennifer Carey, Erica Fletcher, Michael Fosberg, Jonas Hultin, Alison Ridgway, Lyahna Spencer, Angela Tinson, Amanda Williamson, Juan Winata

Index

See also separate subindexes for:
- Eating p221
- Drinking p222
- Entertainment p223
- Shopping p223

A

Abbesses 97
accessible travel 210-11
accommodation 204-5
Agoudas Hakehilos Synagogue 124
air travel 205-6, 207
Arc de Triomphe 54-5
Archaeological Crypt 141
architecture 18-19, 122
Arènes de Lutèce 161
art galleries 16-17, see also individual art galleries
art nouveau 18
Aymé, Marcel 97

B

Bastille 111-31, **116-17**
drinking 127-9
eating 121-7
entertainment 129
shopping 130-1
sights 118-21
transport 111
bathrooms 214
Batobus 210
beer 12
belle époque 100
Bibliothèque Nationale de France 173
boat travel 210

bouquinistes 195
Bourse de Commerce 80
brasseries 191
bus travel 205-6, 207, 208
business hours 211

C

Canal St-Martin 108-9
cell phones 213
Centre Pompidou 112-13
Champs-Élysées 53-65, **56-7**
drinking 64-5
eating 61-4
shopping 65
sights 58-61
transport 53
children, travel with 26
Cimetière de Montmartre 100
Cimetière du Montparnasse 186
Cité de l'Architecture et du Patrimoine 58
climate 204
Clos Montmartre 97
cocktails 12-13
coffee 12
Collection Pinault Paris 80
Colonne de Juillet 121
Conciergerie 144
cooking classes 25
costs 30, 211-12
courses 25
crêpes 155, 190

currency 30, 213
cycling 208-9

D

Dalí, Salvador 99-100
dangers, see safety
de Gaulle, Charles 51
disabilities, travellers with 210-11
drinking 12-13, see also Drinking subindex

E

eating 10-11, see also Eating subindex
Église du Dôme 44
Église St-Eustache 78
Église St-Germain des Prés 184
Église St-Louis en l'Île 145
Église St-Sulpice 184
Eiffel Tower 38-9
electricity 212
emergencies 212
entertainment, see Entertainment subindex
Espace Dalí 99-100
etiquette 212

F

fashion 14
flea markets 106, see also Shopping subindex
Fondation Cartier pour l'Art Contemporain 186

Fondation Louis Vuitton 60
food 10-11, 14, 15 see also Eating subindex
Forum des Halles 80
French language 215-16
French Revolution 20, 149
Funicular de Montmartre 95

G

Galerie Colbert 75
Galerie Véro Dodat 75
gardens 22
gay travellers 27, 128
Gill, André 97
Ginsberg, Allen 181
Girondins 149
Grande Arche 61
Grande Pyramide 71
Grand Palais 59
Guimard, Hector 97

H

Halle St-Pierre 100-1
Hemingway, Ernest 181
highlights 6-9
history 20-1, 51, 100, 149, 160
holidays 213
Hôtel de Ville 120
Hôtel des Invalides 44
Hugo, Victor 118, 146

I

Île aux Cygnes 45

Île de la Cité 135-51, **142-3**
drinking 148
eating 145-8
shopping 150-1
sights 136-40, 144-5
transport 135

Île St-Louis 135-51, **142-3**
drinking 148
eating 145-8
history 150
shopping 150-1
sights 145
transport 135

impressionism 16

Institut du Monde Arabe 158

internet access 212-13

internet resources 204, 216

itineraries 28-9, see also walks

J

Jacobins 149

Jardin des Plantes 91, 159-60

Jardin des Tuileries 78, 91

Jardin du Luxembourg 178-9

Jardin du Palais Royal 79, 91

Jeu de Paume 78

Jewish community 124

Joyce, James 181

K

Kerouac, Jack 181

L

La Boutique Extraordinaire 115

La REcyclerie 106

Sights 000
Map Pages **000**

Lafayette Anticipations 120

language 215-16

L'Atelier des Lumières 119

Latin Quarter 153-71, **156-7**
drinking 167-8
eating 161-6
entertainment 168-9
shopping 169-71
sights 158-61
transport 153
walks 154-5, **154**

Le Grand Musée du Parfum 59-60

Le Marais 111-31, **116-17**
drinking 127-9
eating 121-7
entertainment 129
shopping 130-1
sights 112-13, 118-21
transport 111
walks 114-15, **114**

Le Mur des je t'aime 99

Les Catacombes 185-6

Les Docks 173

Les Invalides 37-51, **42-3**
drinking 49-50
eating 45-9
shopping 50-1
sights 38-41, 44-5
transport 37

lesbian travellers 27, 128

LGBT+ travellers 27, 128

literary sites 180-1

L'Oasis d'Aboukir 82

Louis XVI 149, 198-201

Louvre 68-73

Louvre area 67-89, **76-7**
drinking 84-5
eating 80-3
entertainment 85-7
shopping 87-9
sights 78-80
transport 67

M

Maison de Victor Hugo 118

Marie Antoinette 149, 198-201

markets 14, 106, see also Shopping subindex

Mémorial de la Shoah 118

Mémorial des Martyrs de la Déportation 144-5

Miller, Henry 181

mobile phones 213

Mona Lisa 70

Monet, Claude 46

money 30, 211-12, 213

Monnaie de Paris 184

Montmartre 93-107, **98**
drinking 103-4
eating 101-3
entertainment 105-7
shopping 107
sights 94-5, 99-100
transport 93
walks 96-7, **96**

Montparnasse 175-97, **182-3**
drinking 192-4
eating 187-91
shopping 194-7
sights 176-9, 184-7
transport 175

Mosquée de Paris 158-9

Moulin Blute-Fin 97

Moulin Radet 97

Musée Cognacq-Jay 120-1

Musée d'Art et d'Histoire du Judaïsme 124

Musée d'Art Moderne de la Ville de Paris 61

Musée de la Sculpture en Plein Air 91, 161

Musée de la Vie Romantique 99

Musée de l'Armée 44

Musée de l'Orangerie 78

Musée de Montmartre 97, 99

Musée des Arts Décoratifs 73

Musée des Arts et Métiers 118-19

Musée d'Orsay 176-7

Musée du Quai Branly 44

Musée Guimet des Arts Asiatiques 58

Musée Jacquemart-André 58

Musée Maillol 186-7

Musée Marmottan Monet 46

Musée National du Moyen Âge 158

Musée National Eugène Delacroix 184-5

Musée National Picasso 118

Musée Rodin 40-1

Musée Yves Saint Laurent Paris 58-9

Muséum National d'Histoire Naturelle 160-1

museums 16-17, see also individual museums

N

nightlife 12-13, see also Drinking subindex

Notre Dame 136-41, 146, **140**

Nouvel, Jean 19

O

opening hours 211

Opéra 67-89, **76-7**
drinking 84-5
eating 80-3
entertainment 85-7

shopping 87 9
sights 78-80
transport 67
Orwell, George 181

P

Palais de Chaillot 60
Palais de Tokyo 60-1
Palais Galliera 61
Palais Garnier 79-80
Panthéon 158
Parc des Buttes Chaumont 109
Parc du Champ de Mars 44-5
Parc Rives de Seine 119-20, 185
parks & gardens 22
passages couverts 74-5, **74**
Passe-Muraille 97
Pei, IM 71
Père Lachaise 132-3
Périphérique 165
Petit Palais 60
Picasso, Pablo 118
Pigalle 93-107, **98**
    drinking 103-4
    eating 101-3
    entertainment 105-7
    shopping 107
    sights 99-100
    transport 93
Place de la Bastille 121
Place de la Concorde 79
place de la Madeleine 89
place des Vosges 121
place du Tertre 97
planning 30
Pletzl 124
Point Éphémère 109
Pompidou, Georges 113
Pont Neuf 91, 144
Pound, Ezra 181
Promenade Plantée 120

public holidays 213
Pyramide Inversée 71

R

Reign of Terror 149
Rodin, Auguste 40-1
rue Cler 49
rue Daguerre 188
rue de Lappe 129
rue des Lombards 86
rue des Martyrs 103
rue Montorgueil 81
rue Mouffetard 154-5

S

Sacré-Cœur 94-5
safety 213
Sainte-Chapelle 144
sculptures 17
Seine, the 23, 90-1
shopping 14-15, *see also* Shopping subindex
Sorbonne 161
Square du Vert-Galant 144
Square René Viviani 159
Station F 186
Stein, Gertrude 181
St-Germain des Prés 175-97, **182-3**
    drinking 192-4
    eating 187-91
    shopping 194-7
    sights 176-9, 184-7
    transport 175
    walks 180-1, **180**
swimming 173

T

taxis 210
telephone services 213-14
time zones 30
toilets 214
Tomb of the Unknown Soldier 55
top sights 6-9

tourist information 214
tours 24
train travel 208
transport 31, 205-10
Triangle d'Or 65
Tuileries 67-89, **76-7**
    drinking 84-5
    eating 80-3
    entertainment 85-7
    shopping 87-9
    sights 78-80
    transport 67

V

vacations 213
Van Gogh, Vincent 97
Verlaine, Paul 181
Versailles 198-201
Viaduc des Arts 120
vineyards 97
visas 214

W

walks
    Canal St-Martin 108-9, **108**
    Latin Quarter 154-5, **154**
    Le Marais 114-15, **114**
    Left Bank 180-1, **180**
    Montmartre 96-7, **96**
    Right Bank 74-5, **74**
    Seine, the 90-1, **90**
    southeastern Paris 172-3, **172**
weather 204
websites 204
Wilde, Oscar 133, 181
wine 12, 13
wine tasting 25
WWII 51

⊗ **Eating**

58 Tour Eiffel 39
86 Champs 62-3

A

À la Petite Chaise 187
Abattoir Végétal 101
Abri 101-2
Anicia 190
Arnaud Nicolas 46
Aspic 101
Atelier Vivanda 64
Au Passage 124-5
Au Pied de Fouet 190
Au Rocher de Cancale 81

B

Balagan 82
Bercy Village 173
Berthillon 91, 145-6
Besnier 41
Bontemps Pâtisserie 124
Bouillon Pigalle 102
Bouillon Racine 187
Brasserie Bofinger 125
Breizh Café 122
Broken Biscuits 133
Bustronome 62

C

Café Campana 177
Café Constant 47
Café de la Nouvelle Mairie 162
Café de l'Ours 177
Café La Fusée 113
Café Miroir 103
Café Saint Régis 146
Chambelland 122-3
Chez Dumonet 189
Chez La Vieille 82
Chez Louisette 106
Chez Nicos 155
Chez Paul 126-7
Clover 188-9
Croq' Fac 163

D

Dame Tartine 113
Dans Les Landes 164

F

Framboise 63
Frenchie 81

H

Huré 146-7

K

Karamel 47

L

La Bête Noire 162
La Butte aux Piafs 173
La Closerie des Lilas 191
La Coupole 191
La Maison Plisson 121-2
La Mascotte 102
La Rotonde
    Montparnasse 191
La Salle à Manger 164
La Tour d'Argent 166-7
La Tour de Montlhéry –
    Chez Denise 83
Ladurée 61-2
Ladurée Picnic 47
L'affineur Affiné 101
L'Agrume 166
L'As du Fallafel 124
Lasserre 62
L'Avant Comptoir de la
    Mer 188
Le Baratin 109
Le Bistrot de la Galette
    102
Le Bistrot Paul Bert
    123-4
Le Buisson Ardent 164
Le Cassenoix 46
Le Caveau du Palais 147
Le Chardenoux 127
Le Cochon à l'Oreille 83
Le Comptoir du
    Panthéon 163

Le Coupe-Chou 163
Le Dôme 191
Le Fontaine de Mars 48
Le Grand Véfour 82
Le Grenier à Pain 101
Le Hide 62
Le Jules Verne 39
Le Pantruche 103
Le Petit Pontoise 166
Le Procope 187
Le Restaurant 177
Le Select 191
Le Servan 122
Le Train Bleu 173
Le Violon d'Ingres 47
Les Climats 191
Les Fables de la
    Fontaine 46-7
Les Fous de l'Île 147-8
Les Papilles 163
Les Pipos 166
L'Étable Hugo
    Desnoyer 190
L'Été en Pente
    Douce 95
L'Îlot Vache 148

M

Ma Salle à Manger 148
Maison Maison 80-1
Marché Bastille 121
Marché des Enfants
    Rouges 125
Mococha 155

O

Odette 164
Ore (Versailles) 199

P

Pastelli 123
Philippe & Jean-Pierre
    63-4
Pink Flamingo 109
Plume 48-9
Publicis Drugstore 55

R

Rainettes 126
Restaurant AT 161
Restaurant David
    Toutain 47-8
Restaurant Guy Savoy
    187-8
Richer 81

S

Semilla 189
Septime 125-6
Sequana 146

T

Tomy & Co 45-6

🍷 Drinking

3w Kafé 128
52 Faubourg St-Denis 109

A

Angelina 85
Au Sauvignon 192

B

Bar Hemingway 84
Beans on Fire 127-8
BHV 127
Boot Café 115, 128

C

Café Charbon 109
Café de Flore 193
Café Delmas 168
Café des Deux
    Moulins 97
Candelaria 127
Castor Club 193
Cave La Bourgogne 168
Chez Bouboule 104
Chez Prune 109
Club, The 50
Cod House 192
Coutume Café 49

D

Danico 84
Dirty Dick 105
Dose 155

F

Fitzgerald 49

G

Glass 105

H

Hardware Société 95
Harry's New York Bar 84
Holybelly 109
Honor 64

L

La Belle Hortense 129
La Caféothèque 128-9
La Fourmi 104-5
La Machine du Moulin
    Rouge 105
La Palette 194
La Quincave 193-4
L'Atmosphère 109
Le Bar du Caveau 148
Le Batofar 173
Le Flore en l'Île 148
Le Garde Robe 84
Le Mary Céleste 115
Le Perchoir 127
Le Petit Trianon 104
Le Rex Club 85
Le Tambour 85
Le Tango 128
Le Très Particulier 103
Le Verre à Pied 168
Les Deux Magots 192
Lipstick 105
Little Bastards 167
Little Red Door 128
Lulu White 105

M

Matamata 84-5

Sights 000
Map Pages **000**

N

Nouveau Casino 109

O

Open Café 128

P

Pub St-Hilaire 168

Q

Quetzal 128

R

Rosa Bonheur 109

S

Shakespeare & Company Café 167
St James Paris 64

T

Terres de Café 49-50
Tiger 192

U

Upper Crèmerie 64-5

Z

Zig Zag Club 64

🎭 Entertainment

Bus Palladium 107
Café Universel 168-9
Cave du 38 Riv' 129
Caveau de la Huchette 169
Cinémathèque Française 173
Comédie Française 86
Église St-Julien le Pauvre 169
Forum des Images 86
Kiosque Théâtre Madeleine 87
La Chapelle des Lombards 129

La Cigale 106
Le Balajo 129
Le Champo 169
Le Divan du Monde 106
Le Grand Rex 86
Le Louxor 105-6
L'Epée de Bois 155
Moulin Rouge 105
Opéra Bastille 129
Palais Garnier 85

🛍 Shopping

38 Saint Louis 150

A

À la Mère de Famille 89
Abbey Bookshop 171
Album 170-1
Androuet 155
Arnaud Magistry 75
Au Plat d'Étain 196
Au Vieux Campeur 171

B

Balades Sonores 107
Belle du Jour 107
Bières Cultes Jussieu 170
Boutique Maille 89

C

Cantin 50-1
Chercheminippes 51
Cire Trudon 196
Clair de Rêve 151

D

Delizius 155
Deyrolle 196
Didier Ludot 88

E

E Dehillerin 89
Emilio Robba 75
Empreintes 131

F

Fauchon 89
Fermob 197
Finger in the Nose 115
Fou de Pâtisserie 81
Frivoli 109
Fromagerie Laurent Dubois 171
Fromagerie Quatrehomme 197

G

Gab & Jo 195
Galeries Lafayette 87
Galeries Lafayette – Champs-Élysées 65
Gérard Mulot 195
Guerlain 65

H

Hédiard 89

I

Il Campiello 151

K

Kerzon 130

L

La Dernière Goutte 195
La Grande Épicerie de Paris 196
La Maison de la Truffe 89
La Maison de Poupée 196
La Manufacture de Chocolat 131
La Samaritaine 88
Le Bon Marché 196
Le Bonbon au Palais 169-70
Le Printemps 88
Legrand Filles & Fils 75
Les Caves Augé 65
L'Exception 87-8
L'Habilleur 115

Librairie Ulysse 150
L'Iles aux Images 150-1

M

Magasin Sennelier 196
Maison Chaudun 51
Marché aux Fleurs Reine Elizabeth II 91, 150
Marché aux Puces d'Aligre 125
Marché aux Puces de St-Ouen 106
Marché Beauvau 125
Marché d'Aligre 125
Marché des Enfants Rouges 115
Marché Maubert 171
Marché Monge 171
Marché Mouffetard 155
Marché Raspail 197
Mariage Frères 131
Merci 115, 130
Mesdemoiselles Madeleines 103

P

Pain Pain 103
Paris Rendez-Vous 131
Patrick Roger 89
Pierre Hermé 197
Pigalle 107
Poilâne 196

S

Sabbia Rosa 194
Shakespeare & Company 91, 169, 181
Smallable Concept Store 197
Spree 107
Stohrer 81

W

Wolff et Descourtis 75

Our Writers

Catherine Le Nevez

Catherine's wanderlust kicked in when she roadtripped across Europe from her Parisian base aged four, and she's been hitting the road at every opportunity since, travelling to around 60 countries and completing her Doctorate of Creative Arts in Writing, Masters in Professional Writing, and postgraduate qualifications in editing and publishing along the way. Over the past dozen-plus years she's written scores of Lonely Planet guides and articles covering Paris, France, Europe and far beyond. Her work has also appeared in numerous online and print publications.

Christopher Pitts

Chris' first expedition in life ended in failure when he tried to dig from Pennsylvania to China at the age of six. Hardened by reality but still curious about the other side of the world, he went on to live for several years in Kunming, Taiwan and Shanghai. A chance encounter led to a Paris relocation, where he lived with his wife and two children for more than a decade before succumbing to the lure of Colorado's sunny skies.

Nicola Williams

Border-hopping is a way of life for British writer, runner, foodie, art aficionado and mum of three, Nicola Williams. Nicola has authored more than 50 guidebooks for Lonely Planet, and covers France as a destination expert for the *Telegraph*. She also writes for the *Independent*, the *Guardian*, lonelyplanet.com, *Lonely Planet Magazine*, *French Magazine*, *Camping France* and others. Catch her on Twitter and Instagram @tripal

Published by Lonely Planet Global Limited
CRN 554153
6th edition – December 2018
ISBN 978 1 78657 281 3
© Lonely Planet 2018   Photographs © as indicated 2018
10 9 8 7 6 5 4 3 2 1
Printed in Singapore